Teach Yourself VISUALLY™ Mac® OS X

Visual

From
maranGraphics®

&

Wiley Publishing, Inc.

Teach Yourself VISUALLY™ Mac® OS X

Published by
Wiley Publishing, Inc.
909 Third Avenue
New York, NY 10022

Published simultaneously in Canada

Library of Congress Control Number: 2002109833

ISBN: 0-7645-1802-X

Manufactured in the United States of America

10 9 8 7 6 5 4 3 2

1K/RX/RQ/QS/MG

Trademark Acknowledgments

Important Numbers

For U.S. corporate orders, please call maranGraphics at 800-469-6616 or fax 905-890-9434.

For general information on our other products and services or to obtain technical support, please contact our Customer Care Department within the U.S. at 800-762-2974, outside the U.S. at 317-572-3993 or fax 317-572-4002.

Permissions

Wiley Publishing, Inc.   is a trademark of Wiley Publishing, Inc.

U.S. Corporate Sales	U.S. Trade Sales
Contact maranGraphics at (800) 469-6616 or fax (905) 890-9434.	Contact Wiley at (800) 762-2974 or fax (317) 572-4002.

Some comments from our readers...

"I have to praise you and your company on the fine products you turn out. I have twelve of the *Teach Yourself VISUALLY* and *Simplified* books in my house. They were instrumental in helping me pass a difficult computer course. Thank you for creating books that are easy to follow."

–*Gordon Justin (Brielle, NJ)*

"I commend your efforts and your success. I teach in an outreach program for the Dr. Eugene Clark Library in Lockhart, TX. Your *Teach Yourself VISUALLY* books are incredible and I use them in my computer classes. All my students love them!"

–*Michele Schalin (Lockhart, TX)*

"Thank you so much for helping people like me learn about computers. The Maran family is just what the doctor ordered. Thank you, thank you, thank you."

–*Carol Moten (New Kensington, PA)*

"I would like to take this time to compliment maranGraphics on creating such great books. Thank you for making it clear. Keep up the good work."

–*Kirk Santoro (Burbank, CA)*

"I write to extend my thanks and appreciation for your books. They are clear, easy to follow, and straight to the point. Keep up the good work!"

–*Seward Kollie (Dakar, Senegal)*

"What fantastic teaching books you have produced! Congratulations to you and your staff. You deserve the Nobel prize in Education in the Software category. Thanks for helping me to understand computers."

–*Bruno Tonon (Melbourne, Australia)*

"Over time, I have bought a number of your 'Read Less-Learn More' books. For me, they are THE way to learn anything easily."

–*José A. Mazón (Cuba, NY)*

"I was introduced to maranGraphics about four years ago and YOU ARE THE GREATEST THING THAT EVER HAPPENED TO INTRODUCTORY COMPUTER BOOKS!"

–*Glenn Nettleton (Huntsville, AL)*

"Compliments To The Chef!! Your books are extraordinary! Or, simply put, Extra-Ordinary, meaning way above the rest! THANK YOU THANK YOU THANK YOU! for creating these."

–*Christine J. Manfrin (Castle Rock, CO)*

"I'm a grandma who was pushed by an 11-year-old grandson to join the computer age. I found myself hopelessly confused and frustrated until I discovered the Visual series. I'm no expert by any means now, but I'm a lot further along than I would have been otherwise. Thank you!"

–*Carol Louthain (Logansport, IN)*

"Thank you, thank you, thank you...for making it so easy for me to break into this high-tech world. I now own four of your books. I recommend them to anyone who is a beginner like myself. Now... if you could just do one for programming VCRs, it would make my day!"

–*Gay O'Donnell (Calgary, Alberta, Canada)*

"You're marvelous! I am greatly in your debt."

–*Patrick Baird (Lacey, WA)*

maranGraphics is a family-run business
located near Toronto, Canada.

At **maranGraphics**, we believe in producing great computer books—one book at a time.

Each maranGraphics book uses the award-winning communication process that we have been developing over the last 25 years. Using this process, we organize screen shots, text and illustrations in a way that makes it easy for you to learn new concepts and tasks.

We spend hours deciding the best way to perform each task, so you don't have to! Our clear, easy-to-follow screen shots and instructions walk you through each task from beginning to end.

Our detailed illustrations go hand-in-hand with the text to help reinforce the information. Each illustration is a labor of love—some take up to a week to draw!

We want to thank you for purchasing what we feel are the best computer books money can buy. We hope you enjoy using this book as much as we enjoyed creating it!

Sincerely,

The Maran Family

CREDITS

Author:
Ruth Maran

Copy Development Director:
Wanda Lawrie

**Copy Developer and
Indexer:**
Raquel Scott

Project Manager:
Judy Maran

**Editing and
Screen Captures:**
Roxanne Van Damme
Roderick Anatalio
Megan Robinson

Layout Designer:
Sarah Jang

Illustrators:
Russ Marini
Steven Schaerer

**Screen Artist
and Illustrator:**
Darryl Grossi

**Wiley Vice President and
Executive Group Publisher:**
Richard Swadley

**Wiley Vice President
and Publisher:**
Barry Pruett

Wiley Editorial Support:
Jennifer Dorsey
Sandy Rodrigues
Lindsay Sandman

Post Production:
Robert Maran

ACKNOWLEDGMENTS

Thanks to the dedicated staff of maranGraphics, including
Roderick Anatalio, Darryl Grossi,
Sarah Jang, Wanda Lawrie, Jill Maran, Judy Maran,
Robert Maran, Ruth Maran, Russ Marini,
Megan Robinson, Steven Schaerer,
Raquel Scott and Roxanne Van Damme.

Finally, to Richard Maran who originated
the easy-to-use graphic format of this guide.
Thank you for your inspiration and guidance.

TABLE OF CONTENTS

Chapter 1

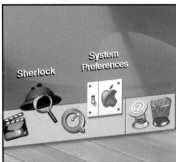

MAC OS X BASICS

Chapter 2

VIEW FILES

Chapter 3

Chapter 4

TABLE OF CONTENTS

Chapter 5

USE MAC OS X APPLICATIONS

Chapter 6

PLAY MUSIC USING iTUNES

Chapter 7

MANAGE PHOTOS USING iPHOTO

Chapter 8

CREATE MOVIES USING iMOVIE

Chapter 9

SHARE YOUR COMPUTER

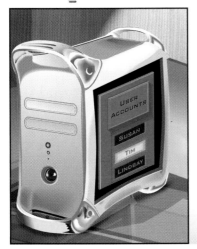

TABLE OF CONTENTS

Chapter 10

WORK ON A NETWORK

Chapter 11

BROWSE THE WEB USING INTERNET EXPLORER

Chapter 12

SEARCH THE INTERNET USING SHERLOCK

Chapter 13

EXCHANGE E-MAIL USING MAIL

Chapter 14

EXCHANGE INSTANT MESSAGES USING iCHAT

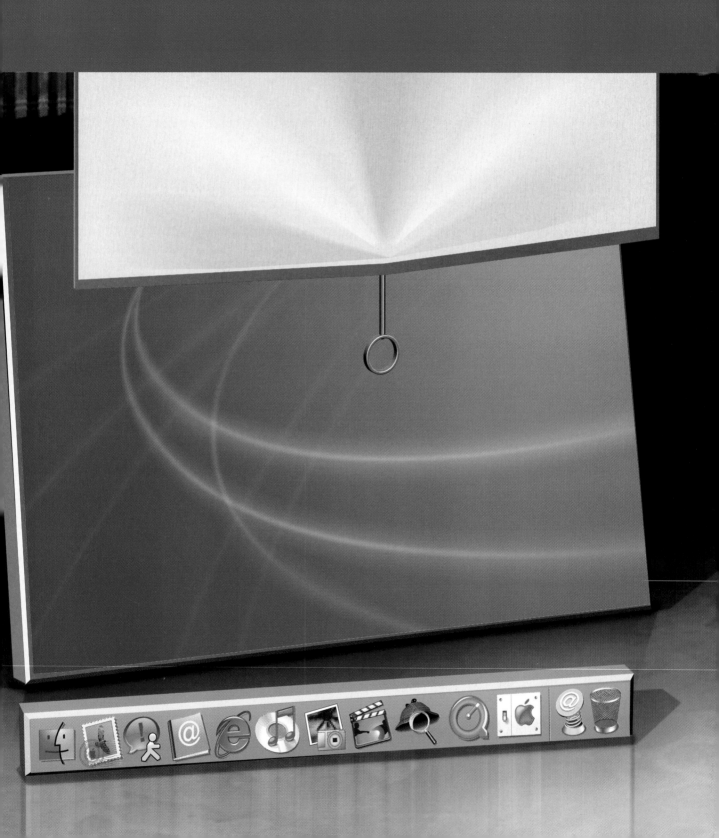

CHAPTER 1

Mac OS X Basics

This chapter teaches you all the basic skills you need to work with Mac OS, such as how to use the Dock, restart your computer and get help.

INTRODUCTION TO MAC OS X

Mac® OS X controls the overall activity of your computer and ensures that all parts of your computer work together smoothly and efficiently.

Work with Files

Mac OS allows you to effectively manage the files stored on your computer. You can open, rename, duplicate, move, delete, print and search for files. You can also copy files to a recordable CD or DVD.

Customize Mac OS

You can customize Mac OS to suit your preferences. You can change the picture used to decorate your desktop, change the way your mouse works, add fonts and turn on speech recognition to use spoken commands to perform tasks on your computer. Mac OS also allows you to change the screen effect that appears when you do not use your computer for a period of time.

Use Mac OS Applications

Mac OS offers many applications you can use to perform tasks on your computer. You can use TextEdit to create documents, Address Book to store information for people you frequently contact and Stickies to create colorful electronic sticky notes. You can also play chess, use an on-screen calculator, play QuickTime movies and watch DVD movies on your computer.

Play and Organize Music

Mac OS allows you to play music CDs and listen to radio stations that broadcast on the Internet. You can also create playlists that contain your favorite songs, create your own music CDs and copy songs from your computer to a portable MP3 player.

Manage Photos and Create Movies

You can use iPhoto to copy photos from a digital camera to your computer so you can view, organize and edit the photos. You can use iMovie to transfer video from a digital video camera to your computer so you can organize and edit the video before sharing it with friends and family.

Share Your Computer

If you share your computer with other people, you can create a separate user account for each person to keep the personal files and settings for each person separate. You can also change the capabilities for a user account, share files with other users and delete a user account you no longer need.

Access the Internet

Mac OS offers several applications you can use to access the Internet. Internet Explorer allows you to browse through information on the Web. You can use Sherlock to search the Internet for information of interest, including stock information and movies playing in your area. You can use Mail to exchange electronic mail and iChat to exchange instant messages and files over the Internet with friends and family.

THE MAC OS X SCREEN

The Mac OS X screen displays various items that allow you to perform tasks on your computer.

MENU BAR

Provides access to lists of commands available in the active application. The menu bar displays the name of the active application, such as Finder.

WINDOW

Displays information such as the contents of a file or folder. A window can usually be moved or resized.

TITLE BAR

Displays the name of an open window.

TOOLBAR

Contains buttons that provide quick access to frequently used commands in a window.

ICON

An item on the desktop, in a window or in the Dock. An icon can represent an item such as a file or folder.

DISK ICONS

Provide quick access to the contents of your hard disk, CDs, DVDs and other types of disks.

DESKTOP

The background area of your screen.

FINDER

Allows you to perform common tasks with the files and folders on your computer, such as moving, deleting and searching for files and folders. Finder starts automatically each time you start your computer. You cannot quit Finder.

DOCK

Provides quick access to commonly used applications, such as Mail ( ), Internet Explorer ( ) and System Preferences ( ). A triangle (▲) appears below the icon for each application that is currently open.

You can display or hide the toolbar in a window. A toolbar contains buttons that help you quickly perform common tasks.

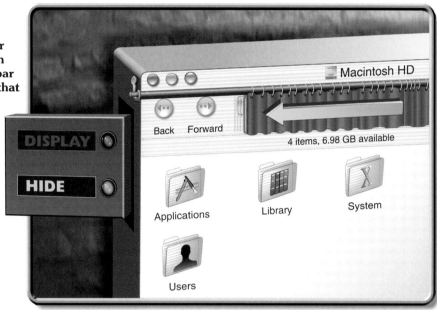

For example, the toolbar in a Finder window contains buttons you can use to move through windows and buttons you can use to change the appearance of items in a window.

Hiding the toolbar reduces clutter in a window.

DISPLAY OR HIDE THE TOOLBAR

1 To display or hide the toolbar in a window, click ⬭ in the window.

Note: If the ⬭ button is not available in a window, you cannot hide the toolbar in the window.

■ The toolbar appears or disappears.

■ If a window is not wide enough to show all the buttons on the toolbar, arrows (≫) appear at the right side of the toolbar. You can click the arrows (≫) to display a menu of the hidden buttons and select the button you want to use.

USING THE DOCK

You can use the Dock to quickly access frequently used applications.

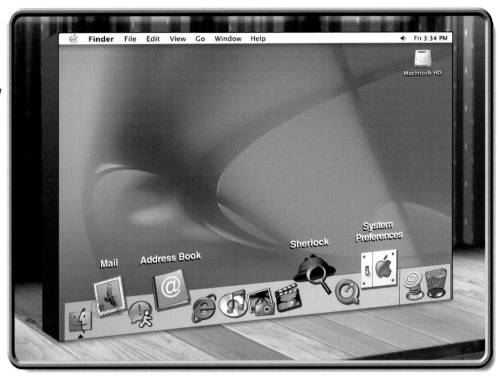

The Dock automatically displays icons for several applications, such as Mail, Address Book, Sherlock and System Preferences.

USING THE DOCK

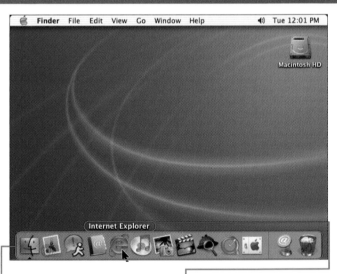

■ By default, the Dock appears at the bottom of your screen and displays the icons for several applications.

■ A triangle (▲) appears below the icon for each application that is currently open.

IDENTIFY A DOCK ICON

1 To identify an icon in the Dock, position the mouse ► over the icon.

■ The name of the icon appears above the Dock.

Will other icons appear in the Dock as I work?

When you open an application that does not appear in the Dock by default, an icon for the application appears to the left of the line in the Dock. The icon for the application will disappear when you quit the application.

When you minimize a window, an icon for the window appears to the right of the line in the Dock. To minimize a window, see page 14.

Open
Application

Minimized
Window

Can I use the Dock to quickly quit an application?

Yes. Press and hold down the `control` key as you click the icon for the application you want to quit. On the menu that appears, click **Quit** to quit the application.

OPEN AN APPLICATION

1 To open an application displayed in the Dock, click the icon for the application.

■ When you open an application, the application's icon bounces while the application opens.

■ The application appears on your screen.

QUIT AN APPLICATION

1 When you finish working with an application, click the icon for the application in the Dock.

■ This area displays the menu bar for the application you selected.

2 Click the name of the application in the menu bar.

3 Click **Quit** to quit the application.

Note: You cannot quit the Finder application.

9

SCROLL THROUGH A WINDOW

You can use a scroll bar to browse through the information in a window. Scrolling is useful when a window is not large enough to display all the information it contains.

SCROLL THROUGH A WINDOW

SCROLL UP OR DOWN

1 Click ▲ or ▼ to scroll up or down through the information in a window.

Note: If all the information in a window is displayed, you cannot scroll through the window.

SCROLL TO ANY POSITION

1 Position the mouse ▶ over the scroller on a scroll bar.

2 Drag the scroller along the scroll bar until the information you want to view appears.

■ The location of the scroller indicates which part of the window you are viewing. For example, when the scroller is halfway down the scroll bar, you are viewing information from the middle of the window.

CLOSE A WINDOW

When you finish
working with a
window, you can
close the window
to remove it from
your screen.

CLOSE A WINDOW

1 Click ⬤ in the window
you want to close.

■ The window disappears
from your screen.

*Note: To close all windows in the
same application at once, such
as all your open word processing
files, press and hold down the*
`option` *key as you click* ⬤ *in
one of the application's windows.*

MOVE A WINDOW

If a window covers items on your screen, you can move the window to a different location on the screen.

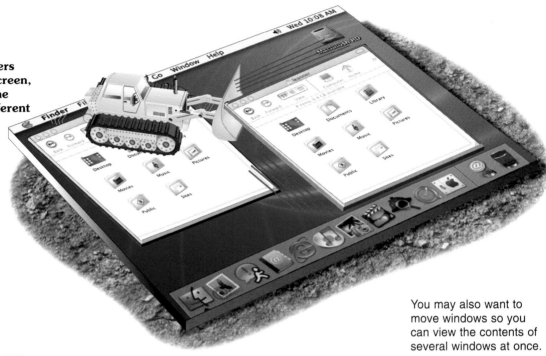

You may also want to move windows so you can view the contents of several windows at once.

MOVE A WINDOW

1 Position the mouse ▶ over the title bar of the window you want to move.

2 Drag the mouse ▶ to where you want to place the window.

■ The window moves to the new location.

RESIZE A WINDOW

You can easily change
the size of a window
displayed on your
screen.

Increasing the size of a
window allows you to
view more information in
the window. Decreasing
the size of a window
allows you to view items
covered by the window.

RESIZE A WINDOW

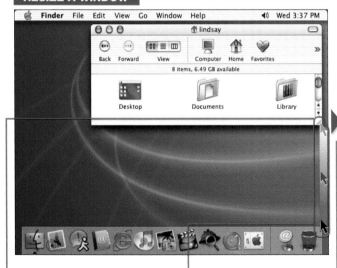

1 Position the mouse ▲
over ▨ at the bottom
right corner of the window
you want to resize.

2 Drag the mouse ▲
until the window displays
the size you want.

■ The window displays
the new size.

MINIMIZE A WINDOW

If you are not using a window, you can minimize the window to temporarily move it out of the way. You can redisplay the window at any time.

Minimizing a window allows you to temporarily put the window aside so you can work on other tasks.

MINIMIZE A WINDOW

1 Click ⬤ in the window you want to minimize.

■ You can also double-click the title bar of a window to minimize the window.

■ The window reduces to an icon in the Dock.

■ To redisplay the window, click its icon in the Dock.

Note: To minimize all windows in the same application at once, such as all your open word processing files, press and hold down the `option` *key as you click ⬤ in one of the application's windows.*

ZOOM A WINDOW

You can zoom a window to display more or less of the window's contents.

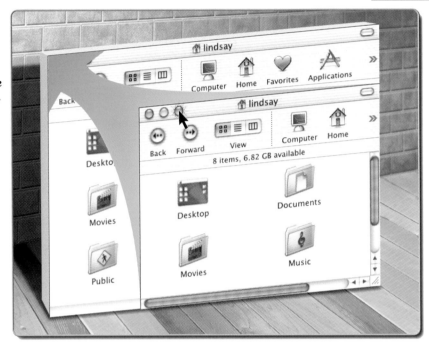

ZOOM A WINDOW

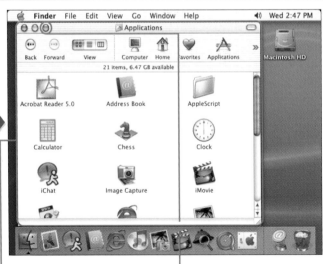

1 Click ⬤ in the window you want to zoom.

■ The window is enlarged to display more of its contents or reduced to display less of its contents.

■ To return the window to its previous size, click ⬤ again.

ARRANGE ICONS IN A WINDOW

You can arrange the icons displayed in a window to help you find files and folders more quickly.

You can arrange icons in a window by name, size, kind or the date the items were last changed or created.

ARRANGE ICONS IN A WINDOW

1 Click a blank area in the window that contains the icons you want to arrange.

Note: To arrange the icons on your desktop, click a blank area on the desktop.

2 Click **View**.

3 Click **Arrange**.

4 Click the way you want to arrange the icons in the window.

Note: The Arrange command is available only when files are displayed as icons. To change the view of files, see page 32.

■ The icons are arranged in the window. In this example, the icons are arranged by name.

CLEAN UP A WINDOW

You can clean up a window by neatly arranging the files and folders in the window.

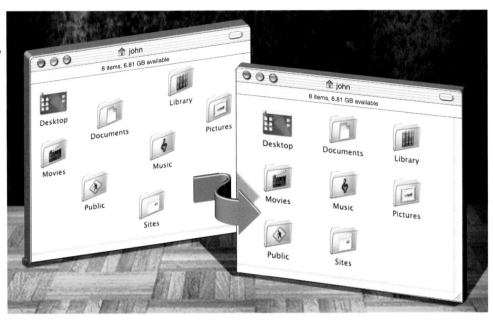

CLEAN UP A WINDOW

1 Click a blank area in the window you want to clean up.

Note: To clean up the icons on your desktop, click a blank area on the desktop.

2 Click **View**.

3 Click **Clean Up**.

Note: The Clean Up command is available only when files are displayed as icons. To change the view of files, see page 32.

■ The icons move to the nearest empty positions in the window's invisible grid.

SWITCH BETWEEN WINDOWS

If you have more than one window open on your screen, you can easily switch between the windows.

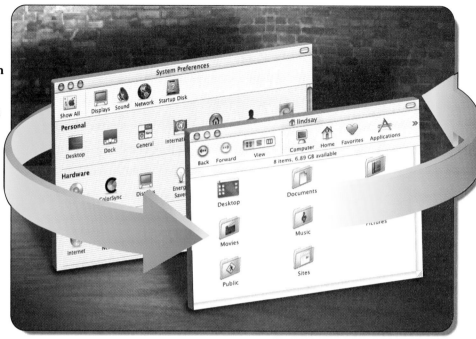

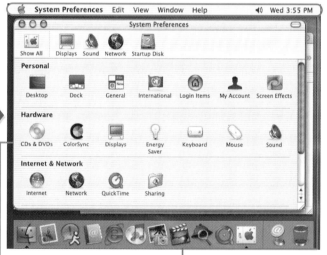

■ You can work in only one window at a time. The active window appears in front of all other windows.

1 Click inside a window you want to make the active window.

■ The window becomes active and appears in front of all other windows. You can now clearly view the contents of the window.

■ This area displays the menu bar for the active window.

Note: The menu bar changes, depending on the active window. You should make sure the window you want to work with is the active window before using the menu bar to perform a task.

FORCE AN APPLICATION TO QUIT

If an application is no longer responding, you can force the application to quit without having to shut down your computer.

When you force an application to quit, you will lose any information you did not save in the application.

Forcing an application to quit should not affect other open applications.

FORCE AN APPLICATION TO QUIT

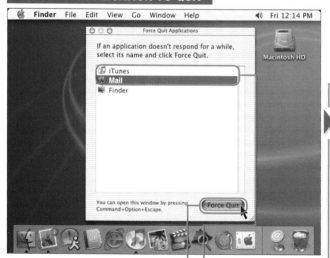

1 To force an application to quit, press and hold down the `option` and `⌘` keys as you press the `esc` key.

■ The Force Quit Applications window appears, listing the applications that are currently open.

2 Click the application you want to quit.

3 Click **Force Quit**.

■ A dialog sheet appears, confirming that you want to quit the application.

4 Click **Force Quit** to quit the application.

5 Click ⬤ to close the Force Quit Applications window.

Note: You can try starting the application again. If you continue to have problems, try re-installing the application or contact the application's manufacturer for help.

RESTART YOUR COMPUTER

If your computer is not operating properly, you can restart the computer to try to fix the problem.

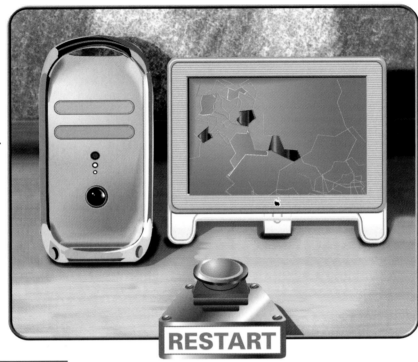

Restarting your computer shuts down the computer and then immediately starts it again.

RESTART YOUR COMPUTER

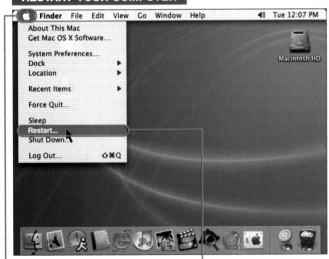

■ Before restarting your computer, make sure you close any files and applications you have open.

1 Click to display the Apple menu.

2 Click **Restart**.

■ A dialog box appears, confirming that you want to restart your computer.

3 Click **Restart** to restart your computer.

SHUT DOWN YOUR COMPUTER

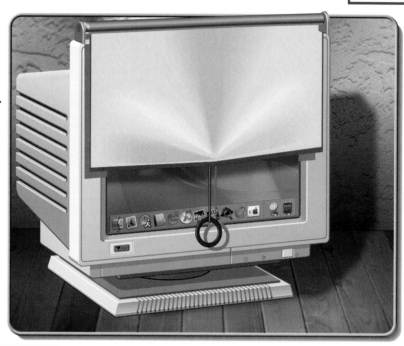

When you finish using
your computer, you
should shut down the
computer to turn it off.

If you turn off the
power to your
computer without
first shutting down
the computer, you
could lose data.

SHUT DOWN YOUR COMPUTER

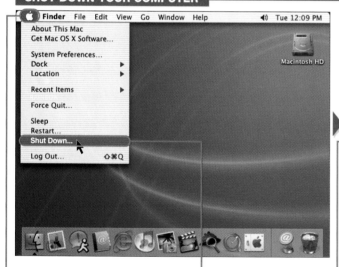

■ Before shutting down
your computer, make sure
you close any files and
applications you have open.

1 Click to display the
Apple menu.

2 Click **Shut Down**.

■ A dialog box appears,
confirming that you want to
shut down your computer.

3 Click **Shut Down** to
shut down your computer.

GETTING HELP

If you do not know how to perform a task on your computer, you can use the Help Viewer to find information on the task.

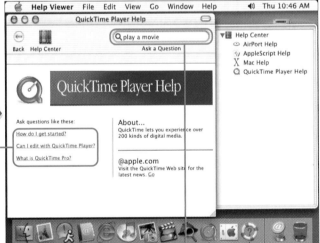

1 Click **Help**.

2 Click the Help command.

Note: The name of the Help command depends on the active application.

■ The Help window appears.

■ This area displays the Help Center drawer, which lists common Help sections and Help sections you have recently viewed. You can click a Help section to display the main page of that section.

■ This area may display a list of frequently asked questions about the active application. You can click a question of interest to display a list of related help topics.

3 To search for specific help information about any Mac OS topic, click this area and type a word or phrase that describes the topic of interest.

4 To start the search, press the return key.

Why does a blue, underlined phrase appear at the bottom of some help topics?

Some help topics display a blue, underlined phrase that you can click to obtain additional help.

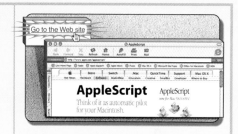

Tell me more

Displays a list of related help topics. You can double-click a help topic of interest to display the help topic.

Open *application or feature* for me

Opens a specific application or feature that allows you to perform the task discussed in the help topic.

Go to the Web site

Displays a Web site in your Web browser so you can find the latest information available for the help topic.

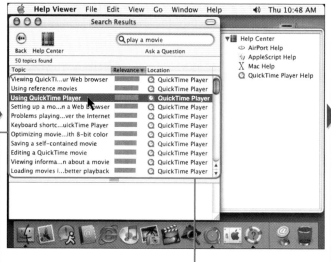

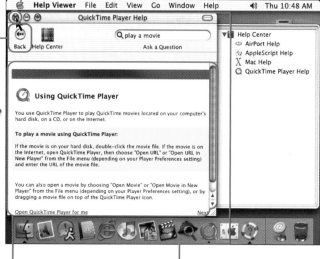

■ This area lists help topics related to the word or phrase you entered. A bar beside each help topic indicates the relevance of the topic to the word or phrase you entered.

5 Double-click a help topic of interest.

■ The information for the help topic you selected appears.

■ To return to the previous help page, you can click the **Back** button.

6 When you finish reviewing help information, click ○ to close the Help window.

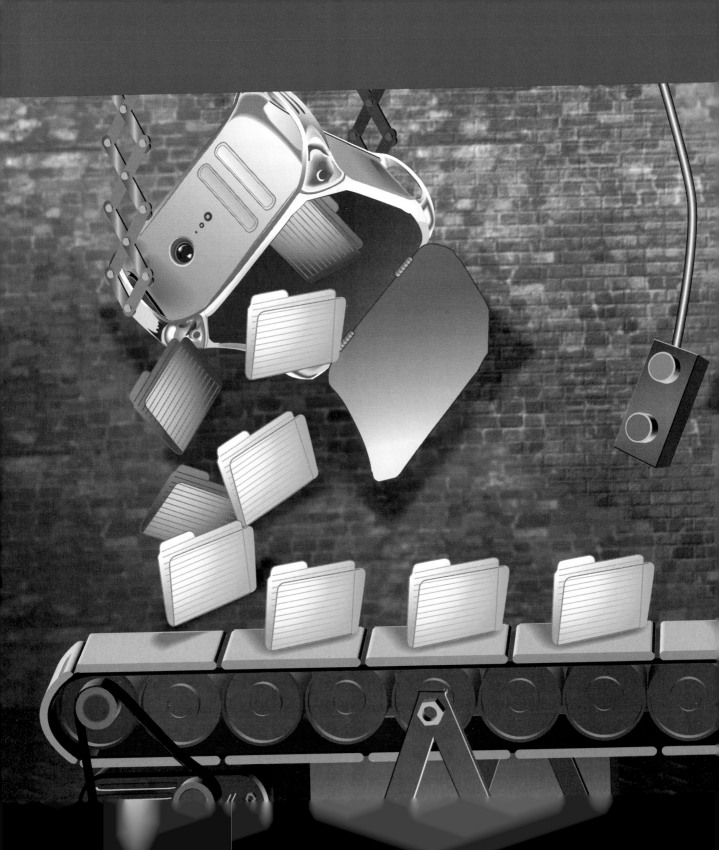

CHAPTER 2

View Files

Read this chapter to learn how to view the files and folders stored on your computer as well as the contents of a CD or DVD.

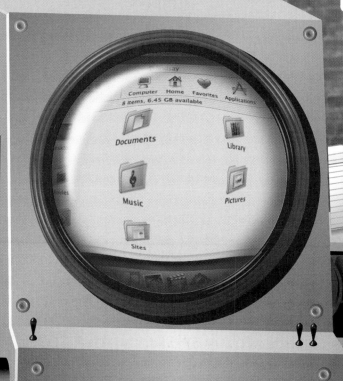

VIEW

VIEW PERSONAL FOLDERS AND APPLICATIONS

You can view the personal folders and applications stored on your computer.

The home folder stores your personal folders, which provide a convenient place for you to store and manage your files.

The Applications folder stores the applications available on your computer. Mac OS comes with many applications that you can use.

VIEW PERSONAL FOLDERS

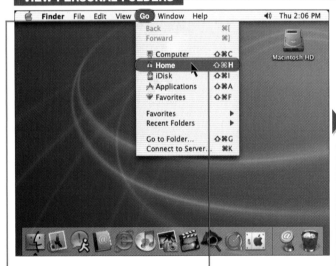

1 Click **Go**.

Note: If Go is not available, click a blank area on your desktop to display the Finder menu bar.

2 Click **Home** to view your personal folders.

■ A window appears, displaying your personal folders.

■ To display the contents of a personal folder, double-click the folder.

■ You can also click **Home** in any open window to view your personal folders.

3 When you finish viewing your personal folders, click ⬤ to close the window.

What personal folders does Mac OS include?

Desktop Stores the items displayed on the desktop.		**Movies, Music and Pictures** Provide convenient places to store your movies, music and pictures.	
Documents Provides a convenient place to store files you create.		**Public** Stores files you want to share with every user on your computer. For more information on the Public folder, see page 225.	
Library Stores items such as fonts, screen savers and sounds for your user account.		**Sites** Stores Web pages you created that you want to make available on the Internet.	

VIEW APPLICATIONS

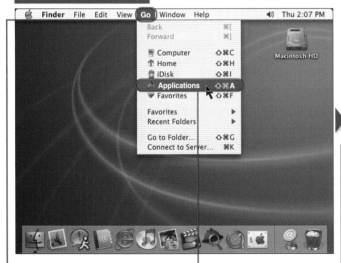

1 Click **Go**.

Note: If Go is not available, click a blank area on your desktop to display the Finder menu bar.

2 Click **Applications** to view the applications available on your computer.

■ The Applications window appears, displaying the applications available on your computer.

■ To start an application, double-click the application.

■ You can also click **Applications** in any open window to view the applications available on your computer.

3 When you finish viewing the applications available on your computer, click ● to close the Applications window.

VIEW THE CONTENTS OF YOUR COMPUTER

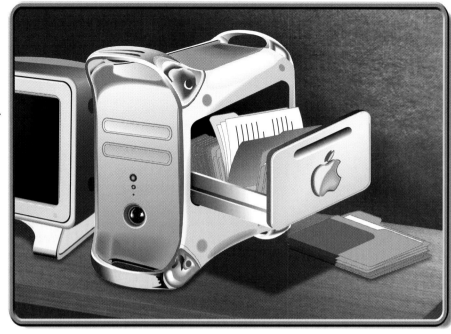

You can browse through the disks, folders and files on your computer.

Mac OS uses folders to organize the information stored on your computer.

VIEW THE CONTENTS OF YOUR COMPUTER

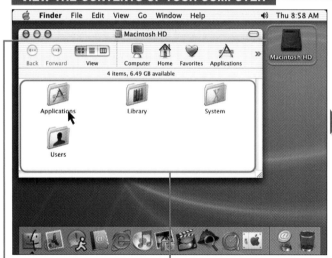

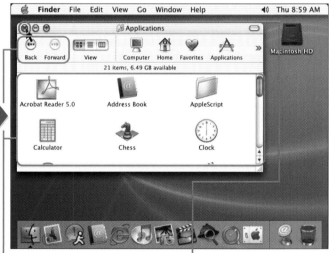

VIEW THE CONTENTS OF YOUR HARD DISK

1 Double-click your hard disk icon on the desktop to view the contents of your hard disk.

■ A window appears, displaying the contents of your hard disk.

2 To display the contents of a folder, double-click the folder.

■ The contents of the folder you selected appear.

■ To display the contents of another folder, double-click the folder.

■ You can click **Back** or **Forward** to move backward or forward through the windows you have viewed.

Note: The Forward button is available only after you click the Back button.

3 When you finish viewing the contents of your hard disk, click ⊙ to close the window.

What folders does Mac OS automatically include on my hard disk?

Applications

Stores the applications available on your computer, such as Internet Explorer and TextEdit.

Library

Stores system items available to every user account on your computer, such as desktop pictures, fonts and screen savers.

System

Stores a Library folder that contains the files Mac OS requires to run.

Users

Stores a home folder for each user account on your computer. For more information on the Users folder, see page 224.

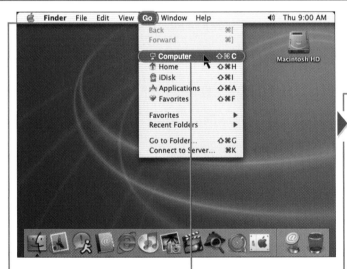

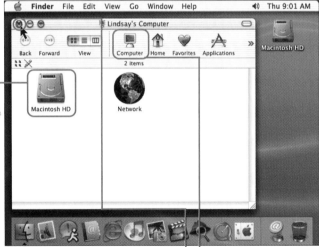

VIEW THE CONTENTS OF YOUR COMPUTER

1 Click **Go**.

Note: If Go is not available, click a blank area on your desktop to display the Finder menu bar.

2 Click **Computer** to view the disks available on your computer.

Note: The desktop also displays the disks available on your computer.

■ The Computer window appears, displaying an icon for each disk available on your computer, including your hard disk and any CD or DVD inserted into a drive on your computer.

■ To display the contents of a disk, double-click the disk.

■ You can also click **Computer** in any open window to view the disks available on your computer.

3 When you finish viewing the contents of your computer, click ⬤ to close the Computer window.

VIEW THE CONTENTS OF A DISC

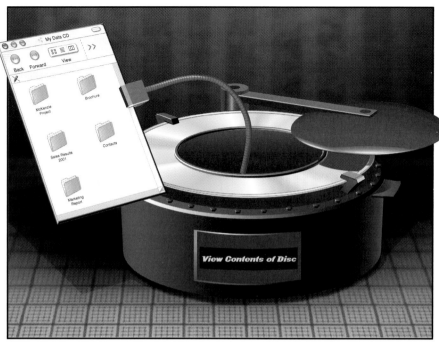

You can view the contents of a CD, DVD or other type of disc. When you finish working with a disc, you can eject the disc from your computer.

The drive(s) available on your computer determine what types of discs you can view. For example, in addition to viewing the contents of CDs or DVDs, you may also be able to view the contents of Jaz or Zip disks.

VIEW THE CONTENTS OF A DISC

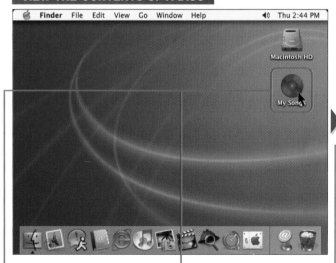

1 Insert a CD, DVD or other type of disc into your computer's drive.

■ An icon for the disc appears on your desktop.

2 Double-click the disc's icon to view the contents of the disc.

■ A window appears, displaying the contents of the disc.

3 When you finish viewing the contents of the disc, click ◯ to close the window.

Why did my computer's drive eject my disc?

Your computer's drive may eject a disc if there is a problem with the disc. For example, you may need to clean the disc or the disc may be unreadable due to scratches.

Why did a dialog box appear when I tried to eject a disc?

A dialog box may appear if one or more files on the disc are open when you try to eject the disc. To close the dialog box, click **OK**. Close the files that are open and quit any applications that may be using files on the disc. Then try to eject the disc again.

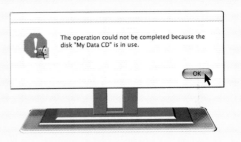

The operation could not be completed because the disk "My Data CD" is in use.

OK

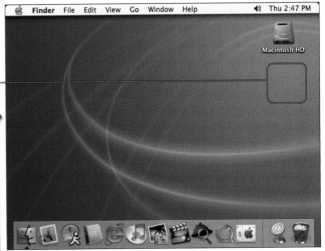

EJECT A DISC

1 To eject a disc, position the mouse ▶ over the disc's icon on your desktop.

2 Drag the disc's icon to the Trash icon (🗑 changes to ⏏).

■ The disc's icon disappears from your desktop and the disc is physically ejected from the drive.

Note: If your keyboard has an Eject key, you can also press the Eject key to eject the disc.

CHANGE THE VIEW OF ITEMS IN A WINDOW

You can change the view of items in a window.

CHANGE THE VIEW OF ITEMS IN A WINDOW

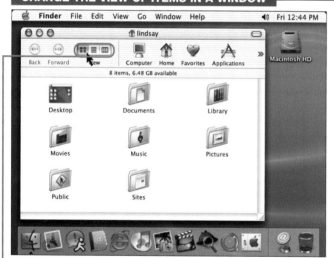

1 Click a button to specify the way you want to view items in the window.

⊞	Icons
≡	List
▥	Columns

ICONS

■ The Icons view displays items as icons.

■ By default, the name of each item appears below each icon.

Can I sort items displayed in the List view?

Yes. You can sort items by name, date last modified, size or kind. Click the heading for the column you want to use to sort the items. To sort the items in the reverse order, you can click the heading again.

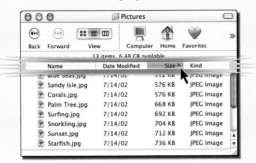

How do I change the width of a column in the List view?

To change the width of a column in the List view, position the mouse ᛏ over the right edge of the column heading (ᛏ changes to ↔) and then drag the column edge until the column displays the width you want.

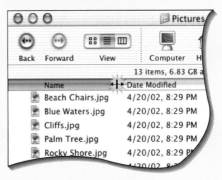

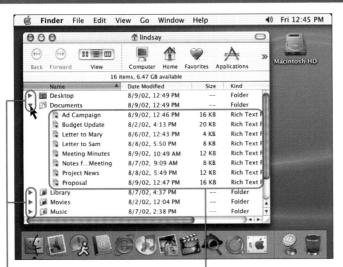

LIST

■ The List view displays items as small icons arranged in a list. This view displays information about each item, including the name, date last modified, size and kind of item.

1 To display the contents of a folder, click ► beside the folder (► changes to ▼).

■ The contents of the folder appear.

Note: To once again hide the contents of a folder, click ▼ beside the folder.

COLUMNS

■ The Columns view shows the location of the current folder in relation to the disks, folders and files on your computer.

Note: The leftmost column shows the disks on your computer. Each of the following columns shows the contents of the item selected in the previous column.

1 To display the contents of a folder, click the folder.

■ The contents of the folder appear in the next column.

DISPLAY FILE INFORMATION

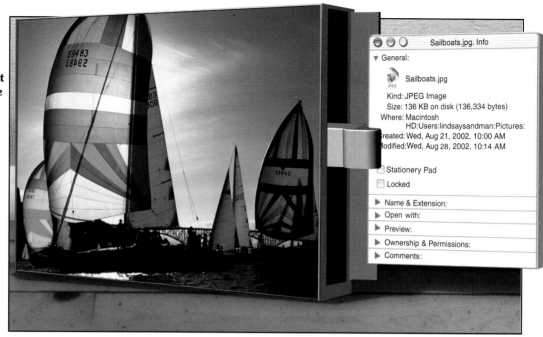

You can display information about a file, such as the file size and date you last modified the file.

You can display information about folders, disks, applications and aliases the same way you display information about files.

DISPLAY FILE INFORMATION

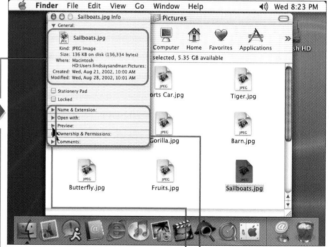

1 Click a file of interest.

2 Click **File**.

3 Click **Get Info**.

■ The Info window appears, displaying general information about the file, including the name, kind, size, location and dates the file was created and last modified.

■ This area displays additional categories of information you can display for the file.

4 To display the information in a category, click ► beside the category of interest (► changes to ▼).

What additional categories of information can I display for a file?

Name & Extension

Allows you to view and change the **file name** and **extension** of a file, such as **Report.rtf**.

Open with

Allows you to view and change the application that opens a file.

Preview

Allows you to preview some types of files, such as pictures, movies and sounds. If a preview is unavailable, a larger version of the file's icon appears.

Ownership & Permissions

Allows you to specify who owns a file and who you want to be able to access the file. This is useful if you share your computer with other people or are connected to a network.

Comments

Allows you to enter and view comments about a file.

■ The information in the category appears. In this example, a preview of the file appears.

■ To once again hide the information in the category, click ▼.

5 When you finish reviewing information about the file, click ⬤ to close the Info window.

■ You can repeat steps **1** to **5** to display information about another file.

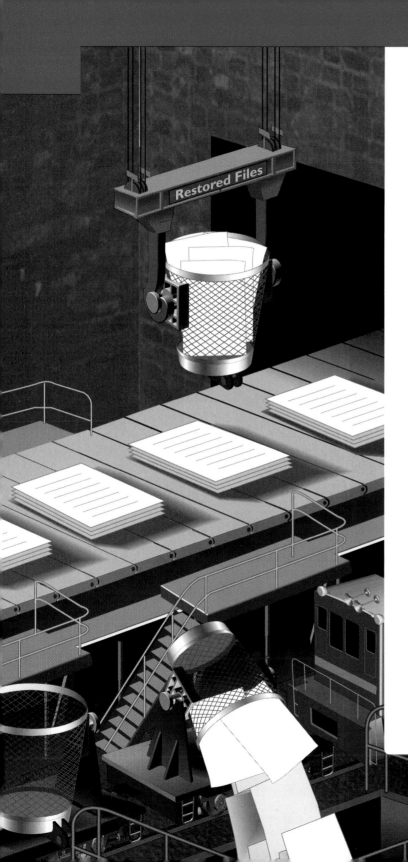

CHAPTER 3

Work With Files

This chapter teaches you how to efficiently manage your files. Learn how to duplicate files, print files, search for files, copy files to a CD or DVD and much more.

SELECT FILES

Before working with files, you often need to select the files you want to work with. Selected files appear highlighted on your screen.

You can select folders the same way you select files.

SELECT A FILE

1 Click the icon for the file you want to select.

■ The file is highlighted.

SELECT A GROUP OF FILES

1 Click the icon for the first file you want to select.

2 Press and hold down the shift key as you click the icon for the last file you want to select.

Note: You can use this method to select a group of files only in the List or Columns view. To change the view of files, see page 32.

■ This area displays the number of files you have selected.

How do I deselect files?

To deselect all the files in a window, click a blank area in the window.

To deselect one or more files from a group of selected files, press and hold down the ⌘ key as you click the icon for each file you want to deselect.

Note: You can deselect folders the same way you deselect files.

How can I select all the files in a window?

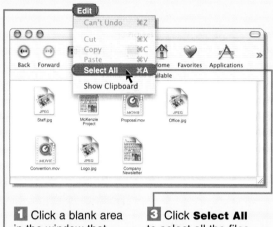

1 Click a blank area in the window that contains the files you want to select.

2 Click **Edit**.

3 Click **Select All** to select all the files in the window.

SELECT A GROUP OF FILES BY DRAGGING

1 Position the mouse ▶ slightly above and to the left of the first file you want to select.

2 Drag the mouse ▶ diagonally across the files you want to select.

■ While you drag the mouse ▶, a box appears around the files that will be selected.

SELECT RANDOM FILES

1 Click the icon for a file you want to select.

2 Press and hold down the ⌘ key as you click the icon for each additional file you want to select.

OPEN A FILE

You can open a file to display its contents on your screen. Opening a file allows you to review and make changes to the file.

You can open a folder the same way you open a file.

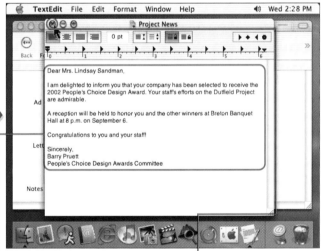

1 Double-click the icon for the file you want to open.

■ The file opens. You can review and make changes to the file.

Note: If you opened a picture, the picture opens in the Preview application. The Preview application allows you to only review the picture. For information on the Preview application, see page 120.

2 When you finish working with the file, click ⬤ to close the file.

OPEN A RECENTLY USED APPLICATION OR FILE

Mac OS keeps track of the applications and files you have recently used. You can quickly open any of these applications or files.

OPEN A RECENTLY USED APPLICATION OR FILE

1 Click to display the Apple menu.

2 Position the mouse ▶ over **Recent Items**.

■ A list of applications and files you have recently used appears.

3 Click the application or file you want to open.

■ The application or file you selected opens.

*Note: To clear the list of applications and files you have recently used, perform steps 1 to 3, selecting **Clear Menu** in step 3. Clearing the list of recently used applications and files will not delete the applications and files from your computer.*

RENAME A FILE

You can rename a file to better describe the contents of the file. Renaming a file can help you more quickly locate the file in the future.

You can rename folders the same way you rename files.

RENAME A FILE

1 Click the name of the file you want to rename.

■ After a moment, a box appears around the file name and the file name is selected.

Note: If a box does not appear around the file name, press the return *key.*

2 Type a new name for the file and then press the return key.

Note: A file name can contain up to 256 letters, spaces and symbols. A file name cannot contain a colon (:) or begin with a period (.). Each file in the same location must have a unique name.

You can quickly create a duplicate of a file.

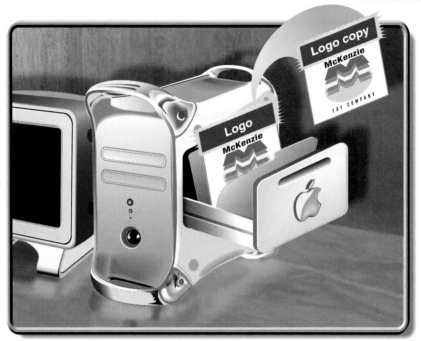

Creating a duplicate of a file is useful if you plan to make major changes to a file, but you want to keep a copy of the original file. Creating a duplicate gives you two copies of a file—the original file and a file that you can change.

You can duplicate a folder the same way you duplicate a file. When you duplicate a folder, all the files in the folder are also duplicated.

DUPLICATE A FILE

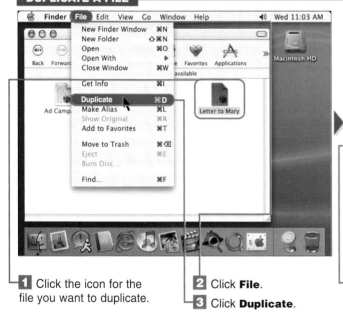

1 Click the icon for the file you want to duplicate.

2 Click **File**.

3 Click **Duplicate**.

■ A duplicate of the file appears. The word "copy" appears in the name of the duplicate file.

Note: To move the duplicate file to another location on your computer, see page 44. To rename the duplicate file, see page 42.

MOVE OR COPY A FILE

You can move or copy a file to a new location on your computer.

You can move or copy a folder the same way you move or copy a file. When you move or copy a folder, all the files in the folder are also moved or copied.

MOVE A FILE

■ Before moving a file, make sure you can clearly see the location where you want to move the file.

1 Position the mouse ▶ over the file you want to move.

2 Drag the file to a new location.

Note: You can move a file to the desktop, a folder or to another disk.

■ The file moves to the new location.

■ The file disappears from its original location.

Can I move or copy more than one file at once?

To move or copy more than one file at once, you need to select all the files you want to move or copy. To select multiple files, see page 38.

To move the selected files, drag one of the files to the new location. To copy the selected files, press and hold down the `option` key as you drag one of the files to the new location. All the selected files will be moved or copied to the new location.

When I drag a file to another disk, why does Mac OS copy rather than move the file?

When you drag a file to another disk displayed on your desktop, Mac OS creates a copy of the file on the other disk. To move a file to another disk instead of copying the file, press and hold down the ⌘ key as you drag the file.

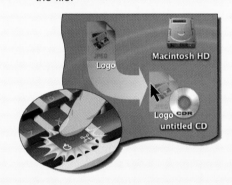

COPY A FILE

■ Before copying a file, make sure you can clearly see the location where you want to place a copy of the file.

1 Position the mouse ▶ over the file you want to copy.

2 Press and hold down the `option` key as you drag the file to a new location (▶ changes to ➕).

Note: You can copy a file to the desktop, a folder or to another disk.

■ A copy of the file appears in the new location.

■ The original file remains in the original location.

DELETE A FILE

You can delete a file you no longer need. The Trash stores all the files you delete.

If you regret deleting a file, you can restore the file from the Trash.

You can delete a folder the same way you delete a file. When you delete a folder, all the files in the folder are also deleted.

DELETE A FILE

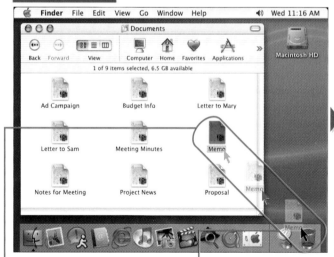

1 Position the mouse ▶ over the file you want to delete.

2 Drag the file to the Trash icon.

Note: To delete a file, you can also click the icon for the file and then press and hold down the ⌘ *key as you press the* delete *key.*

■ The file is moved to the Trash in case you later want to restore the file.

Can I delete or restore more than one file at a time?

To delete more than one file at a time, select all the files you want to delete. Then drag one of the selected files to the Trash icon. All the files you selected will move to the Trash. To select multiple files, see page 38.

To restore more than one deleted file at a time, select all the files in the Trash window that you want to restore. Then drag one of the selected files to the desktop or to a folder.

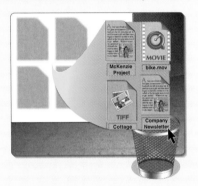

How do I know if the Trash contains deleted files?

The appearance of the Trash icon indicates whether the Trash contains deleted files.

Does not contain deleted files.

Contains deleted files.

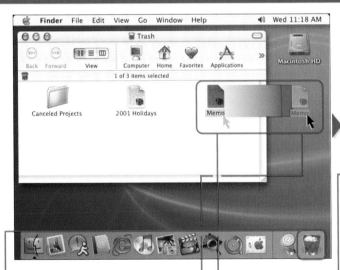

RESTORE A DELETED FILE

1 Click the Trash icon.

■ The Trash window appears, displaying all the files you have deleted.

2 Position the mouse ▶ over the file you want to restore.

3 Drag the file to the desktop or to a folder.

■ The file disappears from the Trash window and moves to the location you specified.

4 Click ⬤ to close the Trash window.

EMPTY THE TRASH

You can empty the Trash to create more free space on your computer. The Trash stores all the files you have deleted.

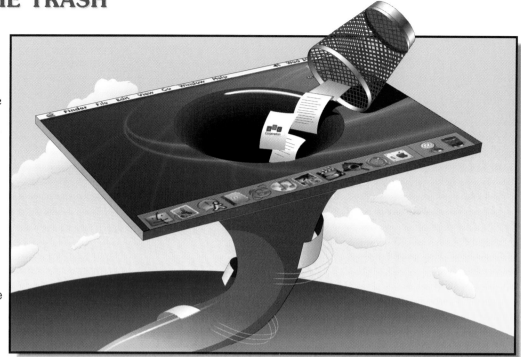

Files you delete remain in the Trash until you empty the Trash.

When you empty the Trash, all the files in the Trash are permanently removed from your computer and cannot be restored.

EMPTY THE TRASH

1 Click the Trash icon.

■ The Trash window appears, displaying all the files you have deleted.

2 Click **Finder**.

3 Click **Empty Trash**.

■ A warning dialog box appears, confirming that you want to permanently remove all the files in the Trash.

4 Click **OK** to permanently remove all the files in the Trash and close the Trash window.

You can create a new folder to help you organize the files stored on your computer.

Creating a new folder is useful when you want to keep related files together, such as the files for a particular project.

After you create a new folder, you can move files and other folders to the new folder. To move files and folders, see page 44.

CREATE A FOLDER

1 Click anywhere in the window for the folder you want to contain a new folder.

■ To create a new folder on your desktop, click a blank area on the desktop.

2 Click **File**.

3 Click **New Folder**.

■ The new folder appears, displaying a temporary name.

4 Type a name for the new folder and then press the `return` key.

Note: If you cannot type a name, press the `return` key and then perform step 4.

■ A folder name can contain up to 256 letters, spaces and symbols. A folder name cannot contain a colon (:) or begin with a period (.). Each folder in the same location must have a unique name.

CREATE AN ALIAS

You can create an alias for a file you frequently use to provide a quick way of opening the file.

An alias points to an original file. If you delete the original file, the alias will no longer work.

You can create an alias for a folder or an application the same way you create an alias for a file. Creating an alias for a folder will give you quick access to all the files in the folder. Creating an alias for an application allows you to quickly start the application.

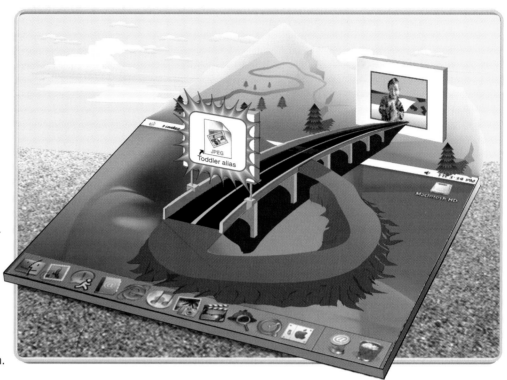

1 Click the icon for the file you want to create an alias for.

2 Click **File**.

3 Click **Make Alias**.

■ The alias appears.

■ The icon for the alias looks like the icon for the original file, but displays an arrow (↗).

How do I rename or delete an alias?

You can rename or delete an alias the same way you rename or delete any file. Renaming or deleting an alias will not affect the original file.

Rename an Alias

Click the name of the alias you want to rename. Type a new name for the alias and then press the return key. The name of an alias does not need to contain the word "alias." For more information on renaming files, see page 42.

Delete an Alias

Position the mouse ▶ over the icon for the alias you want to delete and then drag the alias to the Trash icon in the Dock. For more information on deleting files, see page 46.

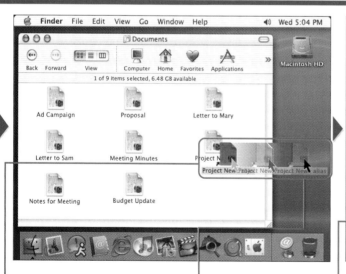

4 To move the alias to the desktop or to another location on your computer, position the mouse ▶ over the alias.

5 Drag the alias to the desktop or to another location.

■ The alias appears in the new location.

■ To use the alias to open the original file, double-click the alias.

PRINT A FILE

You can produce a paper copy of a file stored on your computer.

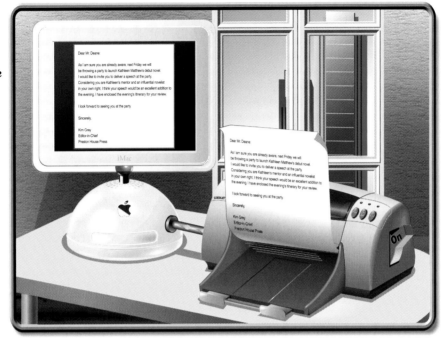

Before printing, make sure your printer is turned on and contains paper.

PRINT A FILE

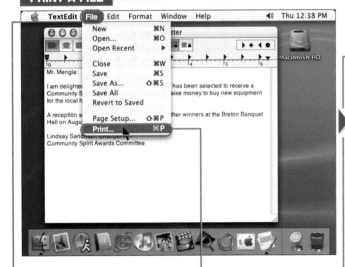

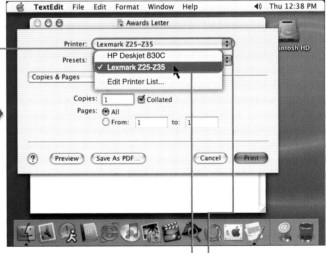

1 Open the file you want to print. To open a file, see page 40.

2 Click **File**.

3 Click **Print** to print the file.

Note: The name of the Print command depends on the active application.

■ A dialog sheet appears.

■ This area displays the printer your computer will use to print the file.

4 To change the printer your computer will use, click this area to display a list of the available printers.

5 Click the printer you want to use to print the file.

Can I preview a file before printing?

Yes. You can preview a file to see how the file will look when printed. To preview a file, perform steps **1** to **3** below. In the dialog sheet that appears, click **Preview**. A window appears, displaying a preview of the file. If the file contains multiple pages, a thumbnail of each page will appear on the side of the window. You can click the thumbnail of a page you want to view. When you finish previewing the file, click ⬤ to close the window.

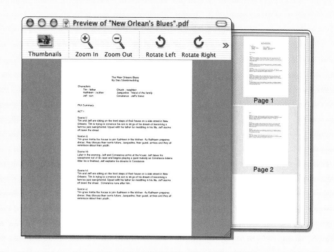

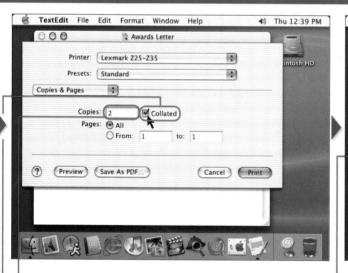

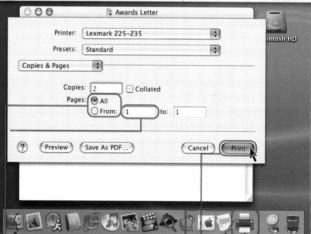

6 Double-click this area and type the number of copies of the file that you want to print.

7 If you chose to print more than one copy of the file, this option collates the copies. You can click this option to turn the option on (☑) or off (☐).

Note: The Collated option prints the pages of each copy in order (1, 2, 1, 2). If you turn off the Collated option, the copies of each page will print together (1, 1, 2, 2).

8 Click an option to specify if you want to print all the pages or a specific range of pages (◯ changes to ⬤).

9 If you selected **From** in step **8**, double-click this area and type the first page you want to print. Then press the **tab** key and type the last page you want to print.

10 Click **Print**.

■ When you print a file, the Print Center icon appears in the Dock until the file has finished printing.

MANAGE FILES WAITING TO PRINT

You can view the status of files waiting to print. You can then stop one file from printing or temporarily stop all files from printing.

Stopping a file from printing is useful if you accidentally printed the wrong file or if you want to make last-minute changes to the file. Temporarily stopping all files from printing is useful when you want to change the toner or add more paper to the printer.

When you print a file, the file is added to the printer's queue, where it waits to be printed.

MANAGE FILES WAITING TO PRINT

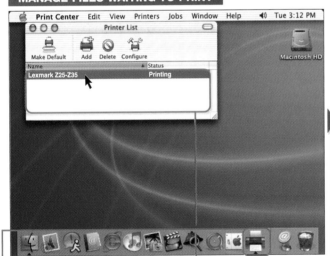

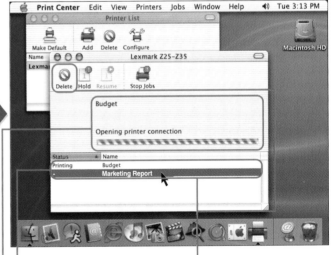

■ When you print a file, the Print Center icon appears in the Dock. The icon disappears when the file has finished printing.

1 Click the Print Center icon to be able to view the status of files waiting to print.

■ The Printer List window appears, displaying the name and status of each printer available on your computer.

2 To view the status of files waiting to print on a printer, double-click the printer.

■ A window appears, displaying the status and name of each file waiting to print. The file at the top of the list will print first.

■ This area displays the status of the printer.

CANCEL A PRINT JOB

1 Click the name of the file you no longer want to print.

2 Click **Delete** to cancel the print job.

■ The file disappears from the window and will no longer print.

Can I cancel the printing of several files at once?

Yes. To cancel the printing of several files at once, perform steps 1 and 2 in the first screen on page 54 to display the files waiting to print. Press and hold down the ⌘ key as you click the name of each file you no longer want to print. Then click **Delete** to cancel the print jobs.

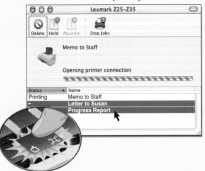

How can I pause the printing of a file?

Pausing the printing of a file is useful when you want to allow more important files to print first. To pause the printing of a file, perform steps 1 and 2 in the first screen on page 54 to display the files waiting to print. Click the name of the file you want to pause and then click **Hold**. To resume printing the file, click the name of the file and then click **Resume**.

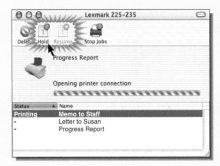

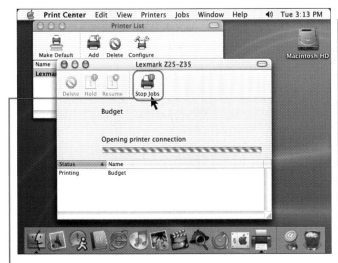

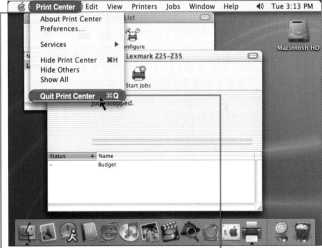

TEMPORARILY STOP ALL PRINT JOBS

1 To temporarily stop the printer from printing, click **Stop Jobs**.

*Note: After you click **Stop Jobs**, the name of the button changes to **Start Jobs** and the status of the printer changes to "Jobs Stopped."*

■ To resume printing, click **Start Jobs** at any time.

QUIT PRINT CENTER

1 When you finish managing the files waiting to print, click **Print Center**.

2 Click **Quit Print Center**.

SEARCH FOR FILES

If you cannot remember the exact name or location of a file you want to work with, you can have Mac OS search for the file on your computer.

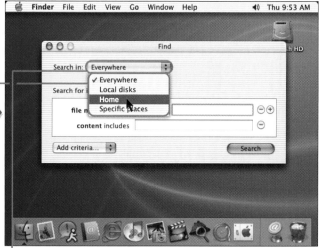

You can search for a file by file name, content and/or date. You should provide as much search information as possible to help narrow your search.

SEARCH FOR FILES

1 Click **File**.

Note: If File is not available, click a blank area on your desktop to display the Finder menu bar.

2 Click **Find** to search for a file on your computer.

■ The Find dialog box appears.

3 To specify the location you want to search, click this area to display a list of locations.

4 Click the location you want to search.

Note: **Everywhere** searches the disks on your computer and all available network disks. **Local disks** searches the disks on your computer. **Home** searches your home folder, which stores your personal files. **Specific places** allows you to specify the location you want to search.

Why do plus (⊕) and minus (⊖) signs appear in the Find dialog box?

You can click a plus sign (⊕) to display an area where you can specify additional search information. For example, you can click the plus sign next to **file name** to specify additional text in the file name you want to search for. To remove an area you do not want to include in your search, click the minus sign (⊖) beside the area.

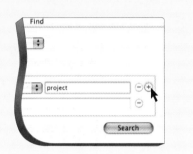

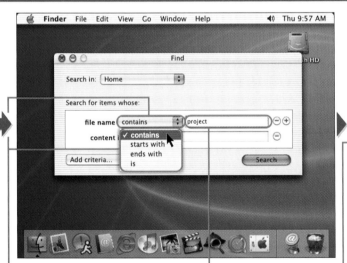

SEARCH BY NAME

5 To search by file name, click this area to display a list of options you can use to search by file name.

6 Click the file name option you want to use.

Note: You can search for a file name that contains, starts with, ends with or exactly matches text you specify.

7 Click this area and type all or part of the file name you want to search for.

SEARCH BY CONTENT

8 To search by file content, click this area and type a word or phrase that appears within the file.

CONTINUED

SEARCH FOR FILES

You can search for a file you changed or created during a specific period of time.

SEARCH FOR FILES (CONTINUED)

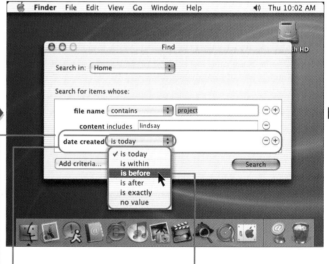

SEARCH BY DATE

9 To search for a file you worked with during a specific time period, click **Add criteria** to display a list of additional criteria you can use.

10 Click **date modified** or **date created** to search for a file you changed or created during a specific time period.

■ An area that allows you to specify a date appears.

11 Click this area to display a list of options you can use to search by date.

12 Click the date option you want to use.

What additional criteria can I use to search for a file?

Mac OS offers four additional criteria you can use to search for a file.

Kind

Searches for a specific kind of file, such as a document, image or movie, or excludes a kind of file you do not want to search for.

Size

Searches for a file based on its size in KB (kilobytes).

Extension

Searches for a file with a specific file name extension. A file name consists of a **name** and an **extension**, separated by a period, such as **Report.rtf**. The extension identifies the type of file.

Visibility

Searches for a file that is visible or invisible. Many of the files that Mac OS requires to run are invisible.

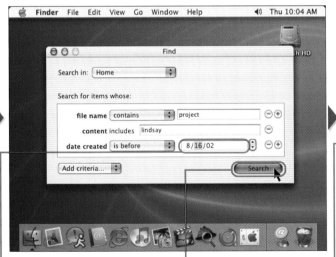

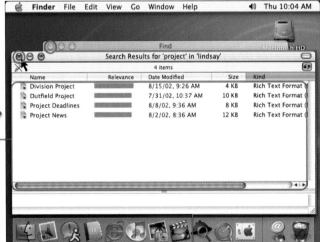

13 If you chose **is before**, **is after** or **is exactly**, click each part of the date you want to change and type the date you want to use.

■ If you chose **is within**, click the area and then select a time period from the menu that appears.

*Note: If you chose **is today** or **no value**, skip to step 14.*

START THE SEARCH

14 Click **Search** to start the search.

■ The Search Results window appears.

■ This area lists the matching files that Mac OS found and information about each file.

■ To open a file, double-click the icon for the file.

15 When you finish viewing the results of your search, click ○ to close the Search Results window.

16 Click ○ to close the Find dialog box.

USING FAVORITES

You can create a list of your favorite files, folders and applications so you can quickly access these items at any time.

USING FAVORITES

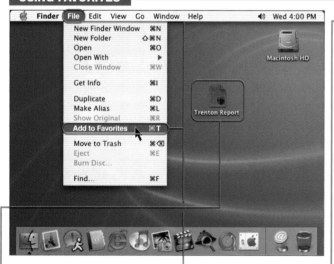

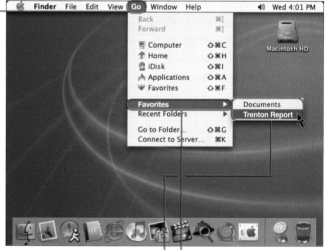

ADD A FAVORITE ITEM

1 Click the icon for the file, folder or application you want to add to your list of favorites.

2 Click **File**.

3 Click **Add to Favorites**.

■ The file, folder or application is added to your list of favorites.

OPEN A FAVORITE ITEM

1 Click **Go**.

Note: If Go is not available, click a blank area on your desktop to display the Finder menu bar.

2 Position the mouse ▶ over **Favorites**.

3 Click the favorite item you want to open.

■ The favorite item you selected opens.

Why does the Documents folder appear in my list of favorites?

Mac OS automatically adds the Documents folder to your list of favorites to give you quick access to the folder. The Documents folder provides a convenient place for storing the documents you create.

Is there another way to access my favorite items?

You can click **Favorites** in any open drive or folder window to display the Favorites window, which contains each item you have added to your list of favorites. To open an item in the Favorites window, double-click the item.

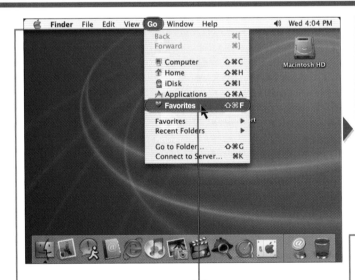

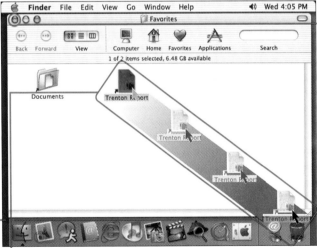

DELETE A FAVORITE ITEM

1 Click **Go**.

Note: If Go is not available, click a blank area on your desktop to display the Finder menu bar.

2 Click **Favorites**.

■ The Favorites window appears, displaying each item you have added to your list of favorites.

3 Position the mouse ▸ over the item you want to delete from your list of favorites.

4 Drag the item to the Trash icon.

■ The item will no longer appear in your list of favorites.

5 Click ⬤ to close the Favorites window.

Note: Deleting a favorite item will not delete the original item on your computer.

COPY FILES TO A CD OR DVD

You can copy files, such as pictures and movies, from your computer to a recordable CD or DVD.

To copy files to a recordable CD, you need a computer with a recordable CD drive. To copy files to a recordable DVD, you need a computer with a recordable DVD drive.

A recordable CD can typically store 650 MB of information. A recordable DVD can typically store 4.7 GB of information.

If you want to copy only songs to a recordable CD, see page 158 for information on using iTunes to create a music CD.

COPY FILES TO A CD OR DVD

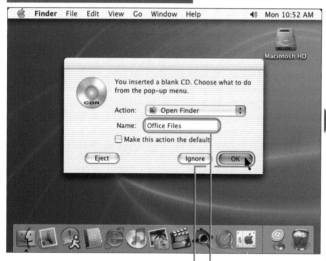

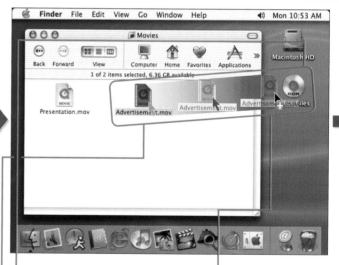

1 Insert a blank, recordable CD or DVD into your computer's recordable CD or DVD drive.

■ A dialog box appears, stating that you inserted a blank CD or DVD.

2 Type a name for the disc.

3 Click **OK** to continue.

■ An icon for the disc appears on the desktop, displaying the name you specified.

4 Position the mouse over a file you want to copy to the disc.

5 Drag the file to the disc's icon on the desktop.

6 Repeat steps **4** and **5** for each file you want to copy to the disc.

What type of disc can I copy files to?

You can copy files to a CD-R (Compact Disc-Recordable) or DVD-R (Digital Versatile Disc-Recordable). You can copy files to a CD-R or DVD-R only once. After you copy files to a CD-R or DVD-R, you cannot erase or change the contents of the disc.

If your computer has a CD-RW drive, you can also copy files to a CD-RW (Compact Disc-ReWritable). You can erase the contents of a CD-RW in order to copy new files to the disc.

Why would I copy files to a recordable CD or DVD?

You can copy files to a recordable CD or DVD to transfer large amounts of information between computers. You can also copy important files stored on your computer to a CD or DVD in case you accidentally erase the files or your computer fails.

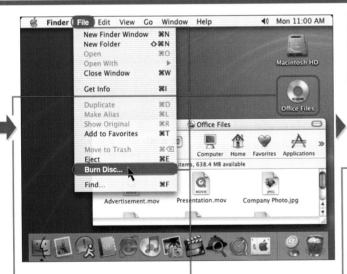

7 To display the files you selected to copy to the disc, double-click the disc's icon.

■ A window appears, displaying the files you selected to copy to the disc.

Note: If the window displays a file you no longer want to copy to the disc, drag the file to the Trash icon in the Dock to no longer copy the file.

8 To copy all the files you selected to the disc, click **File**.

9 Click **Burn Disc**.

■ A dialog box appears, confirming that you want to burn the disc.

10 Click **Burn** to copy the files to the disc.

■ The Burn Disc dialog box will appear on your screen until the copy is complete.

11 When the copy is complete, you can drag the disc's icon to the Trash icon in the Dock to eject the disc.

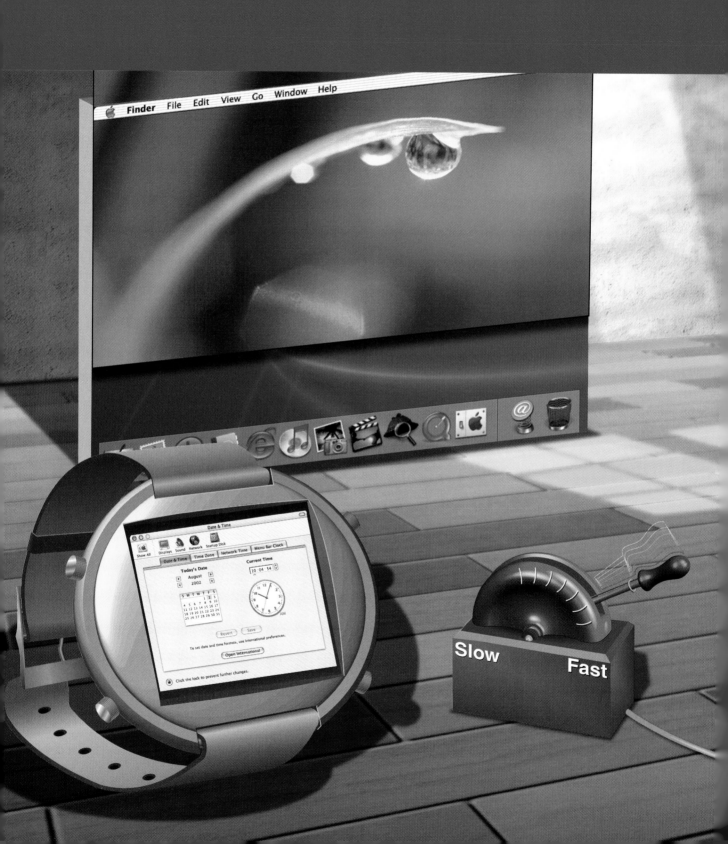

Customize Your Computer

In this chapter, you will learn how to customize your computer by changing the screen effect, desktop picture and mouse settings. You will also learn how to turn on speech recognition so you can use spoken commands to perform tasks on your computer.

ADD OR REMOVE ICONS FROM THE DOCK

You can customize the Dock to include icons for the applications, folders and files you use most often. Adding icons to the Dock gives you quick access to these items at any time.

The Dock automatically displays icons for several applications, such as Mail, Address Book, Sherlock and System Preferences.

ADD AN ICON TO THE DOCK

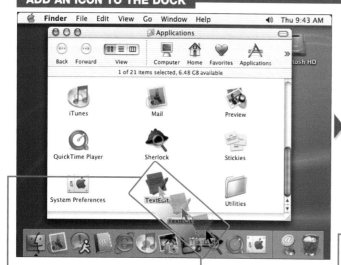

1 Locate the application, folder or file you want to add to the Dock.

2 Position the mouse ▶ over the icon for the application, folder or file.

3 Drag the icon to the Dock.

Note: Drag applications to the left of the line in the Dock. Drag folders and files to the right of the line in the Dock.

■ The icon for the application, folder or file appears in the Dock.

Note: Adding an icon to the Dock does not remove the application, folder or file from its original location on your computer.

■ To open an application, folder or file displayed in the Dock, click its icon in the Dock.

Where can I find applications that I can add to the Dock?

You can find most of the applications available on your computer in the Applications folder.

Note: If Go is not available, click a blank area on your desktop to display the Finder menu bar.

2 Click **Applications**.

1 To display the contents of the Applications folder, click **Go**.

How do I move an icon to a different location in the Dock?

To move an icon in the Dock, position the mouse ▶ over the icon and then drag the icon to a new location. The other icons in the Dock will move to make room for the icon. You cannot move the Finder or Trash icon. You also cannot move icons across the line in the Dock.

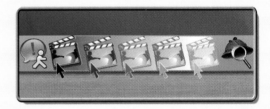

REMOVE AN ICON FROM THE DOCK

1 Position the mouse ▶ over the icon you want to remove from the Dock.

2 Drag the icon out of the Dock.

Note: You cannot remove the Finder ( ) or Trash ( ) icon from the Dock.

■ The icon disappears from the Dock in a puff of smoke.

Note: When you remove the icon for an open application, the icon will not disappear from the Dock until you quit the application.

■ Removing an icon from the Dock does not remove the application, folder or file from your computer.

CUSTOMIZE THE DOCK

You can change
the appearance
of the Dock and
the way the Dock
functions.

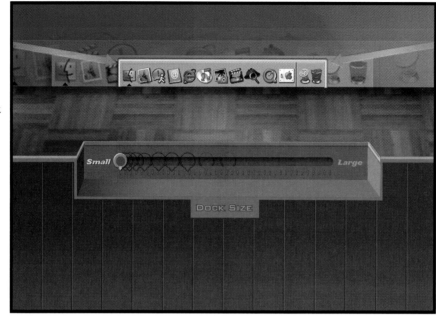

For example, you
can change the size
of the Dock and
have application
icons in the Dock
animate when you
click an icon.

CUSTOMIZE THE DOCK

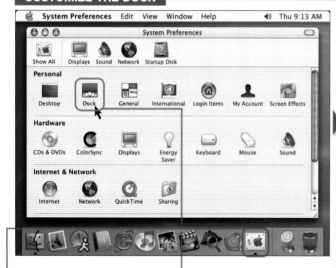

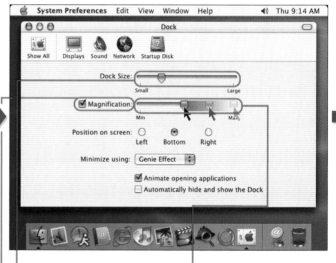

1 Click the System
Preferences icon to
access your system
preferences.

■ The System
Preferences window
appears.

2 Click **Dock** to
customize the Dock.

■ The Dock window
appears.

3 To change the size of the
Dock, drag this slider (⬤)
to decrease or increase the
size of the Dock.

4 This option magnifies
icons in the Dock when
you position the mouse ▶
over the icons. You can
click the option to turn the
option on (☑) or off (☐).

5 To change the amount
of magnification that will be
used, drag this slider (⬤)
to decrease or increase the
amount of magnification.

When the Dock is hidden, how do I redisplay the Dock?

To redisplay the Dock, position the mouse ▶ over the edge of your screen where the Dock last appeared. When you move the mouse ▶ away from the Dock, the Dock will disappear again.

 Why would I use the Magnification option when customizing the Dock?

If you decrease the size of the Dock, you can use the Magnification option to magnify icons in the Dock when you position the mouse ▶ over the icons. This will allow you to clearly view an icon you are about to select in the Dock.

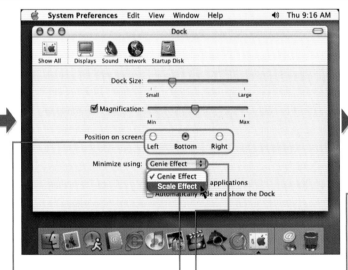

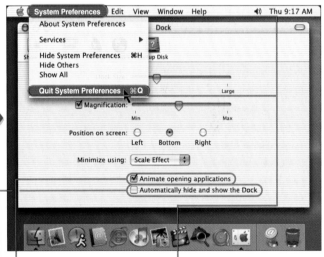

6 To change the position of the Dock on your screen, click the position you want to use (◯ changes to ◉).

7 To specify the way you want windows to minimize to icons in the Dock, click this area to display the available effects.

8 Click the effect you want to use.

Note: To minimize a window to an icon in the Dock, see page 14.

9 This option animates an application's icon in the Dock when you click the icon. You can click the option to turn the option on (☑) or off (☐).

10 This option hides the Dock when you are not using the Dock. You can click the option to turn the option on (☑) or off (☐).

11 To quit System Preferences, click **System Preferences**.

12 Click **Quit System Preferences**.

CHANGE THE SCREEN EFFECT

A screen effect is a picture or pattern that automatically appears on the screen when you do not use your computer for a period of time.

You can use a screen effect to hide your work while you are away from your desk.

By default, a screen effect will appear on your screen when you do not use your computer for 20 minutes.

CHANGE THE SCREEN EFFECT

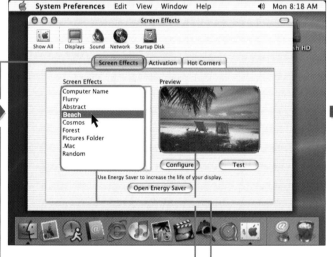

1 Click the System Preferences icon to access your system preferences.

■ The System Preferences window appears.

2 Click **Screen Effects** to change your screen effect.

■ The Screen Effects window appears.

3 Click the **Screen Effects** tab.

4 Click the screen effect you want to use.

■ This area displays a preview of the screen effect.

What are the Pictures Folder, .Mac and Random screen effects?

The Pictures Folder screen effect displays a slide show of the pictures in your Pictures folder. The .Mac screen effect allows you to display a slide show published on the Internet by a .Mac member. You can click **Configure** to specify the .Mac membership name of the person who published the slide show you want to use. The Random screen effect randomly selects a screen effect each time the screen effect starts.

How can I test a screen effect?

After you select a screen effect in step 4 below, you can click **Test** to display the screen effect using your entire screen. To remove the screen effect from your screen, move the mouse or press a key on the keyboard.

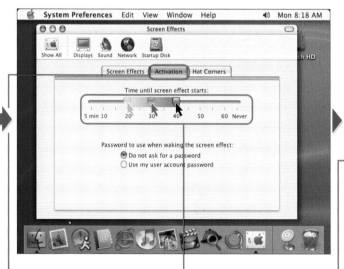

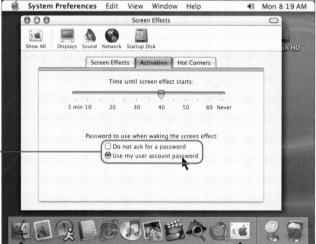

5 Click the **Activation** tab.

6 To specify the number of minutes your computer must be inactive before the screen effect will start, drag this slider ( ) to the desired number of minutes.

*Note: If you never want the screen effect to start, drag the slider to **Never**.*

7 Click an option to specify if you must enter your user account password to remove the screen effect from your screen (changes to).

Note: Requiring a password prevents unauthorized people from removing the screen effect and using your computer while you are away from your desk.

CONTINUED

CHANGE THE SCREEN EFFECT

When selecting a screen effect, you can create hot corners that allow you to move the mouse pointer over a corner of your screen to instantly start or turn off the screen effect.

For example, you may want to instantly start your screen effect if you are playing a game and your boss walks by. You may want to turn off the screen effect when you are reading information on a Web page and you do not want the screen effect to start.

CHANGE THE SCREEN EFFECT (CONTINUED)

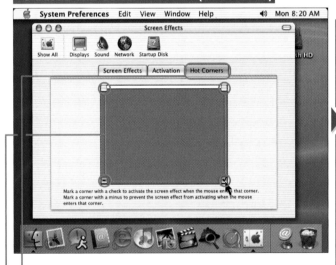

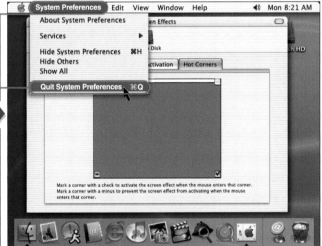

8 Click the **Hot Corners** tab.

9 To create a hot corner on your screen that will start or turn off the screen effect when you position the mouse ▶ over the corner, click the box (☐) in the corner until the box appears the way you want.

☑ Start the screen effect immediately.

⊟ Turn off the screen effect temporarily.

☐ Do not create a hot corner.

10 To quit System Preferences, click **System Preferences**.

11 Click **Quit System Preferences**.

■ The screen effect will start when you do not use your computer for the number of minutes you specified.

■ To remove the screen effect from your screen, you can move the mouse or press a key on the keyboard.

You can change
the picture used
to decorate your
desktop.

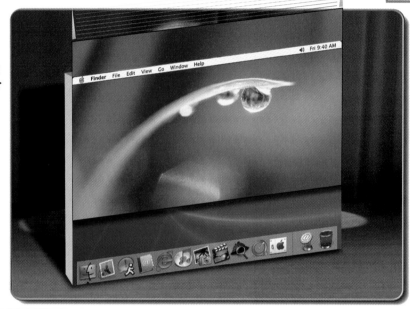

Mac OS comes with
several collections of
pictures that you can
choose from, including
background images,
nature pictures,
abstract pictures and
solid colors. You can
also use your own
pictures by selecting
a picture from your
Pictures folder.

CHANGE THE DESKTOP PICTURE

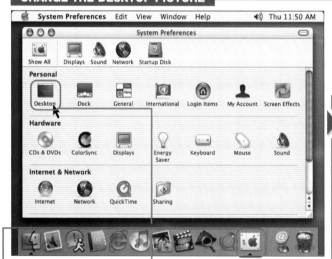

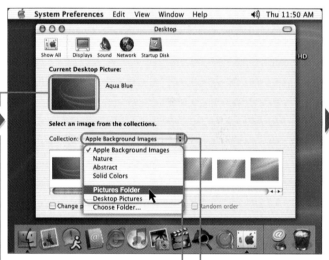

1 Click the System
Preferences icon to
access your system
preferences.

■ The System Preferences
window appears.

2 Click **Desktop** to change
the picture displayed on your
desktop.

■ The Desktop window
appears.

■ This area displays
the picture currently
displayed on your
desktop.

3 Click this area to
display a list of the
available picture
collections.

4 Click the collection
that contains the
pictures you want to
view.

CONTINUED ▶

CHANGE THE DESKTOP PICTURE

You can have Mac OS automatically change the picture displayed on your desktop at a time interval you specify.

CHANGE THE DESKTOP PICTURE (CONTINUED)

■ This area displays the pictures that are available in the collection you selected.

5 Click the picture you want to display on your desktop.

■ The picture you selected immediately appears on your desktop.

6 If you selected a picture from the Pictures Folder collection, click this area to specify how you want to display the picture on your desktop.

7 Click the way you want to display the picture.

How can I display a picture from the Pictures Folder collection on my desktop?

Mac OS offers four ways you can display a picture from the Pictures Folder collection on your desktop.

Fill screen

Enlarges the picture to cover your entire desktop. The top and bottom edges of the picture may be cut off.

Stretch to fill screen

Stretches the picture to cover your entire desktop.

Center

Displays the picture in the middle of your desktop.

Tile

Repeats the picture until it fills your entire desktop.

8 To have Mac OS automatically change the desktop picture to other pictures in the same collection, click this option (□ changes to ☑).

9 To specify how often you want Mac OS to display a new picture, click this area.

10 Click the option you want to use.

11 This option displays the pictures in random order. You can click this option to turn the option off (☑ changes to □).

12 To quit System Preferences, click **System Preferences**.

13 Click **Quit System Preferences**.

■ To return to the original desktop picture, repeat steps **1** to **5**, starting on page 73, selecting the **Apple Background Images** collection in step **4** and the **Aqua Blue** picture in step **5**.

CHANGE THE DISPLAY SETTINGS

You can change the way information appears on your screen.

Resolution

Determines the amount of information displayed on your screen. A higher resolution displays more information on your screen at once.

Colors

Determines the number of colors displayed on your screen.

Refresh Rate

Determines how often the screen is redrawn. A higher refresh rate reduces screen flicker and eyestrain.

CHANGE THE DISPLAY SETTINGS

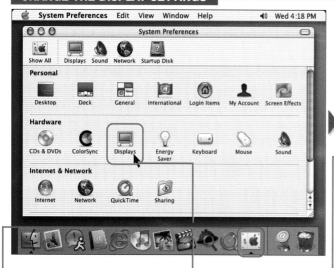

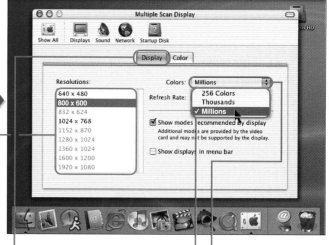

1 Click the System Preferences icon to access your system preferences.

■ The System Preferences window appears.

2 Click **Displays** to change your display settings.

■ A window appears, allowing you to change your display settings.

3 Click the **Display** tab.

4 Click the resolution you want to use.

*Note: A dialog box may appear. Click **OK** to continue. If a confirmation dialog box appears, click **Revert** or **Confirm** to specify if you want to use the new resolution.*

5 To specify the number of colors you want your screen to display, click this area.

6 Click the number of colors you want your screen to display.

Note: The current number of colors displays a check mark (✓).

**Why are my display settings different than
the display settings shown below?**

The available display settings depend on the
monitor you are using. For example, you may
have settings that allow you to change the
contrast and brightness of your display. You
may also have additional tabs, such as a
Color tab that allows you to select a display
profile for your monitor.

**How do I change the display settings using
the icon ( ) in the menu bar?**

Click the icon ( ) in the menu bar to
display a list of available resolutions and
colors. You can select the resolution or
number of colors you want your screen to
display. A check mark (✓) appears beside
the currently selected resolution and number
of colors.

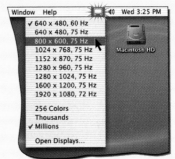

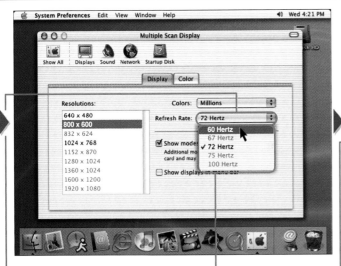

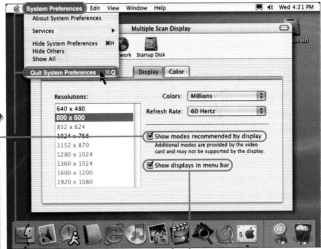

7 To specify the
refresh rate you want
your screen to use,
click this area to
display the available
refresh rates.

8 Click the refresh
rate you want your
screen to use.

*Note: The current refresh
rate displays a check
mark (✓).*

9 To show all the
available resolutions,
colors and refresh
rates, click this option
(✓ changes to).

*Note: Additional options are
provided by your video card
and may not be supported
by the display.*

10 To be able to change
the display settings using
an icon ( ) in the menu
bar, click this option (
changes to ✓).

11 To quit System
Preferences, click **System
Preferences**.

12 Click **Quit System
Preferences**.

CHANGE THE SOUND SETTINGS

You can change your computer's sound settings to suit your preferences. For example, you can change the alert sound your computer uses and adjust the volume of sound on the computer.

Your computer uses the alert sound to get your attention or notify you of a problem.

CHANGE THE SOUND SETTINGS

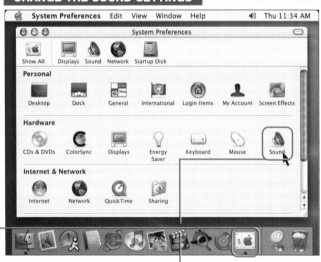

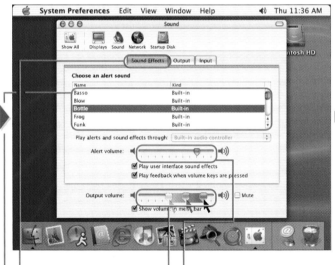

1 Click the System Preferences icon to access your system preferences.

■ The System Preferences window appears.

2 Click **Sound** to change your computer's sound settings.

■ The Sound window appears.

3 Click the **Sound Effects** tab.

4 Click the sound you want to use for alerts. The alert sound you selected plays.

5 To change the alert volume, drag this slider (🔘) to decrease or increase the alert volume. The current alert sound plays at the new volume.

6 To change the computer's volume, drag this slider (🔘) to decrease or increase the computer's volume. The current alert sound plays at the new volume.

How do I change my computer's volume using the speaker icon (◀))) in the menu bar?

To change your computer's volume, click the speaker icon (◀))) in the menu bar. On the volume control bar that appears, drag the slider (⬤) up or down to increase or decrease your computer's volume.

 How can I turn off the sound on my computer?

To turn off the sound on your computer, perform steps 1 and 2 below to display the Sound window. Click **Mute** to turn off the sound on your computer (☐ changes to ☑). To once again turn on the sound, click **Mute** again (☑ changes to ☐).

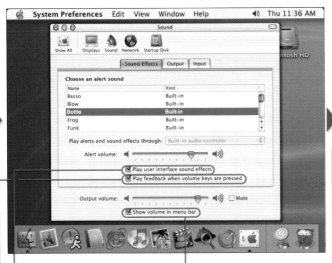

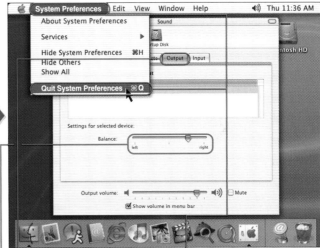

■ This option plays a sound when you perform certain actions on your computer, such as deleting a file.

■ This option plays a sound when you press a volume key on your keyboard.

■ This option allows you to adjust the volume of your computer using a speaker icon (◀))) in the menu bar.

7 You can click an option to turn the option on (☑) or off (☐).

8 Click the **Output** tab.

9 To adjust the balance between your left and right speakers, drag this slider (◯) left or right.

Note: Changing the balance between your speakers increases the volume of one speaker, while decreasing the volume of the other speaker.

10 To quit System Preferences, click **System Preferences**.

11 Click **Quit System Preferences**.

CHANGE THE MOUSE SETTINGS

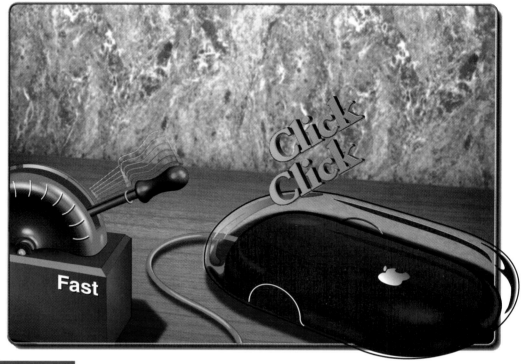

You can change the way your mouse works to make the mouse easier to use.

You can change how fast the mouse pointer moves on your screen and the speed at which you can double-click an item to open the item.

CHANGE THE MOUSE SETTINGS

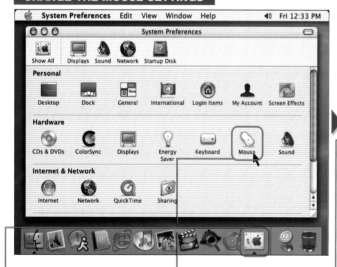

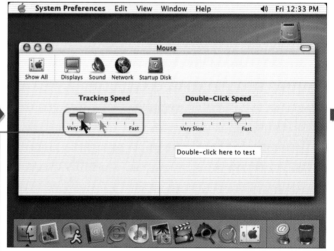

1 Click the System Preferences icon to access your system preferences.

■ The System Preferences window appears.

2 Click **Mouse** to change your mouse settings.

■ The Mouse window appears.

3 To change how fast the mouse ▶ moves on your screen, drag this slider (⬤) to a new position.

Note: If you perform detailed work, you may want to use a slower speed. If you have a large monitor, you may want to use a faster speed.

Should I use a mouse pad?

A mouse pad provides a smooth surface for moving the mouse on your desk. If you use a mechanical mouse with a roller ball, a mouse pad helps reduce the amount of dirt that enters the mouse. If you use an optical mouse, a mouse pad may be necessary when you are working on a highly reflective or transparent surface, such as a glass table. The mouse pad you use with an optical mouse should be a solid color.

Can I make my optical mouse easier to click?

If a ring surrounds the light on the bottom of your optical mouse, you can turn the ring to adjust the click tension and make the mouse easier to click. The **-** setting reduces the click tension, making the mouse easier to click. The **o** setting provides moderate click tension and the **+** setting provides the highest click tension.

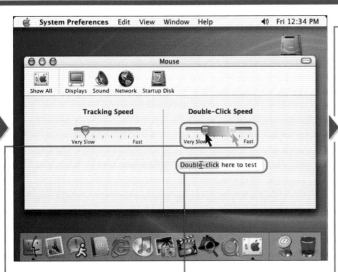

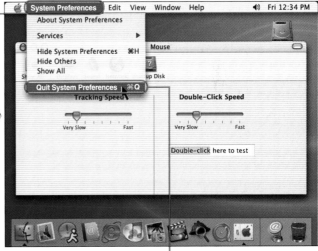

4 To change the amount of time that can pass between two clicks of the mouse button for Mac OS to recognize a double-click, drag this slider () to a new position.

Note: If you have difficulty using the mouse, you may want to use a slower double-click speed.

5 To test the new double-click speed, double-click the text in this area.

6 To quit System Preferences, click **System Preferences**.

7 Click **Quit System Preferences**.

CHANGE THE DATE OR TIME

You can change the date or time set in your computer. You can also customize the appearance of the clock displayed in the menu bar.

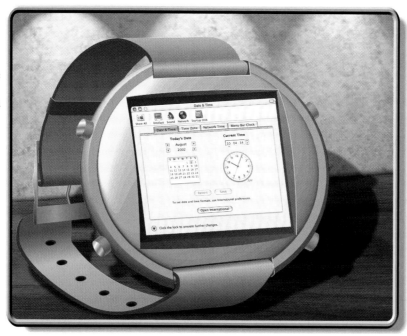

You should make sure the correct date and time are set in your computer. Mac OS uses the date and time to keep track of when you create and update your files.

CHANGE THE DATE OR TIME

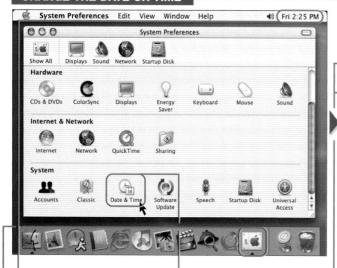

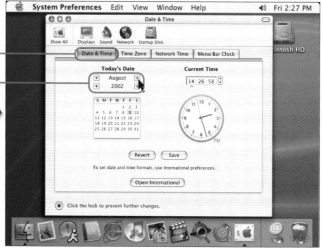

■ By default, the clock appears in the menu bar, displaying the current day and time.

■1 To change the date, time or appearance of the clock, click the System Preferences icon to access your system preferences.

■ The System Preferences window appears.

■2 Click **Date & Time** to change the date or time set in your computer.

■ The Date & Time window appears.

■3 Click the **Date & Time** tab.

■4 This area displays the current month and year. To change the month or year, click ◀ or ▶ to select an earlier or later month or year.

Note: You cannot change the date or time if your computer's clock automatically synchronizes with a time server on the Internet. To stop using a time server, perform steps 12 and 13 on page 84 before performing step 4.

Can I use the analog clock on the Date & Time tab to change the time?

Yes. To change the time, position the mouse ⬆ over the hour, minute or second hand on the analog clock and then drag the hand to a new location.

Is there another way to specify my time zone on the Time Zone tab?

Yes. If you are not sure of your location on the map, you can type the name of your city to specify your time zone. Drag the mouse ⵊ over the text in the Closest City area and then type the first few letters of the name of a major city close to you. Mac OS automatically completes the name of the city for you. Press the return key to keep the city that Mac OS enters or continue typing until Mac OS enters the city you want.

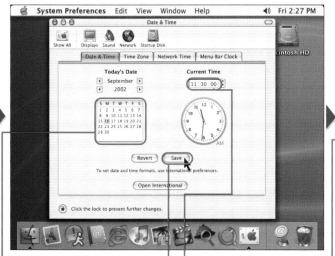

■ This area displays the days in the current month. The current day is highlighted.

5 To change the day, click the correct day.

6 This area displays the current time. To change the time, click the part of the time you want to change and then type the correct time.

7 To save your changes, click **Save**.

Note: To cancel your changes, click Revert.

8 Click the **Time Zone** tab.

9 On the map, click your approximate location.

■ A grey area appears on the map, indicating the time zone you selected.

10 Click ▾ in this area to display a list of major cities in the time zone.

11 Click the major city that is closest to you.

■ A symbol ( ) will appear on the map in the location you selected.

CONTINUED

CHANGE THE DATE OR TIME

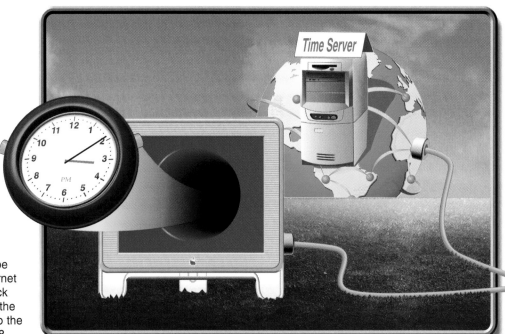

You can have your computer's clock automatically synchronize with a time server on the Internet. This will ensure your clock is always accurate.

Your computer must be connected to the Internet to synchronize its clock with a time server on the Internet. To connect to the Internet, see page 238.

CHANGE THE DATE OR TIME (CONTINUED)

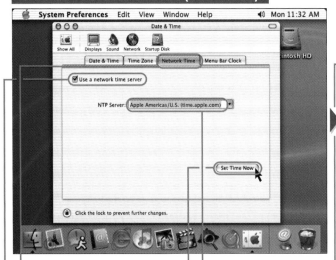

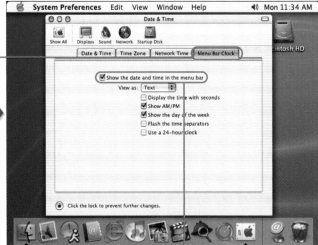

12 Click the **Network Time** tab.

13 This option automatically synchronizes your computer's clock with a time server on the Internet. You can click the option to turn the option on (☑) or off (☐).

■ This area displays the address of the time server on the Internet that your computer will use.

14 To immediately synchronize your computer's clock with the time server, click **Set Time Now**.

15 Click the **Menu Bar Clock** tab.

16 This option shows the clock in the menu bar at the top of your screen. You can click this option to turn the option on (☑) or off (☐).

*Note: The clock in the menu bar immediately displays your change. If you chose not to show the clock in the menu bar, skip to step **20**.*

How can I quickly display the current date?

To display the current date, click the clock in the menu bar. A menu appears, displaying the current date set in your computer. To close the menu, click outside the menu.

Is there another way to display a clock on my screen?

Mac OS includes the Clock application, which allows you to display a clock as an icon in the Dock or as a floating window on your screen. For information on using the Clock application, see page 118.

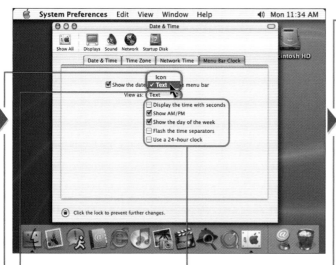

17 To specify if you want to display the clock in the menu bar as an icon ( ) or as text, click this area.

18 Click an option to display the clock as an icon or as text.

19 This area displays options that affect the appearance of the clock in the menu bar. You can click an option to turn the option on ( ) or off ( ).

Note: The options are not available if you selected to view the clock as an icon in step 18.

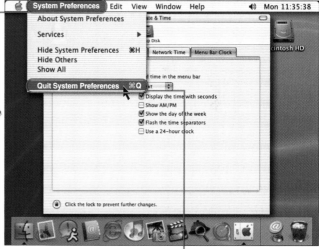

20 To quit System Preferences, click **System Preferences**.

21 Click **Quit System Preferences**.

CHANGE THE ENERGY SAVING SETTINGS

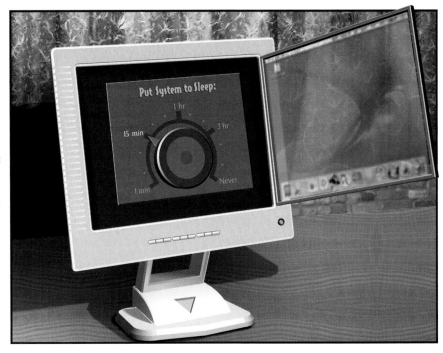

You can change the energy saving settings for your computer. These settings allow you to specify how long your computer must be inactive before automatically going to sleep to conserve power.

By default, your computer automatically goes to sleep when you do not use the computer for 10 minutes. When your computer goes to sleep, your screen will turn black.

CHANGE THE ENERGY SAVING SETTINGS

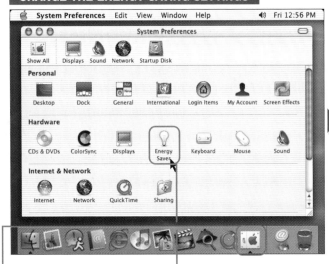

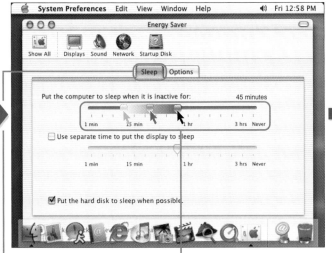

1 Click the System Preferences icon to access your system preferences.

■ The System Preferences window appears.

2 Click **Energy Saver** to change your energy saving settings.

■ The Energy Saver window appears.

3 Click the **Sleep** tab.

4 To specify the amount of time your computer must be inactive before automatically going to sleep, drag this slider (⬤) to the desired amount of time.

*Note: If you never want the computer to automatically go to sleep, drag the slider to **Never**.*

How can I wake a sleeping computer?

To wake a sleeping computer, move the mouse or press a key on your keyboard. When you wake the computer, any open applications and files will appear as you left them. You may have to wait several seconds for the computer to wake.

Why did this warning message appear in the Energy Saver window?

This warning message appears when you specify an amount of time in step 4 or 6 that is shorter than the amount of time your computer must be inactive before the screen effect starts. You may want to change when the screen effect starts so the screen effect will appear before your computer goes to sleep. For information on setting up a screen effect, see page 70.

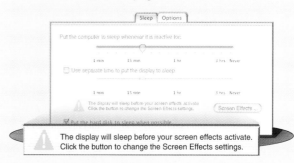

The display will sleep before your screen effects activate. Click the button to change the Screen Effects settings.

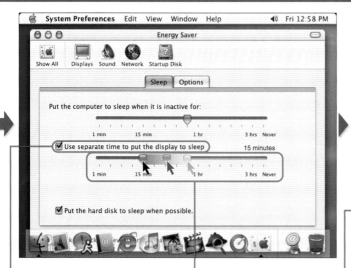

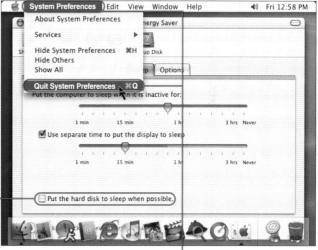

5 This option allows you to put your display to sleep at a different time than the rest of your computer. You can click this option to turn the option on (☑) or off (☐).

6 To specify the amount of time your computer must be inactive before the display goes to sleep, drag this slider (◯) to the desired amount of time.

Note: You cannot specify a longer amount of time for the display than you specified for your computer in step 4.

7 This option puts your hard disk to sleep whenever possible. You can click the option to turn the option on (☑) or off (☐).

8 To quit System Preferences, click **System Preferences**.

9 Click **Quit System Preferences**.

CHANGE UNIVERSAL ACCESS SETTINGS

If you have vision, hearing or mobility impairments, Mac OS offers settings you can select to make your computer easier to use.

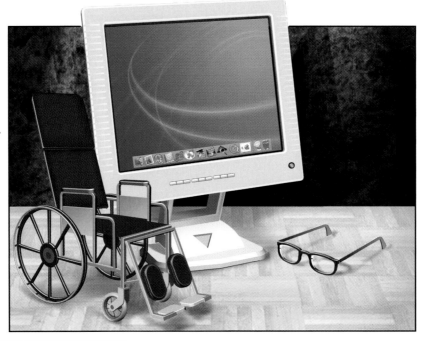

CHANGE UNIVERSAL ACCESS SETTINGS

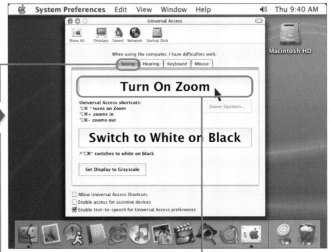

1 Click the System Preferences icon to access your system preferences.

■ The System Preferences window appears.

2 Click **Universal Access** to change your universal access settings.

■ The Universal Access window appears.

Note: Changes you make in the window will immediately affect your computer.

3 If you have difficulty seeing the information on your screen, click the **Seeing** tab.

4 To turn on Zoom so you can magnify an area of your screen, click **Turn On Zoom**.

*Note: To use Zoom to magnify an area of your screen, see the top of page 89. You can click **Turn Off Zoom** to turn off Zoom at any time.*

Why did my computer read aloud options in the Universal Access window?

To help people with vision impairments, your computer automatically reads aloud each word or phrase you position the mouse ➤ over in the Universal Access window. You can click **Enable text-to-speech for Universal Access preferences** at the bottom of the window to turn this feature on (☑) or off (☐).

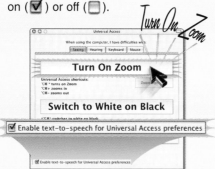

How do I use Zoom to magnify an area of my screen?

To use Zoom to magnify an area of your screen, position the mouse ➤ over the area you want to magnify and then press and hold down the [option] and [⌘] keys as you press the [+] key. You can repeat this step until the area is the size you want. To reduce the magnification of the area, press and hold down the [option] and [⌘] keys as you press the [-] key.

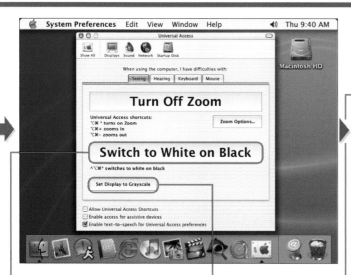

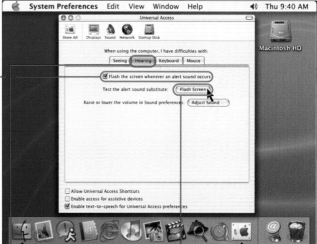

5 To display your screen with white text on a black background, click **Switch to White on Black**.

Note: You can click Switch to Black on White to return to the original screen setting.

6 To display your screen in shades of gray, click **Set Display to Grayscale**.

Note: You can click the option again to return to the original screen setting.

7 If you have difficulty hearing sounds on your computer, click the **Hearing** tab.

8 This option flashes your screen when an alert sound plays. You can click the option to turn the option on (☑) or off (☐).

Note: Your computer uses alert sounds to get your attention or notify you of a problem.

9 To preview how your screen will flash, click **Flash Screen**.

CONTINUED

CHANGE UNIVERSAL ACCESS SETTINGS

Mac OS offers options you can select to help you use the keyboard more effectively.

Sticky Keys

The Sticky Keys option allows you to press the `shift`, `control`, `option` or `⌘` key and have the key remain active while you press another key. This option is useful for people who have difficulty pressing more than one key at a time.

Slow Keys

The Slow Keys option allows you to add a delay between when you press a key and when the key is accepted. This option is useful for people who often press keys for too long.

CHANGE UNIVERSAL ACCESS SETTINGS (CONTINUED)

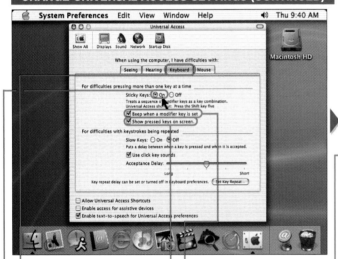

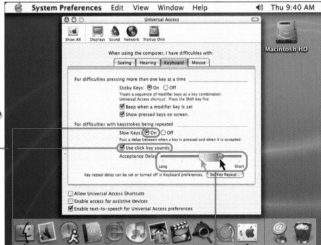

10 If you have difficulty using your keyboard, click the **Keyboard** tab.

11 To turn on Sticky Keys, click **On** (○ changes to ◉).

■ This option plays a sound when you press the `shift`, `control`, `option` or `⌘` key.

■ This option displays the symbol for the `shift`, `control`, `option` or `⌘` key on your screen when you press the key.

12 To turn an option on (✓) or off (☐), click the option.

13 To turn on Slow Keys, click **On** (○ changes to ◉).

14 This option plays a "click" sound when you press a key. To turn the option on (✓) or off (☐), click the option.

15 To change the amount of time the computer must wait before accepting a key you press, drag this slider (▽) to the left or right.

How will the symbol for the [shift], [control], [option] or [⌘] key appear on my screen?

When you press one of these keys, the key's symbol appears and remains on your screen until you complete the keyboard shortcut, such as [⌘] + [Q]. If you no longer want to use the key, press the key twice to remove the key's symbol from your screen.

Key	Symbol
shift	⇧
control	⌃
option	⌥
⌘	⌘

After I turn on the Mouse Keys option, what keys on the numeric keypad can I use to control the mouse ↖ ?

Mouse Action	Key to Press
Move left or right	Press [4] or [6].
Move down or up	Press [2] or [8].
Move diagonally	Press [1], [3], [7] or [9].
Click	Press [5].
Double-click	Press [5] twice.
Hold down the mouse button	Press [0].
Release the mouse button	Press [.].

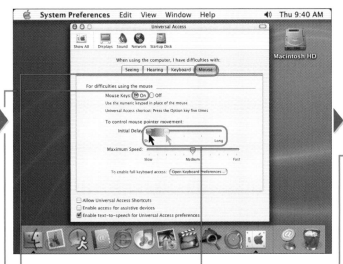

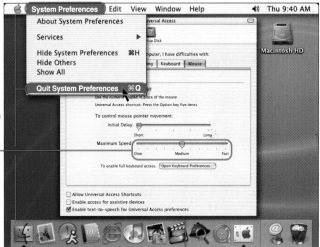

16 If you have difficulty using the mouse, click the **Mouse** tab.

17 To turn on Mouse Keys, click **On** (○ changes to ◉).

Note: Mouse Keys allows you to use the numeric keypad on the right side of your keyboard to control the mouse ↖ on your screen.

18 To change how quickly the mouse ↖ starts moving on your screen when you press a key, drag this slider (◯) to the left or right.

19 To change how quickly the mouse ↖ moves on your screen when you press a key, drag this slider (◯) to the left or right.

20 To quit System Preferences, click **System Preferences**.

21 Click **Quit System Preferences**.

OPEN APPLICATIONS AUTOMATICALLY AT LOG IN

If you use the same applications every day, you can have the applications open automatically each time you log in to Mac OS.

You can set up files and folders to open automatically each time you log in to Mac OS the same way you set up applications.

OPEN APPLICATIONS AUTOMATICALLY AT LOG IN

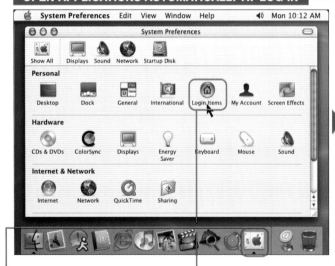

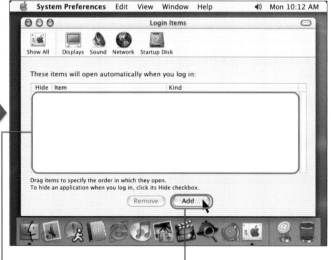

1 Click the System Preferences icon to access your system preferences.

■ The System Preferences window appears.

2 Click **Login Items** to specify the applications you want to open automatically when you log in.

■ The Login Items window appears.

■ This area lists any applications that will open automatically when you log in.

3 To add an application to the list, click **Add**.

■ A dialog sheet appears.

How do I stop an application from opening automatically when I log in?

To stop an application from opening automatically when you log in, you must remove the application from the Login Items window.

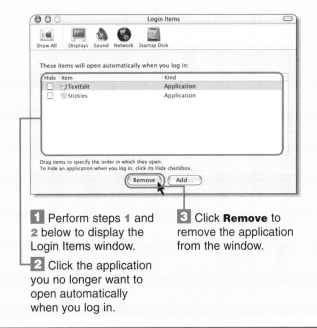

1 Perform steps **1** and **2** below to display the Login Items window.

2 Click the application you no longer want to open automatically when you log in.

3 Click **Remove** to remove the application from the window.

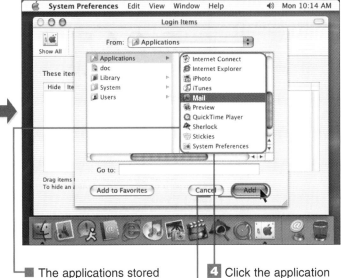

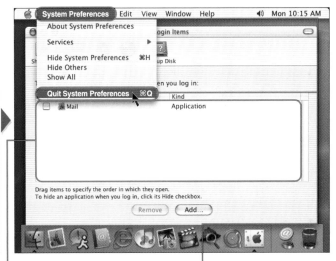

■ The applications stored in the Applications folder automatically appear in the last column.

Note: The leftmost column shows the disks on your computer. Each of the following columns shows the contents of the item selected in the previous column.

4 Click the application you want to open automatically.

5 Click **Add** to add the application to the list.

■ The application appears in the list.

■ A check mark (☑) appears beside each application that Mac OS will automatically hide after the application is opened. You can click a check box to add (☑) or remove (☐) the check mark.

6 To quit System Preferences, click **System Preferences**.

7 Click **Quit System Preferences**.

ADD FONTS

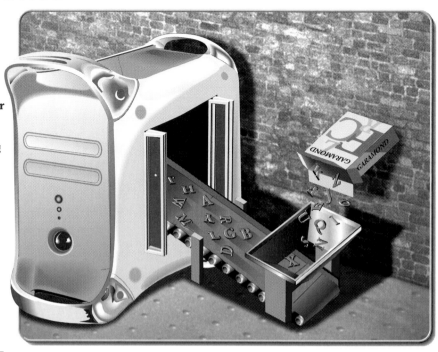

You can add extra fonts to your computer to give you more choices when creating documents.

After you add fonts to your computer, you will be able to use the fonts in all your applications.

1 Double-click your hard disk icon on the desktop to view the contents of your hard disk.

■ A window appears, displaying the contents of your hard disk.

2 Double-click **Library** to view the contents of the Library folder.

■ The Library window appears, displaying the contents of the Library folder.

3 Double-click **Fonts** to view the fonts available on your computer.

Where can I find fonts that I can add to my computer?

You can find fonts at computer stores and on the Web. For example, you can find fonts at the www.macfonts.com/fonts and www.fontfiles.com Web sites. Make sure the fonts you choose are designed for Macintosh computers. Fonts available on the Web are usually compressed to reduce the time required to download the fonts to your computer. When you download a font, Mac OS automatically stores a decompressed version of the font in a folder on your desktop.

How do I delete a font from my computer?

To delete a font, perform steps 1 to 3 below to view the fonts on your computer. Position the mouse ➤ over the font you want to delete and then drag the font to the Trash icon in the Dock. You should delete only fonts that you added to your computer.

■ The Fonts window appears. Each icon in the window represents a font installed on your computer.

4 Locate the font you want to make available on your computer.

5 Position the mouse ➤ over the font.

6 Drag the font to the Fonts window.

■ The icon for the font appears in the Fonts window.

7 Repeat steps 4 to 6 for each font you want to add to your computer.

8 When you finish adding fonts to your computer, click ○ to close the Fonts window.

■ The new fonts are now available on your computer.

Note: You can use Key Caps to view the characters that are available for each font you have added to your computer. To use Key Caps, see page 138.

ADD A PRINTER

Before you can use
a printer, you need
to add the printer
to your computer.
You need to add a
printer only once.

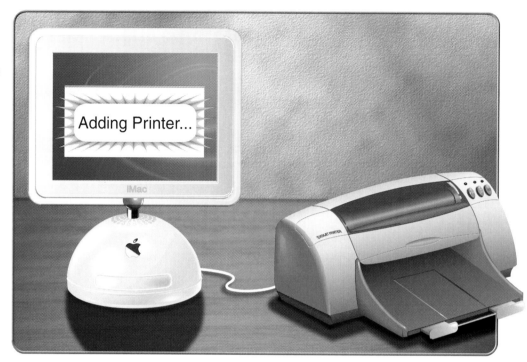

Adding Printer...

ADD A PRINTER

1 Click **Go**.

*Note: If Go is not
available, click a blank
area on your desktop
to display the Finder
menu bar.*

2 Click **Applications**
to view the applications
available on your computer.

■ The Applications window
appears.

3 Double-click **Utilities** to
view the utility applications
available on your computer.

■ The Utilities
window appears,
displaying the
utility applications
available on your
computer.

4 Double-click **Print
Center** to manage
your printers.

*Note: You can click ◯
in the Utilities window to
close the window.*

Which connection type should I choose for my printer?

Mac OS offers four connection types you can choose from.

AppleTalk

Allows you to connect to a printer on an AppleTalk network. An AppleTalk network is commonly used to connect older Macintosh computers.

Directory Services

Allows you to connect to a printer attached to a network server. Network servers are commonly used on large networks. Contact your network administrator for information on adding a printer using this connection type.

IP Printing

Allows you to connect to a printer on a TCP/IP network. A TCP/IP network uses the TCP/IP protocol to connect Macintosh computers or Windows-based computers. The printer will have a specific TCP/IP address, such as 192.168.253.252.

USB

Allows you to connect to a printer plugged directly into a USB port on your computer.

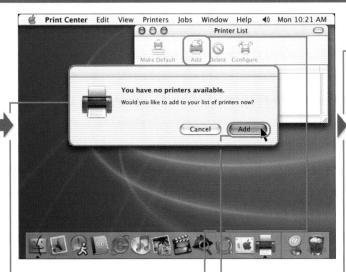

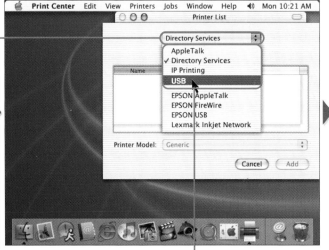

■ The Printer List window appears.

■ If you do not have any printers installed on your computer, a dialog box appears, stating that you have no printers available on your computer.

5 Click **Add** to add a printer.

■ If the dialog box does not appear, click **Add** in the Printer List window to add a printer.

■ A dialog sheet appears.

6 To specify how the printer connects to your computer, click this area to display a list of the available connection types.

7 Click the type of connection the printer uses to connect to your computer.

CONTINUED

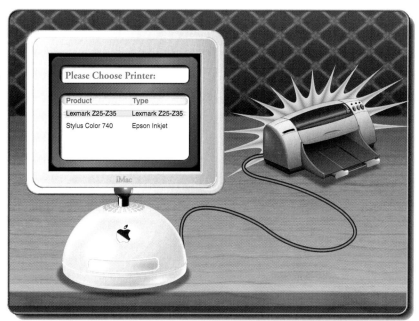

When you add a printer, Print Center can locate the printers available to your computer and then display the printers in a list for you to choose from.

ADD A PRINTER (CONTINUED)

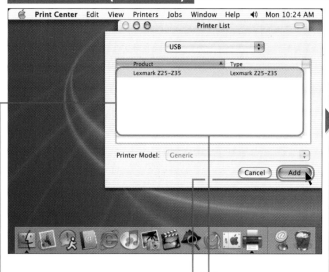

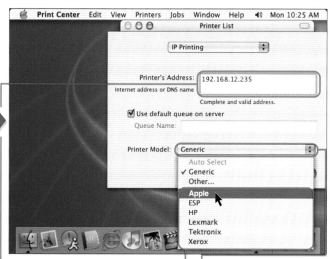

If you selected **AppleTalk**, **Directory Services** or **USB** in step **7**, this area displays the names of the printers that your computer found.

Note: If you selected IP Printing in step 7, skip to step 10.

8 Click the printer you want to add.

9 Click **Add** to add the printer. To continue, skip to step **15**.

10 If you selected **IP Printing** in step **7**, click this area and type the Internet Protocol (IP) address or domain name of the printer.

Note: If you do not know the IP address or domain name of the printer, ask your network administrator.

11 To specify the printer model for the printer, click this area to display a list of the available printer models.

12 Click the printer model for the printer.

I am having trouble adding a printer. What should I do?

If you are having trouble adding a printer, Mac OS may not have the software required to communicate with the printer. To add the printer, install the software included with the printer. If your printer did not come with software, you may be able to download the correct software from the printer manufacturer's Web site. You may also have to perform steps 1 to 16 starting on page 96 to add the printer.

How do I change the default printer?

The default printer automatically prints all your files. To change the default printer, perform steps 1 to 4 on page 96 to display the Printer List window. Click the name of the printer you want to make the default printer and then click **Make Default**. The name of the default printer appears in **bold** type.

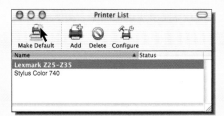

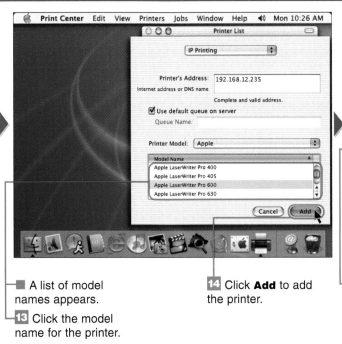

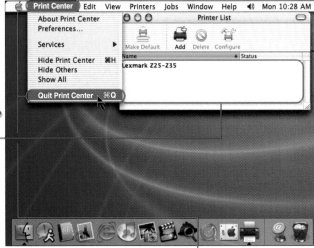

■ A list of model names appears.

13 Click the model name for the printer.

14 Click **Add** to add the printer.

■ The printer appears in the Printer List window.

■ You can now use the printer to print documents on your computer.

15 To quit Print Center, click **Print Center**.

16 Click **Quit Print Center**.

USING SPEECH RECOGNITION

You can turn on speech recognition to use spoken commands to control your computer.

Using spoken commands can help save you time when performing tasks on your computer since one spoken command often performs several steps.

Some applications, such as Chess, automatically allow you to use spoken commands to control the application.

TURN ON SPEECH RECOGNITION

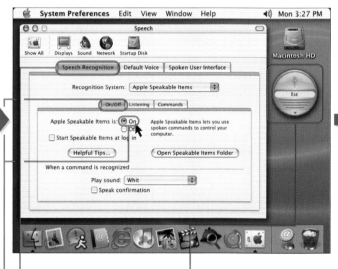

1 Click the System Preferences icon to access your system preferences.

■ The System Preferences window appears.

2 Click **Speech** to turn on speech recognition.

■ The Speech window appears.

3 Click the **Speech Recognition** tab.

4 Click the **On/Off** tab.

5 To turn on speech recognition, click **On** (○ changes to ●).

*Note: The first time you turn on speech recognition, a dialog sheet appears, displaying tips on using speech recognition. You can click **Continue** to close the dialog sheet.*

■ When speech recognition is turned on, the Speech Feedback window appears on your screen.

What spoken commands can I use?

To view spoken commands you can use, perform steps **1** to **4** below and then click **Open Speakable Items Folder**. The Speakable Items window appears, displaying icons for spoken commands you can use. Each icon name represents a spoken command. The Speakable Items window also displays the Application Speakable Items folder, which contains subfolders for applications that offer additional spoken commands you can use. The commands in an application subfolder are specific to the application. To open a folder, double-click the folder.

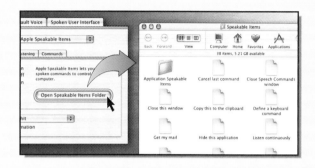

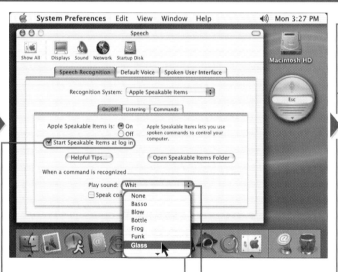

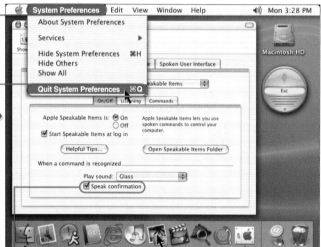

6 To turn on speech recognition each time you log in to your computer, click this option (changes to).

Note: Mac OS automatically turns off speech recognition each time you log out or shut down your computer.

7 To specify the sound you want to play each time your computer recognizes a spoken command, click this area to display a list of the available sounds.

8 Click the sound you want to play. The sound you selected plays.

9 To have your computer repeat your spoken commands, click this option (changes to).

10 To quit System Preferences, click **System Preferences**.

11 Click **Quit System Preferences**.

■ To turn off speech recognition, perform steps **1** to **5**, selecting **Off** in step **5**. Then perform steps **10** and **11**.

■ You can now use spoken commands to control your computer. To use spoken commands, see page 102.

CONTINUED

USING SPEECH RECOGNITION

When speech recognition is turned on, you can use spoken commands to perform tasks on your computer, such as closing a window, opening an application or starting your screen saver.

You need to connect a microphone to your computer to use spoken commands to perform tasks on the computer.

USE SPOKEN COMMANDS

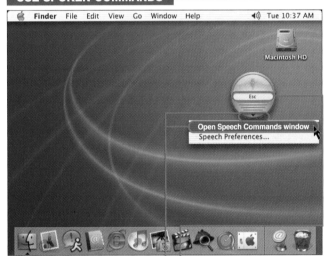

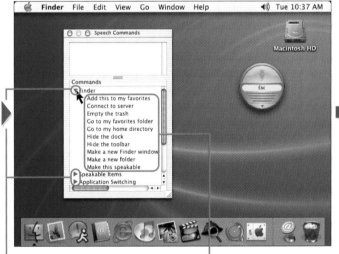

■ When speech recognition is turned on, the Speech Feedback window appears on your screen.

Note: To turn on speech recognition, see page 100.

■ The Speech Feedback window displays the name of the key you can press and hold down to have your computer listen to your spoken commands. By default, this is the `esc` key.

1 To display a list of commands you can use, click ▼.

2 Click **Open Speech Commands window**.

■ The Speech Commands window appears, displaying the categories of commands you can use.

Note: The available categories depend on the active application.

3 You can click ► beside a category to display the commands in the category (► changes to ▼).

■ The commands in the category appear.

■ You can click ▼ to once again hide the commands in the category.

How should I speak to my computer when using spoken commands?

You should speak to your computer in your normal tone of voice, pronouncing words clearly and not pausing between words. You should also speak at a consistent volume so the bars in the Speech Feedback window are primarily green. If you speak too softly or too loudly, the computer may not be able to recognize your commands.

Can I minimize the Speech Feedback window?

Yes. To minimize the Speech Feedback window to an icon in the Dock, double-click the window or press and hold down the `esc` key as you say "Minimize Speech Feedback window." To redisplay the window, click the icon for the window in the Dock.

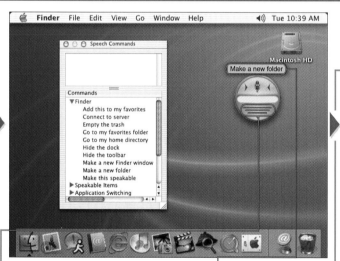

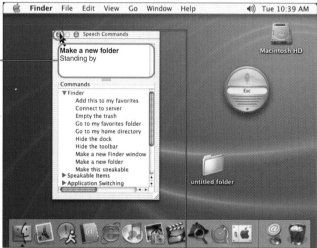

4 Press and hold down the `esc` key and then speak a command into your microphone.

■ While you speak, bars in the Speech Feedback window indicate the sound level of your voice.

Note: The bars should be green. If a red bar appears, you are speaking too loudly.

■ Your spoken command appears in a yellow box above the Speech Feedback window and a sound plays.

Note: Your computer may also repeat your spoken command.

■ This area of the Speech Commands window displays your spoken commands in bold and actions taken by the computer in regular type.

■ You can repeat step 4 for each spoken command you want to use.

5 To close the Speech Commands window, click ◯.

■ To turn off speech recognition, you can say "Quit speakable items."

CHANGE THE WAY YOUR COMPUTER SPEAKS

You can change the voice your computer uses to speak and when the computer will speak.

CHANGE THE WAY YOUR COMPUTER SPEAKS

1 Click the System Preferences icon to access your system preferences.

■ The System Preferences window appears.

2 Click **Speech** to change the way your computer speaks.

■ The Speech window appears.

3 To change the voice your computer uses to speak, click the **Default Voice** tab.

■ This area displays the voices your computer can use to speak.

4 Click the voice you want your computer to use.

■ Your computer speaks using the voice you selected.

Note: To have your computer speak in another voice, repeat step 4.

When will my computer use the voice I select?

Your computer will use the voice you select in step **4** below to read aloud text in applications such as TextEdit. To have your computer read aloud text in a TextEdit document, see the top of page 127. Your computer will also use the voice to speak when you use features such as speech recognition. For information on using speech recognition, see page 100.

Which phrase should I have my computer speak when an alert appears?

If you cannot decide which phrase you want your computer to speak in step **10** below, you can select the Next in the list or the Random from the list option. Click **Next in the list** to have your computer choose a phrase in order from the list each time an alert appears. Click **Random from the list** to have your computer randomly choose a phrase from the list each time an alert appears.

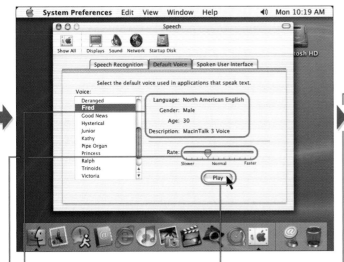

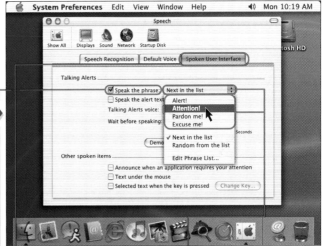

■ This area displays information about the voice you selected, including the language and gender of the voice.

5 To change how fast your computer speaks, drag this slider ( ) left or right to have the computer speak slower or faster.

6 Click **Play** to hear your computer speak using the new speed.

7 To specify when your computer will speak, click the **Spoken User Interface** tab.

8 This option instructs your computer to speak a phrase when an alert appears. You can click the option to turn the option on ( ) or off ( ).

Note: Your computer uses alerts to get your attention or notify you of a problem.

9 If you turned the option on, click this area to display a list of the available phrases.

10 Click the phrase you want your computer to use.

CONTINUED

CHANGE THE WAY YOUR COMPUTER SPEAKS

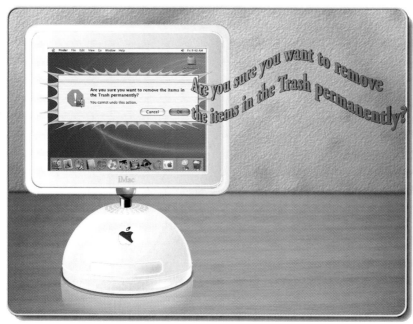

You can have your computer read the text in alerts that appear on your screen.

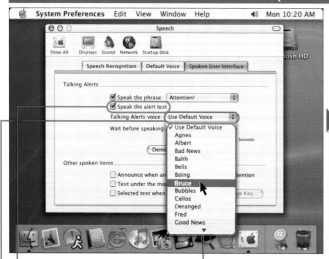

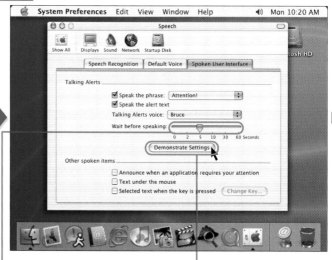

11 This option instructs your computer to read the text in alerts. You can click the option to turn the option on (☑) or off (☐).

12 To specify the voice you want your computer to use to read alerts, click this area to display a list of the available voices.

13 Click the voice you want your computer to use.

Note: The Use Default Voice option uses the voice you selected in step 4 on page 104.

14 To specify how long your computer should wait before speaking when an alert appears, drag this slider (⬤) left or right to decrease or increase the amount of time the computer should wait.

15 To have your computer demonstrate the settings you selected, click **Demonstrate Settings**.

Can my computer read aloud text I select in an application?

Yes. You can have your computer read aloud selected text in an application such as Internet Explorer or Mail when you type a keyboard shortcut. To have your computer read aloud selected text, click **Selected text when the key is pressed** (☐ changes to ☑). The first time you turn the option on, a dialog sheet appears, allowing you to type the keyboard shortcut you want to use to tell the computer to read selected text (example: control + A). Click **OK** to confirm the keyboard shortcut you entered.

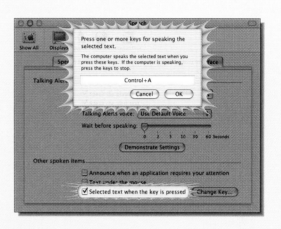

■ A dialog box appears and your computer demonstrates the settings you selected.

16 Click **OK** to close the dialog box.

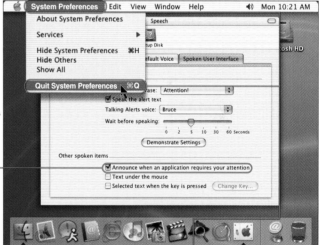

17 This option instructs your computer to announce when an application needs your attention. You can click the option to turn the option on (☑) or off (☐).

18 To quit System Preferences, click **System Preferences**.

19 Click **Quit System Preferences**.

UPDATE SOFTWARE

You can keep
your computer
up to date by
having the
computer
automatically
check for new
and updated
software.

You need to be connected
to the Internet to update
software on your computer.
To connect to the Internet,
see page 238.

UPDATE SOFTWARE

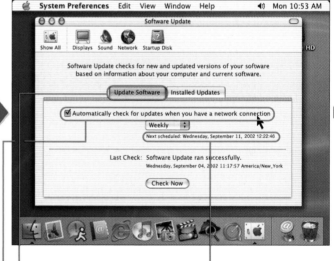

1 Click the System
Preferences icon to
access your system
preferences.

■ The System
Preferences window
appears.

2 Click **Software
Update** to change your
software update settings.

■ The Software Update
window appears.

3 Click the **Update
Software** tab.

4 This option automatically
checks for software updates
when you are connected
to the Internet through a
network. You can click this
option to turn the option
on (✔) or off (☐).

■ This area displays
the date and time of the
next scheduled check
for software updates.

What happens if new software updates are not available?

If new software updates are not available, the message "No new software updates were available" will appear in the Software Update window. To quit System Preferences, press and hold down the `control` key as you click the System Preferences icon in the Dock. Then click **Quit** on the menu that appears.

Will my computer notify me when it automatically detects new software updates?

Yes. If you chose to have your computer automatically check for software updates in step 4 below, the Software Update window will appear on your screen when new software updates are available. To install the updates, perform steps 8 to 13 starting below.

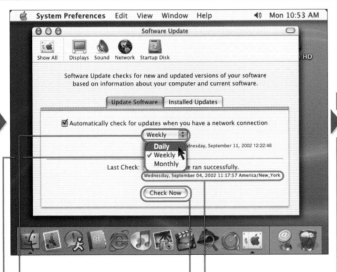

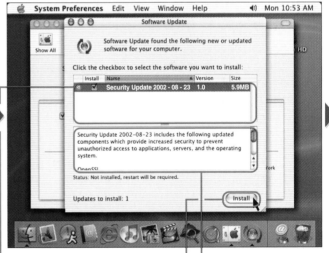

■5 To specify how often you want your computer to automatically check for software updates, click this area.

■6 Click the option you want to use.

■ This area displays the date and time your computer last checked for software updates.

■7 To immediately check for new software updates, click **Check Now**.

■ If software updates are available, the Software Update window appears.

■8 Your computer will install each software update that displays a check mark. To add (☑) or remove (☐) a check mark for a software update, click the box (☐) beside the software update.

■ This area displays a description of the highlighted software update.

■9 Click **Install** to install the software updates.

CONTINUED

UPDATE SOFTWARE

When updating
software on your
computer, you will
need to type the
password for your
user account.

You must have
an administrator
account to update
software on your
computer. An
administrator has
greater control over
a computer than a
regular user.

UPDATE SOFTWARE (CONTINUED)

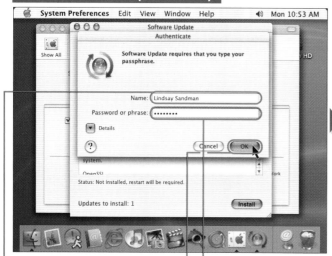

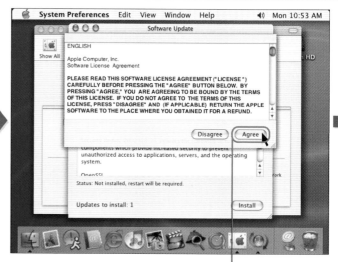

■ The Authenticate
dialog box appears.

■ This area displays
the name of your user
account.

10 Click this area and
type the password for
your user account.

*Note: A bullet (●) appears
for each character you type to
prevent other people from
seeing your password.*

11 Click **OK** to continue.

■ A dialog sheet may
appear, displaying a
license agreement for the
software updates.

*Note: If the license agreement
does not appear, skip to step 13.*

12 To accept the
agreement, click
Agree.

Can I see which software updates I have installed on my computer?

Yes. Displaying the list of installed software updates is useful if you want to confirm that an update was installed correctly. To view the list of previously installed software updates, perform steps 1 and 2 on page 108 to display the Software Update window. Then click the **Installed Updates** tab.

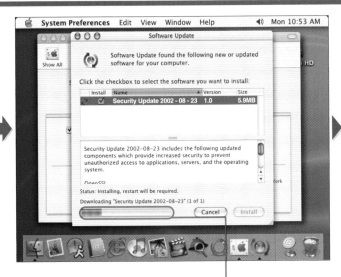

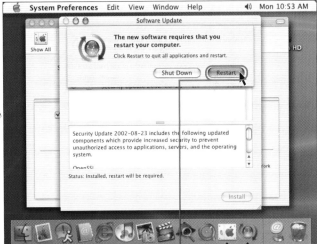

■ Your computer downloads and installs the software updates on your computer.

■ This area shows the progress of the installation.

■ When the installation is complete, a dialog sheet may appear, asking you to restart your computer.

■ Before restarting your computer, make sure you quit all applications.

13 Click **Restart** to restart your computer.

CHAPTER 5

Use Mac OS X Applications

You can use the applications included with Mac OS to perform many tasks on your computer. In this chapter, you will learn how to use Mac OS applications to create documents, work with electronic sticky notes and play DVD movies.

PLAY CHESS

You can play a game of chess on your computer.

When you play a game of chess, the computer is your opponent.

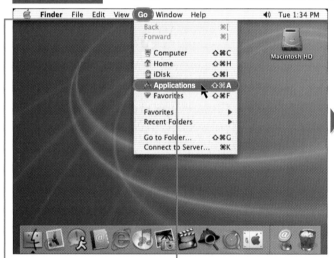

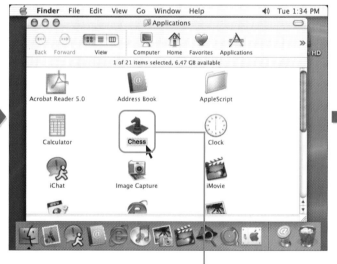

1 Click **Go**.

Note: If Go is not available, click a blank area on your desktop to display the Finder menu bar.

2 Click **Applications** to view the applications available on your computer.

■ The Applications window appears, displaying the applications available on your computer.

3 Double-click **Chess** to play a game of chess.

How can I use spoken commands to play chess?

You must have a microphone connected to your computer to use spoken commands to play chess. To have your computer listen to your spoken commands, press and hold down the esc key as you speak into the microphone. To tell your computer where to move a chess piece, use the numbers and letters along the left and bottom edges of the chessboard, such as "E2 to E4."

"E2 to E4"

Can I get help with my next chess move?

If you are not sure what your next chess move should be, you can select the **Move** menu and then click **Hint** to have Chess suggest a move. The move Chess suggests will flash briefly on the chessboard.

■ The Chess window appears, displaying a three-dimensional chessboard.

■ The Speech Feedback window also appears, allowing you to use spoken commands to play chess.

Note: To use spoken commands to play chess, see the top of this page.

■ To start the game, you must move a chess piece. Your chess pieces are white.

4 To move a chess piece, drag the chess piece to a new location on the chessboard.

Note: If you move a chess piece to an invalid location, an alert will sound and the chess piece will return to its original location.

■ After you move a chess piece, the computer will automatically move a chess piece.

5 When you finish playing chess, click **Chess**.

6 Click **Quit Chess** to close the Chess window.

USING THE CALCULATOR

You can use the Calculator to perform simple mathematical calculations.

The Calculator allows you to perform the same calculations you would perform on a handheld calculator.

USING THE CALCULATOR

1 Click **Go**.

Note: If Go is not available, click a blank area on your desktop to display the Finder menu bar.

2 Click **Applications** to view the applications available on your computer.

■ The Applications window appears.

3 Double-click **Calculator** to start the Calculator.

■ The Calculator appears.

Note: You can click ○ in the Applications window to close the window.

4 To enter information into the Calculator, click each button as you would press the buttons on a handheld calculator.

Note: You can also use the keys on your keyboard to enter information into the Calculator.

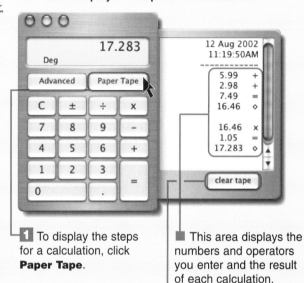

How can I display the steps for a calculation?

■ To once again hide the paper tape area, repeat step **1**.

Note: You can print the paper tape as you would print a file. To print a file, see page 52.

1 To display the steps for a calculation, click **Paper Tape**.

■ This area displays the numbers and operators you enter and the result of each calculation.

■ You can click **clear tape** to clear the paper tape.

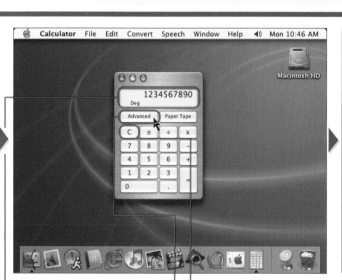

■ This area displays the numbers and operators you enter and the result of each calculation.

■ You can click C to start a new calculation at any time.

5 To perform advanced calculations, click **Advanced**.

■ The advanced view of the calculator appears. This view offers additional features that allow you to perform advanced calculations.

■ To return to the basic view of the calculator, click **Basic**.

6 When you finish using the Calculator, click ○ to close the Calculator.

USING THE CLOCK

You can display a clock in the Dock or in a window on your screen at all times.

You can choose to display an analog or digital clock.

USING THE CLOCK

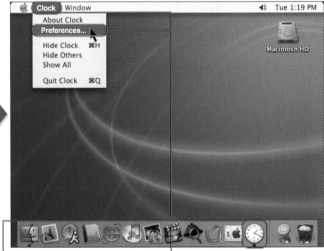

1 Click **Go**.

Note: If Go is not available, click a blank area on your desktop to display the Finder menu bar.

2 Click **Applications** to view the applications available on your computer.

■ The Applications window appears.

3 Double-click **Clock** to display the Clock.

■ By default, the Clock appears as an icon in the Dock.

Note: You can click ⬡ in the Applications window to close the window.

SET CLOCK PREFERENCES

1 Click the Clock.

2 Click **Clock**.

3 Click **Preferences**.

■ The Clock Preferences dialog box appears.

How do I remove the Clock from my screen?

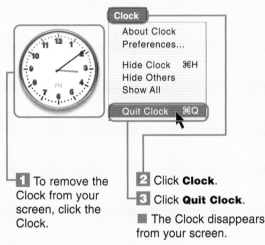

1 To remove the Clock from your screen, click the Clock.

2 Click **Clock**.

3 Click **Quit Clock**.

■ The Clock disappears from your screen.

 Can I change the settings for the clock that appears in the menu bar?

Yes. You can change the settings for the clock that appears in the menu bar at the top of your screen. For example, you can remove the clock from the menu bar or change the appearance of the clock. To change the settings for the clock in the menu bar, see page 84.

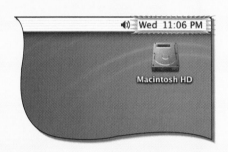

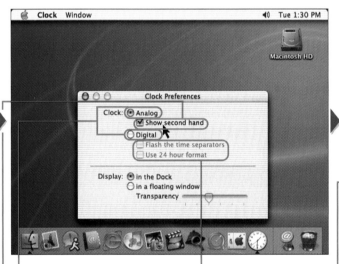

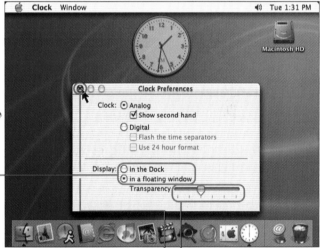

4 Click an option to specify if you want to display an analog or digital clock (○ changes to ●).

Note: The Clock immediately displays any new settings you select.

5 If you selected Analog, you can click this option to show the second hand (☐ changes to ☑).

■ If you selected Digital, these options allow you to flash the time separators (:) each second and display the time in the 24 hour format. You can click an option to turn the option on (☐ changes to ☑).

6 Click an option to specify if you want to display the Clock as an icon in the Dock or as a floating window (○ changes to ●).

Note: When you display the Clock as a floating window, an icon for the application also appears in the Dock.

7 If you chose to display the Clock as a floating window, drag this slider (🔘) to change the transparency of the window.

8 Click 🔘 to confirm your changes and close the Clock Preferences dialog box.

119

USING PREVIEW

You can use Preview to view pictures and Portable Document Format (PDF) files on your computer.

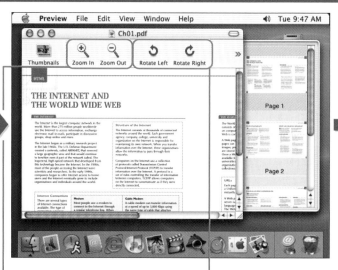

1 Double-click the picture or PDF file you want to view.

■ A window appears, displaying the picture or a page of the PDF file.

2 To magnify or reduce the size of the picture or page, click **Zoom In** or **Zoom Out**.

3 To rotate the picture or page 90 degrees to the left or right, click **Rotate Left** or **Rotate Right**.

What are PDF files?

A Portable Document Format (PDF) file is a popular file type that preserves a document's original layout and formatting. Books, product catalogues and support information for software are often distributed as PDF files, since this file type displays information exactly as it appears in printed form. PDF files are commonly found on the Web and on CDs included with books.

■ If you are viewing a PDF file that contains more than one page, this area displays a miniature version of each page in the file.

■ To hide or display the area at any time, click **Thumbnails**.

4 To view a different page, click the page you want to view.

5 When you finish viewing the picture or the contents of the PDF file, click **Preview**.

6 Click **Quit Preview**.

*Note: If you rotated the picture or page in step 3, a dialog sheet appears, asking if you want to save the changes you made. Click **Don't Save** or **Save** to specify if you want to save your changes.*

USING TEXTEDIT

You can use TextEdit to create and edit documents, such as letters and memos.

TextEdit offers only basic word processing features. If you require more advanced features, you may want to obtain a more sophisticated word processor, such as Microsoft Word.

USING TEXTEDIT

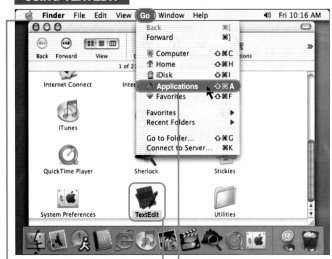

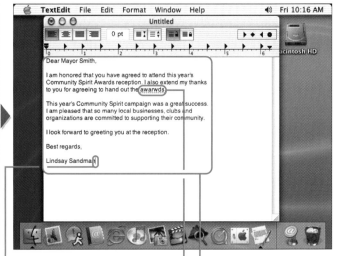

1 Click **Go**.

Note: If Go is not available, click a blank area on your desktop to display the Finder menu bar.

2 Click **Applications** to view the applications available on your computer.

■ The Applications window appears.

3 Double-click **TextEdit** to start TextEdit.

■ A new document window appears.

Note: You can click ⭕ in the Applications window to close the window.

■ The flashing insertion point indicates where the text you type will appear.

4 Type the text for the document.

■ TextEdit checks your spelling as you type and displays a dotted red underline under potential spelling errors. The dotted red underlines will not appear when you print the document.

Can TextEdit help me correct a spelling error in a document?

Yes. To get help correcting a spelling error in a document, press and hold down the `control` key as you click the misspelled word. A menu appears, displaying suggestions to correct the spelling error. Click the suggestion you want to use to correct the spelling error.

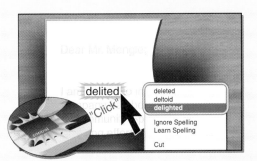

Can I change how TextEdit wraps text?

Yes. By default, TextEdit wraps text based on the width of the document window. To have TextEdit wrap text based on the width of the paper you will print on, select the **Format** menu and then click **Wrap to Page**. Wrapping text to the width of the paper you will print on helps prevent unexpected results when printing a document.

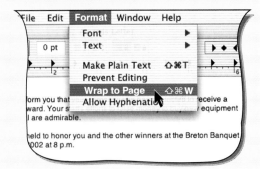

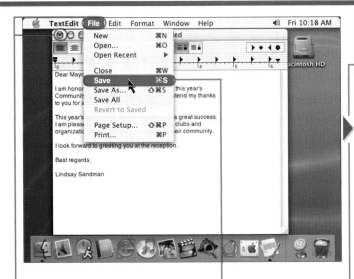

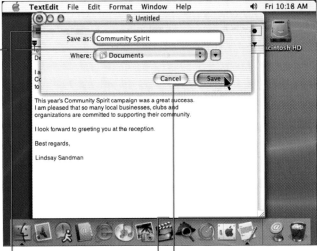

SAVE A DOCUMENT

■1 Click anywhere in the document you want to save.

■ If you have not yet saved changes to the document, the Close button displays a dot (◉).

■2 To save the document, click **File**.

■3 Click **Save**.

■ A dialog sheet appears.

Note: If you previously saved the document, the dialog sheet will not appear since you have already named the document.

■4 Type a name for the document.

■ This area shows the location where TextEdit will store the document. You can click this area to change the location.

■5 Click **Save** to save the document.

■6 When you finish working with the document, click ◯ to close the document.

CONTINUED

USING TEXTEDIT

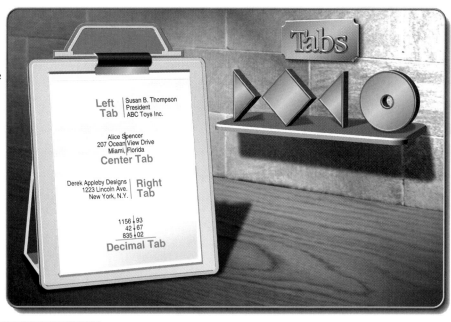

You can change the font of text to enhance the appearance of the text. You can also use tabs to line up information in a document.

TextEdit allows you to add left, center, right or decimal tabs to the ruler. By default, TextEdit places a left tab every .5 inches on the ruler.

USING TEXTEDIT (CONTINUED)

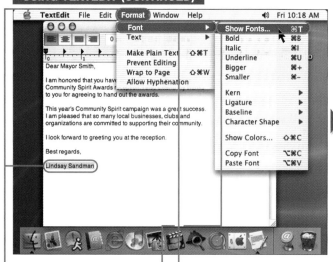

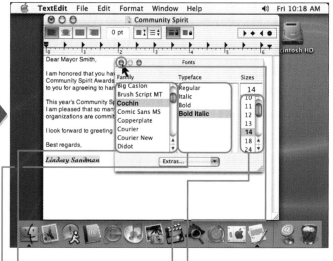

CHANGE THE FONT

1 To select the text you want to change, drag the mouse I over the text until the text is highlighted.

2 Click **Format**.

3 Position the mouse over **Font**.

4 Click **Show Fonts**.

■ The Fonts window appears.

5 Click the font family you want to use.

6 Click the typeface you want to use.

7 Click the size you want to use.

■ Changes you make in the Fonts window immediately affect the selected text in the document.

8 When you finish making changes to the text, click ⬤ to close the Fonts window.

How can I change the alignment of text?

To change the alignment of text, drag the mouse ⌶ over the text you want to change to a new alignment until the text is highlighted. Then click the Align left (☰), Center (☰), Justify (☰) or Align right (☰) button.

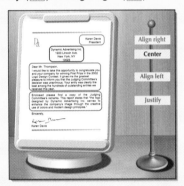

Can I change the line height of text?

Yes. Changing the line height decreases or increases the amount of space between lines of text. Drag the mouse ⌶ over the text you want to change to a new line height until the text is highlighted. Click ▪⌶ or ≡♦ to decrease or increase the line height. You may not notice any change in the line height until you click the button several times.

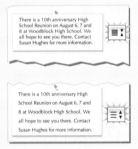

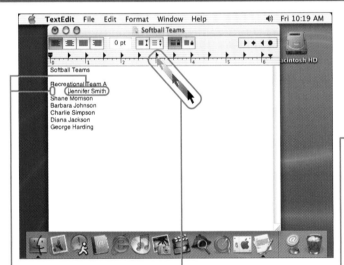

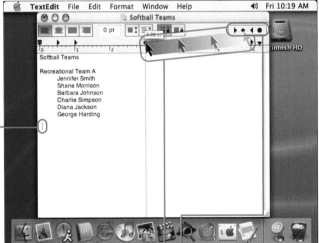

USING TABS

1 To use a tab, click the beginning of the line you want to move to the right and then press the tab key.

■ The insertion point and any text that follows move to the first tab.

DELETE A TAB

1 To delete a tab, position the mouse ▶ over the tab (▶) and then drag the tab off the ruler.

ADD A TAB

1 To add a tab for text you are about to type, click where you want to type the text.

Note: To add a tab for existing text, drag the mouse ⌶ over the text until the text is highlighted.

2 Position the mouse ▶ over the type of tab you want to add.

Note: You can add a left (▶), center (◆), right (◀) or decimal (●) tab.

3 Drag the tab to a location on the ruler.

CONTINUED ▶

USING TEXTEDIT

You can open a saved TextEdit document to display the document on your screen. This allows you to review and make changes to the document.

OPEN A DOCUMENT

1 Click the TextEdit icon to make TextEdit the active application.

Note: If the TextEdit icon does not appear in the Dock, see page 122 to start the application. When you click the TextEdit icon, a new document window may appear.

2 Click **File**.

3 Click **Open**.

■ The Open dialog box appears.

■ This area displays the location of the current folder in relation to the disks, folders and files on your computer. The current folder is highlighted.

Note: The leftmost column shows the disks on your computer. Each of the following columns shows the contents of the item selected in the previous column. You can use the scroll bar to browse through the columns.

■ To display the contents of a different folder, click the folder.

How do I create a new TextEdit document?

To create a new TextEdit document, select the **File** menu and then click **New**. A new document window will appear on your screen.

Can TextEdit read the text in an open document aloud?

3 Click **Start speaking**.

■ TextEdit reads the text in the document aloud.

*Note: To stop TextEdit from reading the text in the document aloud, repeat steps 1 to 3, selecting **Stop speaking** in step 3.*

1 To have TextEdit read the text in a document aloud, click **Edit**.

2 Position the mouse ➤ over **Speech**.

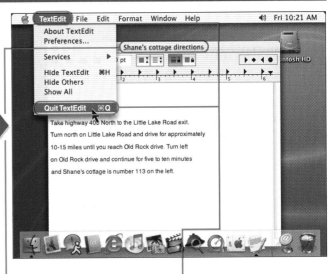

4 Click the document you want to open.

■ Information about the document appears in the last column.

5 Click **Open** to open the document.

■ The document appears on your screen. You can now review and make changes to the document.

■ This area displays the name of the document.

QUIT TEXTEDIT

1 When you finish using TextEdit, click **TextEdit**.

2 Click **Quit TextEdit**.

USING ADDRESS BOOK

You can use Address Book to store information for people you frequently contact.

Mail and other applications can use the information in Address Book. For example, when you compose an e-mail message, Mail can quickly fill in the e-mail address of a person you have added to Address Book.

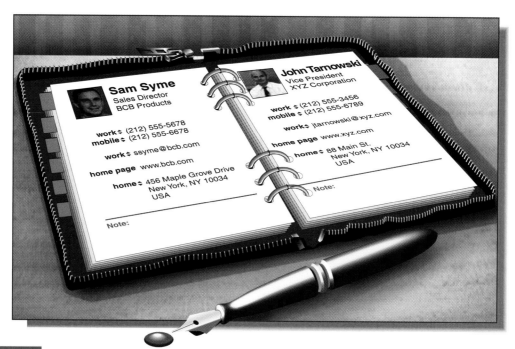

USING ADDRESS BOOK

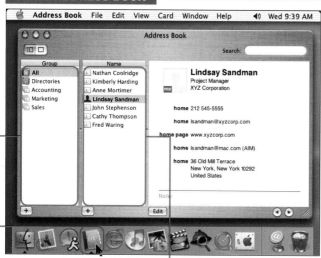

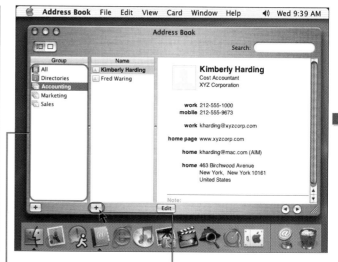

DISPLAY ADDRESS BOOK

■1 Click the Address Book icon to display Address Book.

■ The Address Book window appears.

■ This area displays the groups in Address Book.

■ This area displays the people in the highlighted group.

Note: Your name automatically appears in the All group and displays the 👤 *symbol.*

ADD A PERSON

■1 To add a person to Address Book, click the group you want to add the person to. The group is highlighted.

*Note: If you have not added groups to Address Book, select the **All** group. To add groups to Address Book, see page 132.*

■2 Click ⊕ to add a new person to Address Book.

Why does a plus sign (⊕) appear when I enter information for a person?

A plus sign appears if Address Book can display another area where you can enter information. To display the other area, click the plus sign (⊕). For example, after you enter a mobile phone number, you can click the plus sign (⊕) beside **mobile** to display an area where you can enter a home phone number.

When entering information for a person, can I change the label for an area?

Yes. You may want to change the label for an area to better describe the information you want to enter in the area. For example, you can change the label "mobile" to "pager."

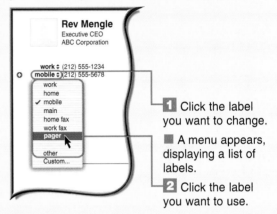

■ **1** Click the label you want to change.

■ A menu appears, displaying a list of labels.

■ **2** Click the label you want to use.

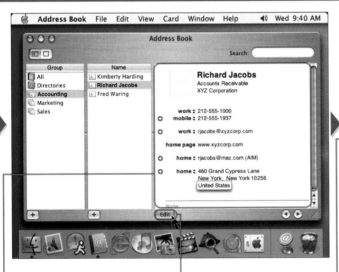

■ Address Book displays areas where you can enter information for the person.

3 Click an area and type the appropriate information for the person. Then press the return key.

4 Repeat step 3 for each area where you want to enter information for the person.

Note: You do not need to enter information into every area.

5 When you finish entering the information for the person, click **Edit** to save the information.

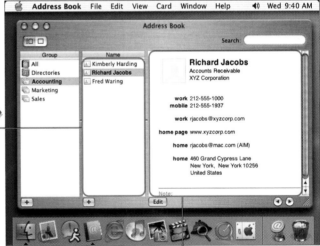

■ The name you entered for the person appears in this area.

■ This area displays the information you entered for the person.

CONTINUED

USING ADDRESS BOOK

You can browse through Address Book to find information for a specific person. You can also edit the information for a person or delete a person you no longer contact.

USING ADDRESS BOOK (CONTINUED)

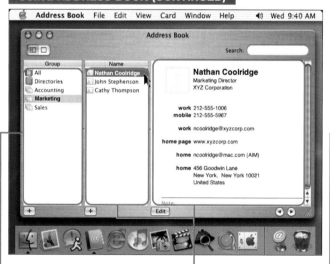

DISPLAY A PERSON'S INFORMATION

1 Click the group that contains a person of interest.

Note: The All group contains all the people you have added to Address Book.

■ This area displays the people in the group you selected.

2 Click the name of a person of interest.

■ This area displays the information for the person.

EDIT A PERSON'S INFORMATION

1 To edit the information for a person, click the name of the person.

■ This area displays the information for the person.

2 Click **Edit** to edit the person's information.

Can I add a picture to a person's information in Address Book?

Yes. Click the name of the person whose information you want to add a picture to. Locate the picture on your computer that you want to add to the person's information and then drag the picture into the box beside the person's name in the Address Book window.

How do I search for a person in Address Book?

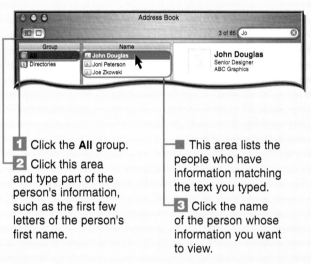

1 Click the **All** group.

2 Click this area and type part of the person's information, such as the first few letters of the person's first name.

■ This area lists the people who have information matching the text you typed.

3 Click the name of the person whose information you want to view.

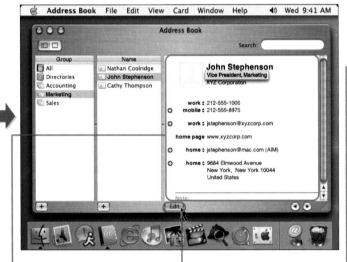

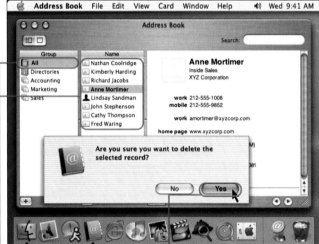

3 Click the information you want to edit. The information is highlighted.

4 Type the new information and then press the return key.

5 Repeat steps 3 and 4 for each area of information you want to edit.

6 Click **Edit** to save your changes.

DELETE A PERSON

1 Click **All** to display all the people you have added to Address Book.

2 Click the name of the person you want to remove from Address Book.

3 Press the delete key.

■ A confirmation dialog sheet appears.

4 Click **Yes** to remove the person from Address Book.

CONTINUED

USING ADDRESS BOOK

You can create groups to organize the people in Address Book. For example, you can create groups such as Family, Friends, Clients and Colleagues.

You can create as many groups as you need. A person can belong to more than one group.

Mail and other applications can use a group you create in Address Book. For example, Mail can use a group you added to Address Book to quickly address an e-mail message to each person in the group.

USING ADDRESS BOOK (CONTINUED)

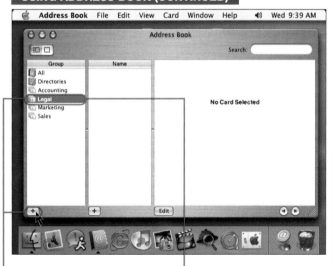

CREATE A GROUP

1 Click ⊕ to create a new group.

■ A new group appears, displaying a temporary name.

2 Type a name for the new group and then press the return key.

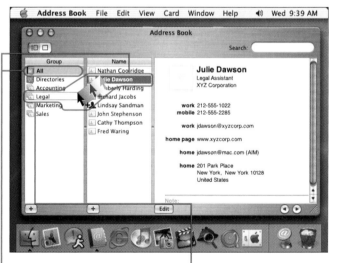

ADD PEOPLE TO A GROUP

1 Click **All** to display all the people you have added to Address Book.

2 Position the mouse over the person you want to add to a specific group.

3 Drag the person to the group.

Note: When you drag a person to a group, a box appears around the group.

■ The person's information is copied to the group.

Can I remove a person from a group?

Yes. Click the group that contains a person you want to remove. Click the name of the person you want to remove from the group and then press the `delete` key. In the confirmation dialog sheet that appears, click **Yes** to remove the person. Removing a person from a group will not remove the person from Address Book.

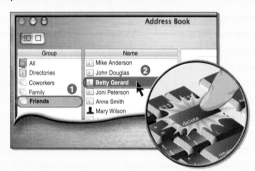

How do I rename a group in Address Book?

Double-click the name of the group you want to rename. A box appears around the name of the group. Type a new name for the group and then press the `return` key. You cannot rename the All group.

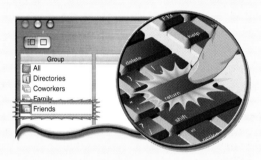

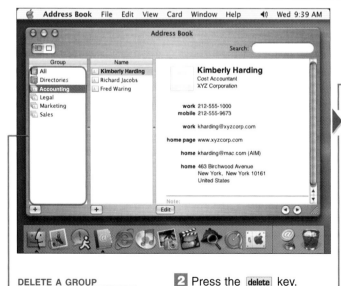

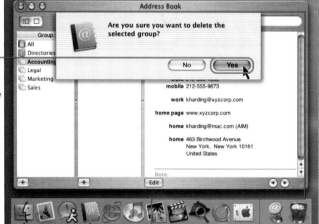

DELETE A GROUP

1 Click the group you want to remove from Address Book.

2 Press the `delete` key.

■ A confirmation dialog sheet appears.

3 Click **Yes** to remove the group from Address Book.

CLOSE ADDRESS BOOK

1 When you finish using Address Book, click ○ to close Address Book.

USING STICKIES

You can create colorful, electronic sticky notes that are similar to paper sticky notes.

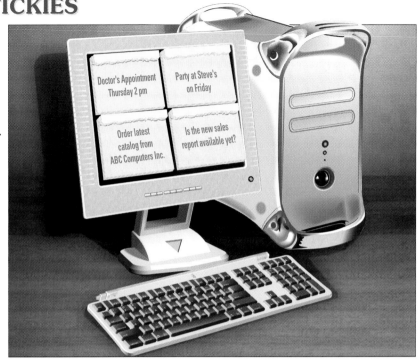

Sticky notes are useful for storing small pieces of information, such as to-do lists, phone numbers, reminders, questions or ideas.

USING STICKIES

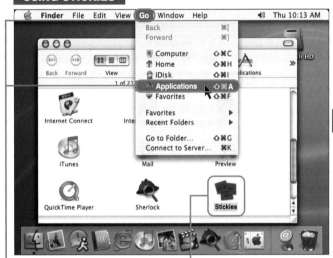

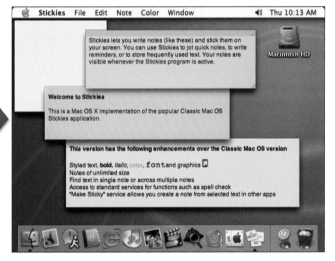

■1 Click **Go**.

Note: If Go is not available, click a blank area on your desktop to display the Finder menu bar.

■2 Click **Applications** to view the applications available on your computer.

■ The Applications window appears.

■3 Double-click **Stickies** to start Stickies.

■ All your sticky notes appear on your screen. Stickies comes with several sample sticky notes that describe some of the application's features.

Note: You can click ⬤ in the Applications window to close the window.

Can I resize a sticky note?

Yes. Click the sticky note you want to resize. Position the mouse ⬆ over ⬐ at the bottom right corner of the sticky note and then drag ⬐ until the sticky note displays the size you want.

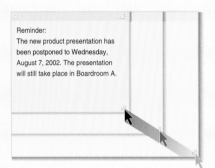

Reminder:
The new product presentation has been postponed to Wednesday, August 7, 2002. The presentation will still take place in Boardroom A.

How can I change the color of a sticky note?

Reminder:
The new product presentation has been postponed to Wednesday, August 7, 2002. The presentation will still take place in Boardroom A

Color
✓ Yellow
Blue
Green
Pink
Purple
Gray

1 Click the sticky note you want to change to a different color.

2 Click **Color** to display a list of the available colors.

3 Click the color you want to use for the sticky note.

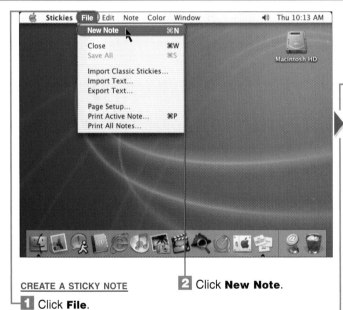

CREATE A STICKY NOTE

1 Click **File**.

2 Click **New Note**.

■ A new sticky note appears.

■ The flashing insertion point indicates where the text you type will appear in the sticky note.

3 Type the text for the new sticky note.

Note: You do not have to save the sticky notes you create. Stickies automatically saves your sticky notes for you.

CONTINUED ▶

USING STICKIES

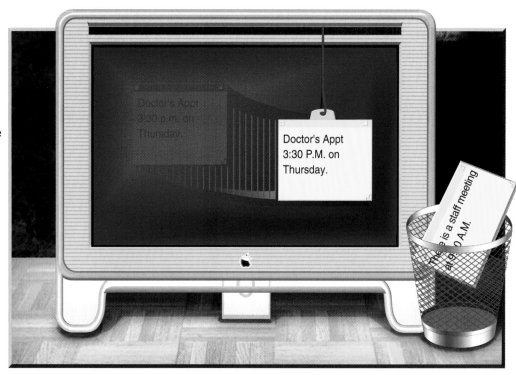

You can move a
sticky note to a
different location
on your screen.
You can also delete
a sticky note you
no longer need.

Doctor's Appt
3:30 P.M. on
Thursday.

USING STICKIES (CONTINUED)

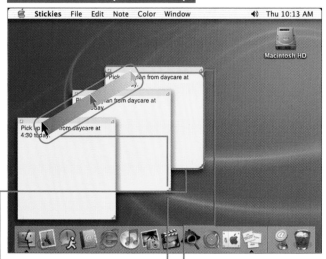

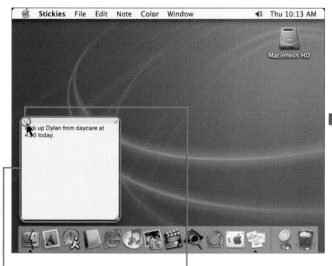

MOVE A STICKY NOTE

1 Click anywhere
in the sticky note
you want to move.

2 Position the mouse ▶
over the bar at the top
of the sticky note.

3 Drag the sticky note
to where you want to
place the sticky note
on your screen.

DELETE A STICKY NOTE

1 Click anywhere in
the sticky note you
want to delete from
your computer.

2 Click ⊡ to delete the
sticky note.

How can I quickly reduce the size of a sticky note?

You can quickly shrink or collapse a sticky note to view other items on your screen more easily.

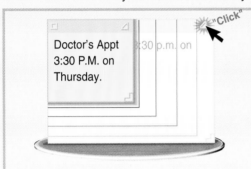

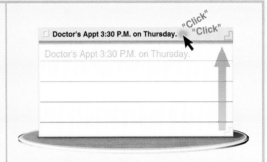

Shrink a Sticky Note

Click the sticky note you want to shrink and then click ◿ at the top right corner of the sticky note. To once again display the entire sticky note, click ◿ again.

Collapse a Sticky Note

Double-click the bar at the top of the sticky note you want to collapse. The sticky note collapses to show only the first line of text in the note. To once again display the entire sticky note, double-click the bar again.

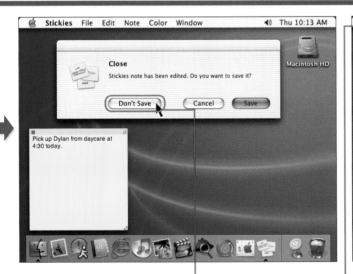

■ A dialog box appears, asking if you want to save the sticky note.

3 Click **Don't Save** to permanently delete the sticky note.

Note: If you decide you want to keep the sticky note, click **Cancel**.

QUIT STICKIES

1 When you finish reviewing and working with your sticky notes, click **Stickies**.

2 Click **Quit Stickies**.

■ When you quit Stickies, all your sticky notes are automatically saved on your computer and will reappear the next time you start Stickies.

USING KEY CAPS

You can use Key Caps to view the characters that are available for each font installed on your computer.

Key Caps allows you to review the characters a font offers before choosing to use the font in your documents.

1 Click **Go**.

Note: If Go is not available, click a blank area on your desktop to display the Finder menu bar.

2 Click **Applications** to view the applications available on your computer.

■ The Applications window appears.

3 Double-click **Utilities** to view the utility applications available on your computer.

■ The Utilities window appears, displaying the utility applications available on your computer.

4 Double-click **Key Caps** to start Key Caps.

■ The Key Caps window appears, displaying an on-screen keyboard. The on-screen keyboard displays the characters available for the current font.

Note: You can click ◯ in the Utilities window to close the window.

How do I enlarge the Key Caps window to make the on-screen keyboard easier to view?

To enlarge the Key Caps window, you can zoom the window. To zoom a window, click ⬤ in the top left corner of the window. You can click ⬤ again to return the window to its previous size.

Can Key Caps help me determine the special characters that are available for a font?

Yes. You can press the option key to have the on-screen keyboard display the special characters available for the current font, such as © or ™. To type a special character, press and hold down the option key as you press the keyboard key that corresponds to the special character you want to enter.

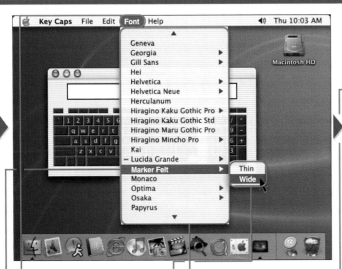

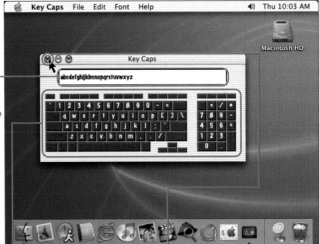

5 To display the characters available for a different font, click **Font**.

■ A list of the fonts installed on your computer appears. The current font displays the — or ✓ symbol.

6 Position the mouse ▶ over a font of interest. If the font displays an arrow (▶), a list of styles for the font appears.

Note: If the font does not display an arrow (▶), you can click the font to select the font.

7 Click a font style of interest.

■ This area displays the characters available for the font you selected.

8 Click this area and then press keys on your keyboard to see how the characters you type will appear.

Note: As you type, the corresponding keys on the on-screen keyboard are highlighted.

9 When you finish using Key Caps, click ⬤ to close Key Caps.

USING QUICKTIME PLAYER

You can use QuickTime Player to play QuickTime movies on your computer.

You can play QuickTime movies you obtained on the Internet or created using iMovie. For information on using iMovie, see pages 186 to 205.

USING QUICKTIME PLAYER

■1 Double-click the QuickTime movie you want to play. QuickTime movies display the icon and .mov extension.

■ A QuickTime Player window opens.

Note: The first time you play a QuickTime movie, a dialog box appears, allowing you to purchase QuickTime Pro, an advanced version of QuickTime. You can click an option in the dialog box to purchase the program now or later.

■2 Click (▶) to start playing the movie ((▶) changes to (⏸)).

■ The movie plays in this area.

■ This area displays the amount of time the movie has been playing and a slider (▼) that indicates the progress of the movie.

140

Is there another way to play a QuickTime movie?

Yes. You can find QuickTime movies on the Web that you can play in your Web browser. For example, the www.apple.com/trailers and www.comingsoon.net/trailers Web sites offer QuickTime movies that you can play. When the movie is playing, you can click **❚❚** to pause the movie (**❚❚** changes to **▶**). To once again play the movie, click **▶** .

3 To adjust the volume, drag this slider (⬤) left or right to decrease or increase the volume.

Note: To quickly turn off the sound, click 🔊 (🔊 changes to ◀-). To once again turn on the sound, click ◀- .

4 To rewind or fast forward through the movie, position the mouse ▶ over ◀◀ or ▶▶ and then press and hold down the mouse button.

5 To quickly move to the beginning or end of the movie, click ◀ or ▶ .

6 To pause the play of the movie, click ❚❚ (❚❚ changes to ▶).

■ You can click ▶ to resume the play of the movie.

7 When you finish playing the movie, click **QuickTime Player**.

8 Click **Quit QuickTime Player**.

USING DVD PLAYER

You can use DVD Player to play DVD movies on your computer.

Your computer must have a DVD drive to play DVD movies. You can usually play DVD movies only on a computer with an Apple DVD drive.

USING DVD PLAYER

1 Insert the DVD movie you want to play into your computer's DVD drive.

■ DVD Player starts and the movie automatically begins to play.

■ You can use the playback controller to control the movie.

Note: If the playback controller does not appear, move the mouse on your desk to display the controller.

■ Most DVD movies display a main menu that lists options you can select to play the movie or access special features.

2 To select an option in the menu, click an arrow in this area to move through the options until you highlight the option you want to select.

3 Click (enter) to select the highlighted option.

Note: You can also select an option by clicking the option on your screen.

Can I play a DVD movie in a window?

Yes. To play a DVD movie in a window, press and hold down the ⌘ key as you press the ① (half size), ② (normal size) or ③ (maximum size) key. To once again play the movie using the entire screen, press and hold down the ⌘ key as you press the ⓪ key.

Are there other ways to browse through a DVD movie?

Yes. You can click ⓵ or ⓶ to display the previous or next chapter in the movie. To display the main menu at any time, click menu. You can click menu again to return to the part of the movie you were last viewing. The menu button may not work for some DVD movies.

4 To adjust the volume of the movie, drag this slider (◯) left or right to decrease or increase the volume.

5 To rewind or fast forward through the movie, position the mouse ▸ over ⓵ or ⓶ and then press and hold down the mouse button.

6 To pause the play of the movie, click ⓘ (ⓘ changes to ▸).

■ You can click ▸ to resume playing the movie.

7 To stop playing the movie at any time, click ■ .

8 To eject the DVD when you finish playing the movie, click eject .

9 To quit DVD Player, move the mouse ▸ over the top of the screen and then click **DVD Player** on the menu bar that appears.

10 Click **Quit DVD Player**.

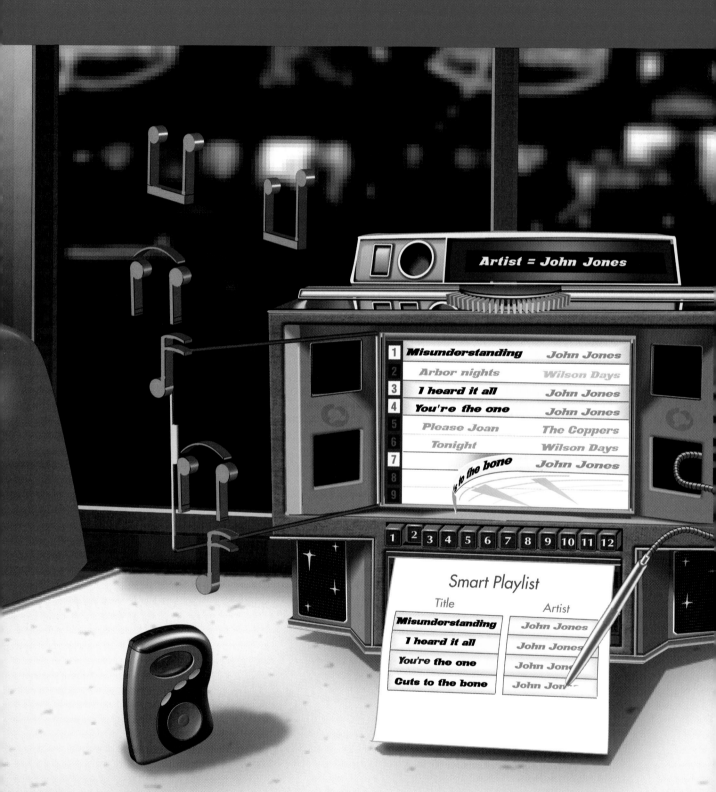

CHAPTER 6

Play Music Using iTunes

In this chapter, you will learn how to use iTunes to play music CDs, listen to radio stations on the Internet, organize your songs and copy songs to a CD or MP3 player.

LISTEN TO A MUSIC CD

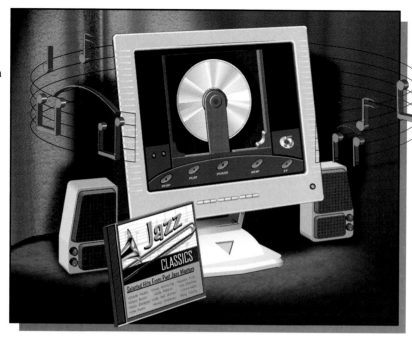

You can use your computer to listen to music CDs while you work.

The first time you start iTunes, a dialog box appears on your screen, displaying a license agreement. Follow the instructions on your screen to accept the agreement and set up iTunes.

LISTEN TO A MUSIC CD

1 Insert a music CD into your computer's CD drive.

■ After a moment, the iTunes window appears.

2 Click the name of the CD in this area.

*Note: If the name of the CD is not displayed, click **Audio CD**.*

3 Click ▶ to start playing the CD.

■ This area lists the songs on the CD and the amount of time each song will play. The song that is currently playing displays a speaker icon (🔊).

■ To play a specific song in the list, double-click the name of the song.

■ iTunes will play each song that displays a check mark. To add (☑) or remove (☐) a check mark for a song, click the box (☐) beside the song.

How does iTunes know the name of each song on my music CD?

If you are connected to the Internet when you insert a music CD, iTunes attempts to obtain information about the CD from the Internet. If you are not connected to the Internet or information about the CD is unavailable, iTunes displays the track number of each song instead. If iTunes is able to obtain information about the CD, iTunes will recognize the CD and display the appropriate information each time you insert the CD.

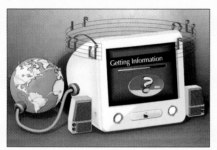

Can I play the songs on my music CD in random order?

Yes. You can shuffle the songs to play the songs in random order. Click 🔀 in the iTunes window to shuffle the songs. To once again play the songs on the CD in order, click 🔀 again.

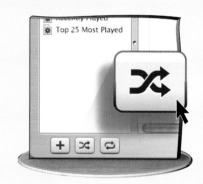

■ This area displays the name of the song that is currently playing and the amount of time the song has been playing.

4 To adjust the volume, drag this slider (○) left or right to decrease or increase the volume.

5 To pause the play of the CD, click ⏸ (⏸ changes to ▶).

Note: You can click ▶ to resume the play of the CD.

6 When you finish listening to the CD, click ⏏ to eject the CD.

7 When you finish listening to CDs, click **iTunes**.

8 Click **Quit iTunes**.

You can listen to radio stations from around the world that broadcast on the Internet.

You need to be connected to the Internet to listen to radio stations that broadcast on the Internet. To connect to the Internet, see page 238.

The first time you start iTunes, a dialog box appears on your screen, displaying a license agreement. Follow the instructions on your screen to accept the agreement and set up iTunes.

LISTEN TO RADIO STATIONS ON THE INTERNET

1 Click the iTunes icon to start iTunes.

■ The iTunes window appears.

2 Click **Radio** to listen to radio stations that broadcast on the Internet.

■ This area lists the categories of available radio stations.

3 To display the radio stations in a category, click ► beside the category (► changes to ▼).

■ The name, bit rate and description of each radio station in the category appear.

Note: The higher the bit rate, the better the sound quality.

■ You can click ▼ beside a category to once again hide the radio stations in the category (▼ changes to ►).

4 Double-click the radio station you want to play.

Note: If you use a modem to connect to the Internet, you should select a radio station with a bit rate of less than 56 kbps for the best results.

Can I display visual effects while listening to a radio station?

Yes. You can click ❋ in the iTunes window to display visual effects while listening to a radio station. To once again display the categories of radio stations, click ❋ again.

How can I reduce the size of the iTunes window?

You can reduce the size of the iTunes window so you can easily view other items on your screen while listening to a radio station. Click ⬤ in the top left corner of the iTunes window to reduce the size of the window. To return the iTunes window to its previous size, click ⬤ again.

■ The radio station begins to play. The selected radio station displays a speaker icon (🔊).

■ This area displays information about the currently playing radio station and the amount of time the radio station has been playing.

5 To adjust the volume, drag this slider (⭕) left or right to decrease or increase the volume.

6 To stop playing the radio station, click (⏹) (⏹ changes to ▶).

Note: You can click ▶ to resume the play of the radio station.

■ To play another radio station, double-click the radio station you want to play.

7 When you finish listening to radio stations on the Internet, click **iTunes**.

8 Click **Quit iTunes**.

USING THE iTUNES LIBRARY

The Library in iTunes acts like an electronic jukebox, providing a central location where you can view and play songs on your computer.

The first time you start iTunes, a dialog box appears on your screen, displaying a license agreement. Follow the instructions on your screen to accept the agreement and set up iTunes.

USING THE iTUNES LIBRARY

1 Click the iTunes icon to start iTunes.

■ The iTunes window appears.

2 Click **Library** to view all the songs in the Library.

■ This area lists all the songs in the Library.

Note: When you first started and set up iTunes, you may have selected to have iTunes automatically add existing songs on your computer to the Library.

ADD A SONG TO THE LIBRARY

1 Locate the song on your computer that you want to add to the Library.

2 Position the mouse ▶ over the song.

3 Drag the song to the list of songs in the Library.

■ iTunes adds the song to the Library.

Are there other ways to add songs to the iTunes Library?

Yes. When you double-click a song on your computer that plays in iTunes, iTunes automatically adds the song to the Library. Songs you copy from a music CD are also automatically added to the Library. To copy songs from a music CD, see page 152. To quickly add all the songs in a folder to the Library, position the mouse ▶ over the folder and then drag the folder to the list of songs in the Library.

How can I remove a song from the iTunes Library?

To remove a song from the Library, click the song and then press the `delete` key. In the confirmation dialog box that appears, click **Yes** to remove the song. An additional dialog box may appear, asking if you want to remove the song from the iTunes Music folder. Click **Yes** or **No** to specify if you want to remove the song from this folder.

PLAY SONGS IN THE LIBRARY

1 Double-click the name of the song you want to play.

2 To adjust the volume, drag this slider (⬤) left or right to decrease or increase the volume.

Note: To quickly turn off the sound, click ◀. To quickly turn the volume to full capacity, click ◀))) .

3 To pause the play of the song, click ⏸ (⏸ changes to ▶).

■ You can click ▶ to resume the play of the song.

■ This area displays the name of the song that is currently playing and the amount of time the song has been playing.

■ When a song finishes playing, iTunes will automatically play the next song in the list that displays a check mark (☑). To add (☑) or remove (☐) a check mark for a song, click the box (☐) beside the song.

4 When you finish playing songs in iTunes, click **iTunes**.

5 Click **Quit iTunes**.

COPY SONGS FROM A MUSIC CD

You can copy songs from your favorite music CD onto your computer.

Copying songs from a music CD allows you to play the songs at any time without having to insert the CD into your computer.

The first time you start iTunes, a dialog box appears on your screen, displaying a license agreement. Follow the instructions on your screen to accept the agreement and set up iTunes.

COPY SONGS FROM A MUSIC CD

1 Insert a music CD into your computer's CD drive.

■ After a moment, the iTunes window appears.

2 Click the name of the CD in this area.

Note: If the name of the CD is not displayed, click **Audio CD**.

■ This area lists the songs on the CD and the amount of time each song will play.

Note: For information on how iTunes determines the name of each song on a CD, see the top of page 147.

■ iTunes will copy each song that displays a check mark. To add (☑) or remove (☐) a check mark for a song, click the box (☐) beside the song.

3 Click 🔄 to copy the songs to your computer.

Where can I find the songs I copied from a music CD?

The Library

Songs you copy from a music CD are listed in the iTunes Library. You can click **Library** in the iTunes window to display all the songs in the Library. To play a song in the Library, see page 151.

The iTunes Music folder

Songs you copy from a music CD are stored in a subfolder of the Music folder called iTunes Music. To view the contents of the Music folder, see page 26. The iTunes Music folder contains a folder for each CD you have copied songs from. You can double-click a song you copied from a CD to open iTunes and play the song.

■ iTunes begins playing the first song you selected to copy.

■ This area displays the name of the song that iTunes is currently copying and the amount of time remaining to complete the copy.

■ The song that iTunes is currently copying displays the ◎ symbol. Each song that iTunes has finished copying displays the ◉ symbol.

■ To stop the copy at any time, click 🔘.

■ When iTunes has finished copying songs from the CD, a sound plays. iTunes will continue to play the songs you selected to copy.

4 To eject the CD, click ▲.

5 When you finish copying songs from a music CD, click **iTunes**.

6 Click **Quit iTunes**.

CREATE A PLAYLIST

My Favorite Songs

You can create a personalized playlist that contains your favorite songs.

You can create as many playlists as you want. For example, you can create one playlist that contains your favorite jazz songs and another playlist that contains your favorite songs by a specific artist.

CREATE A PLAYLIST

1 Click the iTunes icon to start iTunes.

■ The iTunes window appears.

2 Click ＋ to create a new playlist.

■ A new, untitled playlist appears. Playlists display the ♫ symbol.

3 Type a name for the new playlist and then press the return key.

4 To add a song to the playlist, click **Library** to view all the songs in the Library.

■ This area lists all the songs in the Library.

Note: For information on the Library, see page 150.

5 Position the mouse ▶ over a song you want to add to the new playlist.

6 Drag the song to the playlist.

■ The song is added to the playlist.

Can I change the order in which songs will play in a playlist?

Yes. Click the icon for the playlist that contains the songs you want to reorder. Position the mouse ⤹ over a song you want to move and then drag the song to a new location in the playlist. A black line indicates where the song will appear.

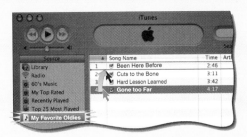

How do I delete a playlist?

To delete a playlist, click the icon for the playlist you want to delete and then press the `delete` key. In the confirmation dialog box that appears, click **Yes** to delete the playlist. Deleting a playlist will not remove the songs in the playlist from the Library.

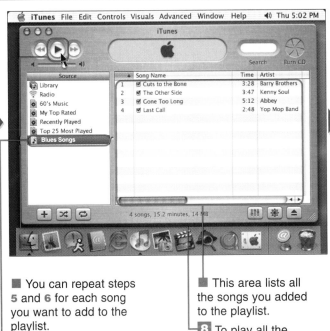

■ You can repeat steps **5** and **6** for each song you want to add to the playlist.

7 When you finish adding songs to the playlist, click the playlist.

■ This area lists all the songs you added to the playlist.

8 To play all the songs in the playlist, click ▶.

■ To play a specific song in the playlist, double-click the song.

9 When you finish working with your playlists, click **iTunes**.

10 Click **Quit iTunes**.

CREATE A SMART PLAYLIST

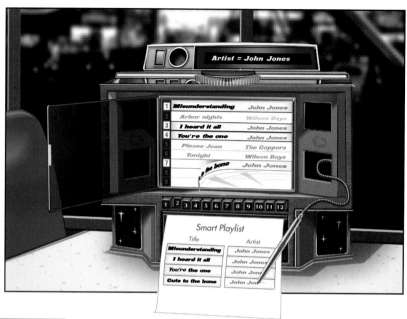

You can create a
Smart Playlist that
will automatically
display songs
from the iTunes
Library that match
information you
specify.

For example, you can
create a Smart Playlist
that displays all the
songs from a specific
artist or genre.

By default, the songs
in a Smart Playlist will
continually update
as you add songs to
the iTunes Library.
For information on the
Library, see page 150.

For information on the
Library, see page 150.

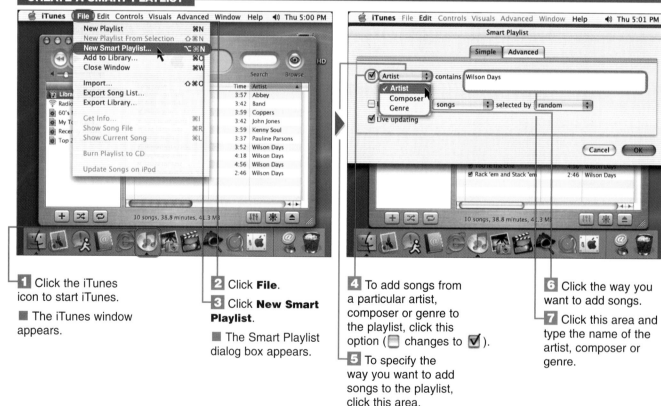

1 Click the iTunes
icon to start iTunes.

■ The iTunes window
appears.

2 Click **File**.

3 Click **New Smart
Playlist**.

■ The Smart Playlist
dialog box appears.

4 To add songs from
a particular artist,
composer or genre to
the playlist, click this
option (☐ changes to ✓).

5 To specify the
way you want to add
songs to the playlist,
click this area.

6 Click the way you
want to add songs.

7 Click this area and
type the name of the
artist, composer or
genre.

What Smart Playlists are automatically included in iTunes?

By default, iTunes includes four Smart Playlists.

Smart Playlist	Contains
60's Music	Songs recorded between 1960 and 1969.
My Top Rated	Songs rated higher than 3 stars.
Recently Played	Songs you have played within the last 2 weeks.
Top 25 Most Played	The 25 songs you have played most often.

How do I delete a Smart Playlist?

To delete a Smart Playlist, click the icon for the Smart Playlist and then press the delete key. In the confirmation dialog box that appears, click **Yes** to delete the Smart Playlist. Deleting a Smart Playlist will not remove the songs in the playlist from the iTunes Library.

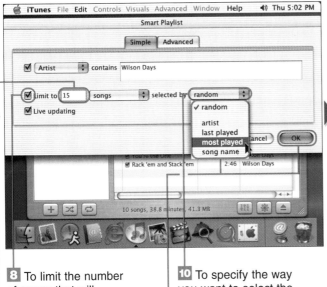

8 To limit the number of songs that will appear in the playlist, click this option (⬜ changes to ☑).

9 Double-click this area and type the maximum number of songs you want to appear in the playlist.

10 To specify the way you want to select the songs for the playlist, click this area.

11 Click the way you want to select the songs.

12 Click **OK** to create the Smart Playlist.

■ The Smart Playlist appears in this area. Smart Playlists display the ❄ symbol.

13 Type a name for the playlist and then press the return key.

■ This area displays the songs iTunes automatically added to the playlist. To play a specific song, double-click the song.

Note: To play all the songs in the Smart Playlist, click ▶ .

14 When you finish working with your Smart Playlists, click **iTunes**.

15 Click **Quit iTunes**.

CREATE YOUR OWN MUSIC CDS

You can create a music CD that contains your favorite songs.

You need a computer with a recordable CD drive to create your own music CDs. A CD can typically store about 74 minutes of audio, which is about 20 songs.

CREATE YOUR OWN MUSIC CDS

■ Before you can create your own music CD, you must create a playlist that contains all the songs you want to include on the CD. To create a playlist, see pages 154 to 157.

1 Click the iTunes icon to start iTunes.

■ The iTunes window appears.

2 Click the playlist that contains the songs you want to copy to a recordable CD.

■ This area lists the songs in the playlist.

3 iTunes will copy each song that displays a check mark. To add (☑) or remove (☐) a check mark for a song, click the box (☐) beside the song.

■ This area displays the total number of songs, the total amount of time the songs will play and the total file size of all the songs in the playlist.

4 To copy the songs you selected to a recordable CD, click ✹ (✹ changes to ✹).

What type of CD should I use to create my music CD?

You should use a CD-R (Compact Disc-Recordable) to create your music CD. Most CD players can play CD-Rs. You cannot erase or change the contents of a CD-R.

If your computer has a CD-RW drive, you can also use a CD-RW (Compact Disc-ReWritable) to create your music CD, but CD-RWs may not play in some CD players. You can erase the contents of a CD-RW in order to copy new music to the disc.

Can I stop iTunes from copying songs to a CD?

Yes. To stop iTunes from copying songs, click ⊗ in the iTunes window. In the confirmation dialog box that appears, click **Yes** to stop the copy. If you are copying songs to a CD-R, keep in mind that you can record data to a CD-R only once.

5 Insert a blank, recordable CD into your computer's recordable CD drive.

■ This area indicates the number of songs you selected and the total amount of time the songs will play.

6 Click 🔘 to start copying the songs.

■ 🔘 spins as iTunes copies the songs to the CD.

■ When the copy is complete, the CD appears in this area, displaying the same name as the playlist.

■ This area lists the songs on the CD.

7 Click ⏏ to eject the CD.

8 To quit iTunes, click **iTunes**.

9 Click **Quit iTunes**.

COPY SONGS TO AN MP3 PLAYER

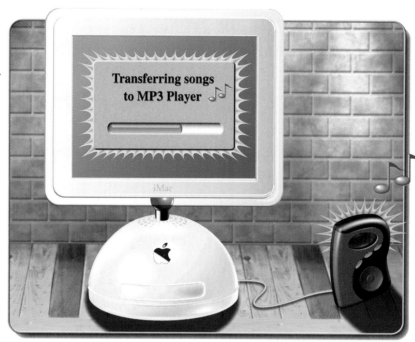

Transferring songs to MP3 Player

You can transfer songs from the iTunes Library to a portable MP3 player.

An MP3 player is a device that can store and play MP3 files.

When transferring songs to your MP3 player, make sure your computer will not go to sleep. To check when your computer will automatically go to sleep, see page 86.

COPY SONGS TO AN MP3 PLAYER

1 Connect the MP3 player to your computer.

2 Click the iTunes icon to start iTunes.

■ The iTunes window appears.

■ The name of the MP3 player appears in this area.

3 Click **Library** to view all the songs in the Library.

Note: For information on the Library, see page 150.

■ To copy songs in a playlist, click the playlist. To create a playlist, see pages 154 to 157.

■ This area lists all the songs in the Library or playlist you selected.

4 To copy a song to your MP3 player, drag the song to the player.

Can I use iTunes to remove a song from my MP3 player?

To use iTunes to remove a song from your MP3 player, perform steps 1 and 2 below and then click the name of the MP3 player in the iTunes window. Click the song you want to remove and then press the delete key. In the confirmation dialog box that appears, click **Yes** to remove the song from your MP3 player.

 How do I copy songs to my iPod?

When you connect the iPod to your computer, the songs in the iTunes Library are automatically transferred to the iPod. If you later change the songs in the Library, the songs on the iPod will be updated automatically the next time you connect the iPod to your computer. This ensures the songs in iTunes always match the songs on your iPod.

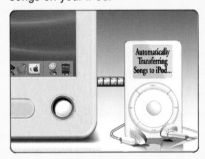

▪ After you drag a song to the MP3 player, this area displays the name of the song you selected to copy and the progress of the copy.

5 You can repeat step 4 for each song you want to copy to the MP3 player.

6 When the copy is complete, click the name of the MP3 player.

▪ This area lists all the songs on the MP3 player.

7 When you finish copying songs to your MP3 player, click **iTunes**.

8 Click **Quit iTunes**.

Scuba Diving in the Bahamas

The Annual Regatta

CHAPTER 7

Manage Photos Using iPhoto

This chapter teaches you how to use iPhoto to copy photos from a digital camera to your computer so you can view, organize and edit the photos.

Summer Vacation

COPY PHOTOS FROM A DIGITAL CAMERA

You can copy photos from a digital camera to your computer so you can view, organize and edit the photos.

Before you start copying photos, make sure the digital camera is connected to your computer and is turned on. You may also need to set the camera to a specific mode, such as the Connect mode.

COPY PHOTOS FROM A DIGITAL CAMERA

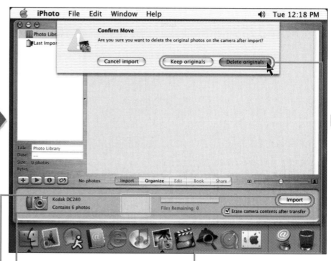

1 Click the iPhoto icon to start iPhoto.

■ The iPhoto window appears.

Note: The first time you start iPhoto, a dialog box appears, asking if you want iPhoto to open automatically when you attach a camera to your computer. Click an option in the dialog box to specify if you want iPhoto to open automatically.

■ This area displays the name of the camera and the number of photos stored on the camera.

2 This option will erase the photos on the camera after the photos are copied to your computer. You can click the option to turn the option on (☑) or off (☐).

3 Click **Import** to start copying the photos to your computer.

■ If you selected to erase the photos in step 2, a confirmation dialog sheet appears.

4 Click an option to keep or delete the photos on the camera after the copy is complete.

How can I quickly display the last photos I copied from my digital camera?

To quickly display the last photos you copied from your digital camera, click **Last Import** in the top left corner of the iPhoto window.

How do I delete a photo I copied from my digital camera?

To delete a photo, click **Photo Library** to view all your photos. Click the photo you want to delete and then press the delete key. In the confirmation dialog box that appears, click **OK** to delete the photo. iPhoto will remove the photo from your photo library and from any albums that contain the photo. For information on albums, see page 166.

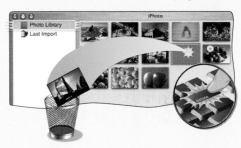

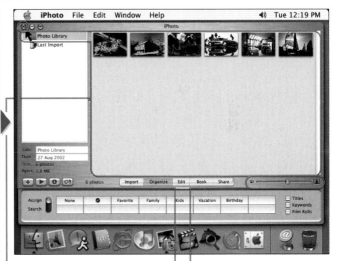

■ This area shows the photo that iPhoto is currently copying.

■ This area shows the progress of the copy.

■ You can click **Stop** to stop copying the photos at any time.

■ When the copy is complete, the photos appear in your photo library. The photo library contains all the photos you have copied to your computer.

5 To decrease or increase the size of the photos, drag this slider (●) left or right.

6 When you finish working with iPhoto, click ● to close the iPhoto window.

CREATE AN ALBUM

You can create an album that contains photos you want to keep together.

You can create as many albums as you want. For example, you can create an album that contains pictures of your summer vacation and another album that contains pictures of your pet.

CREATE AN ALBUM

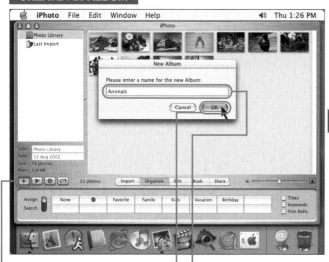

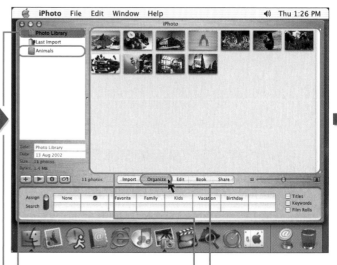

1 Click ⊞ to create a new album.

■ The New Album dialog box appears.

2 Type a name for the new album.

3 Click **OK** to create the album.

■ The album appears in this area. Albums display the 📖 symbol.

4 To add a photo to the album, click **Photo Library** to view all the photos in your photo library.

5 Click **Organize**.

■ This area displays all the photos in your photo library.

Can I change the order of photos in an album?

Yes. Click the name of the album that contains the photos you want to reorder and then click the **Organize** button. Position the mouse ▶ over a photo you want to move and then drag the photo to a new location in the album. A black line indicates where the photo will appear.

How do I delete an album?

To delete an album, click the name of the album you want to delete and then press the delete key. In the confirmation dialog box that appears, click **OK** to delete the album. Deleting an album will not remove the photos in the album from your photo library.

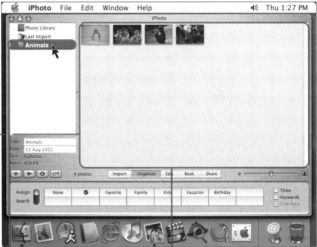

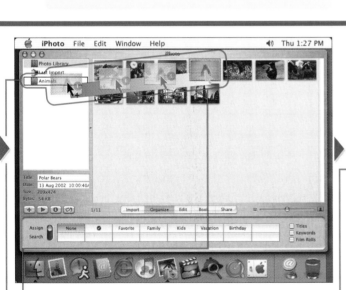

6 Position the mouse ▶ over a photo you want to add to the album.

7 Drag the photo to the album.

Note: When you drag a photo over an album, an outline appears around the album.

■ The photo is added to the album.

8 You can repeat steps **6** and **7** for each photo you want to add to the album.

9 When you finish adding photos to the album, click the album.

■ This area displays all the photos you added to the album.

■ If you no longer want a photo to appear in the album, you can click the photo and then press the delete key to delete the photo.

Note: Deleting a photo from an album will not remove the photo from your photo library.

ADD A TITLE AND COMMENTS TO A PHOTO

You can add a title and comments to a photo to provide a name and description for the photo.

iPhoto uses the film roll and photo number as a photo's title until you provide a new title.

Adding a title and comments to a photo adds the information to every album that contains the photo. To create an album, see page 166.

ADD A TITLE AND COMMENTS TO A PHOTO

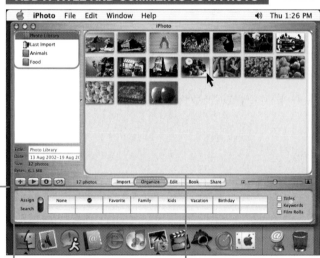

1 Click **Photo Library** to view all your photos or click the album that contains the photo you want to add a title and comments to.

2 Click **Organize**.

■ This area displays the photos in your photo library or the album you selected.

3 Click the photo you want to add a title and comments to.

■ This area displays the current title of the photo.

4 To change the title, drag the mouse ▶ over the current title until the title is highlighted. Then type a new title.

5 To add comments, click 🛈 to display an area where you can enter comments.

6 Click this area and type comments for the photo.

Note: You can click 🛈 again to hide the title and comments. To redisplay the title, click 🛈 again.

168

You can organize your photos by assigning photos to different categories, such as Family, Vacation and Birthday. Organizing your photos by category can help you quickly locate photos of interest.

Each photo can belong to more than one category.

ORGANIZE PHOTOS

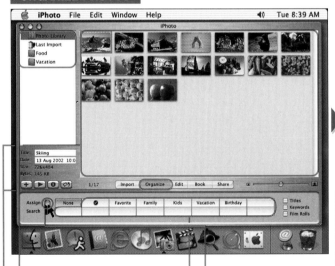

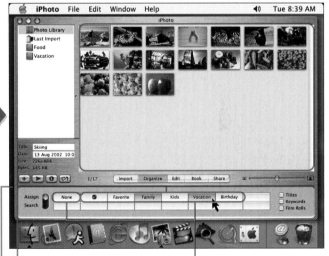

1 Click **Photo Library** to view all your photos or click the album that contains the photos you want to organize.

2 Click **Organize** to organize your photos.

■ This area displays the photos in your photo library or the album you selected.

3 Click the area beside **Assign** (⬤ moves beside **Assign**).

■ This area displays the categories to which you can assign your photos.

4 Click a photo you want to categorize.

5 Click each category the photo belongs to. Each category you select is highlighted.

Note: If you select the ✅ category, a check mark (✅) appears in the photo.

■ To deselect a category, click the category again. To deselect all the categories, click **None**.

6 You can repeat steps 4 and 5 for each photo you want to categorize.

CONTINUED ▷

ORGANIZE PHOTOS

You can create your
own categories that
you can use to
organize your photos.

ORGANIZE PHOTOS (CONTINUED)

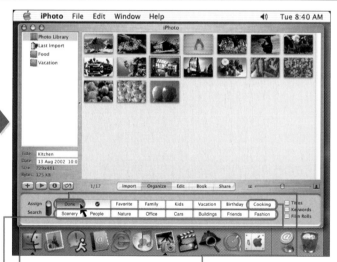

CREATE A CATEGORY

1 To create a new
category, click **Edit**.

2 Click **Edit Keywords**.

3 Click an empty button
and then type a new
category name.

4 You can repeat step **3**
for each new category
you want to create.

*Note: To replace an existing
category name, drag the
mouse I over the category
name until you highlight
the name. Then type a new
category name.*

5 When you finish
creating categories,
click **Done** to save
your changes.

When organizing my photos, can I change the way photos are displayed?

Yes. To change the way photos are displayed, you can click the **Titles**, **Keywords** or **Film Rolls** option at the bottom right corner of the iPhoto window (☐ changes to ☑).

Titles

Displays the title of each photo. To add or change the title for a photo, see page 168.

Keywords

Displays the categories you assigned to each photo.

Film Rolls

Displays your photos arranged according to the date you copied the photos from your digital camera. The Film Rolls option is not available if you are viewing the photos in an album.

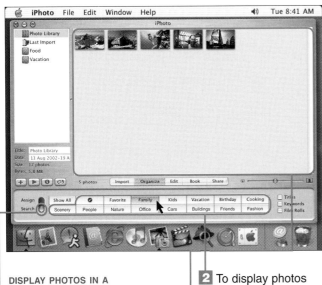

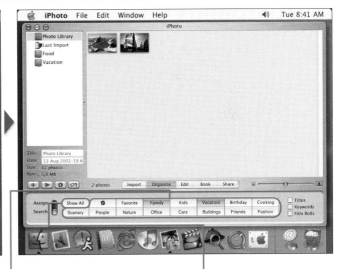

DISPLAY PHOTOS IN A CATEGORY

1 Click the area beside **Search** (◯ moves beside **Search**).

2 To display photos in a specific category, click the category of interest. The category is highlighted.

■ This area displays the photos in the category you selected.

■ To display photos that belong to more than one category, click each additional category of interest.

■ To once again show all the photos, click **Show All**.

EDIT A PHOTO

You can edit a photo to enhance the appearance of the photo. For example, you can crop a photo to remove parts of the photo you do not want to show or change the brightness of a photo.

Editing a photo will change the appearance of the photo in your photo library and in every album that contains the photo.

EDIT A PHOTO

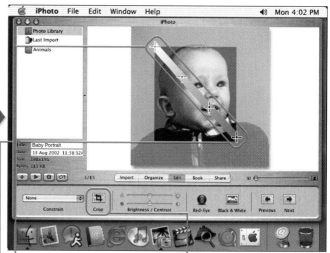

■ **1** Click **Photo Library** to view all your photos or click the album that contains the photo you want to edit.

■ **2** Click **Organize**.

■ This area displays the photos in your photo library or the album you selected.

■ **3** Click the photo you want to change.

■ **4** Click **Edit** to edit the photo.

■ **5** To crop the photo to show only part of the photo, position the mouse ▶ over a corner of the area you want to show (▶ changes to ┼).

■ **6** Drag the mouse ┼ over the photo until you select the entire area you want to show.

■ A square indicates the area you selected.

■ **7** Click **Crop** to crop the photo.

Can I change a photo back to its original appearance?

If you do not like the changes you made to a photo, you can change the photo back to its original appearance. Perform steps **1** to **3** below to select the photo you want to change back to its original appearance. Click the **File** menu and then select **Revert to Original**. In the dialog box that appears, click **OK** to confirm your change.

Can I make a copy of a photo?

Yes. Making a copy of a photo is useful if you want to edit a photo without changing the original photo in your photo library. To make a copy of a photo, perform steps **1** to **3** below and then press and hold down the ⌘ key as you press the D key. If you make a copy of a photo in an album, iPhoto will also add a copy of the photo to your photo library.

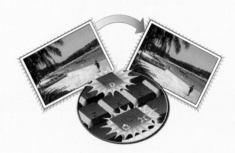

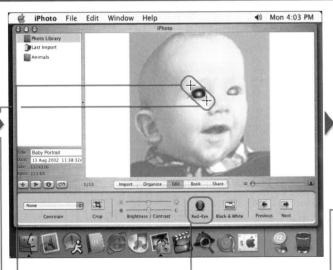

8 To reduce red-eye for a person in the photo, position the mouse ▶ over a corner of the person's eye (▶ changes to ⊹).

9 Drag the mouse ⊹ over the eye until you select the entire eye.

Note: Make sure you select only the eye area since the Red-Eye tool affects all shades of red in the area you select.

10 Click **Red-Eye**.

11 To reduce red-eye in the other eye, repeat steps **8** to **10** for the other eye.

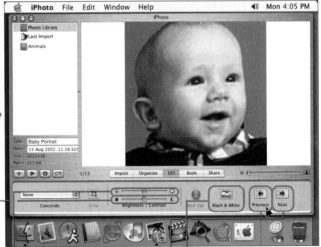

12 To decrease or increase the brightness of the photo, drag this slider (⬤) left or right.

13 To decrease or increase the contrast in the photo, drag this slider (⬤) left or right.

14 To change the photo to black and white, click **Black & White**.

15 To display the previous or next photo in your photo library or album, click **Previous** or **Next**.

DESIGN A BOOK

After you create an album, you can design a book that neatly arranges photos and text in the album.

When you create an album, iPhoto automatically assigns a standard book theme to the album. You can choose a different theme for the book and customize the design of individual pages in the book.

DESIGN A BOOK

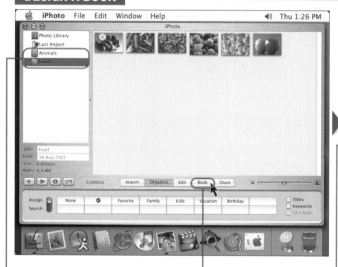

1 Click the album that contains the photos you want to arrange in a book.

Note: To create an album, see page 166.

2 Click **Book** to design a book that arranges the photos in the album.

■ This area displays a miniature version of each page in the book.

Note: You can use the scroll bar to browse through the pages.

3 To view a larger version of a page, click the page.

■ This area displays a larger version of the page you selected.

How can I change the order in which photos appear on the pages in a book?

To change the order of photos in a book, you must reorder the photos in the album for the book. This is useful if you want to display a different photo on the Cover page. To change the order of photos in an album, see the top of page 167.

The photos in my book moved when I changed the design of a page. How can I make sure photos remain on a particular page?

You can lock a page to ensure the photos on the page do not move to other pages when you change the design of a page. To lock a page, click the page and then select the **Lock Page** option (changes to ☑). A lock icon (🔒) appears below the locked page. You can click the Lock Page option again to unlock the page.

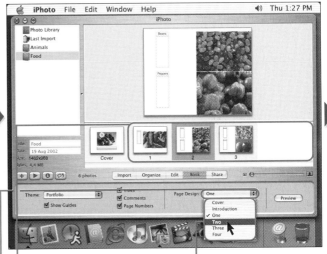

4 To select a theme for all the pages in the book, click this area to display a list of the available themes.

5 Click the theme you want to use for all the pages in the book.

Note: A theme determines the way photos and text appear on the pages in a book.

■ The pages in the book immediately display the new theme.

6 To change the page design of a page in the book, click the page you want to change.

Note: You cannot change the design of the Cover page.

7 Click this area to display a list of the available page designs.

8 Click the page design you want to use.

Note: The available page designs depend on the theme you selected in step 5.

■ The page immediately displays the new page design.

CONTINUED

DESIGN A BOOK

You can choose to display or hide titles, comments and page numbers on each page in a book.

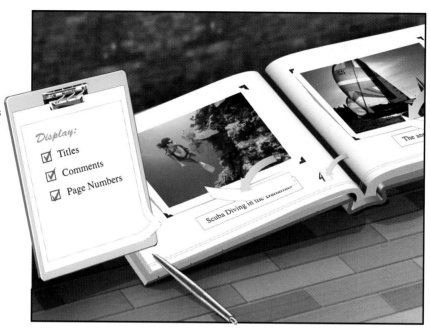

You cannot hide the title on the Cover page of a book.

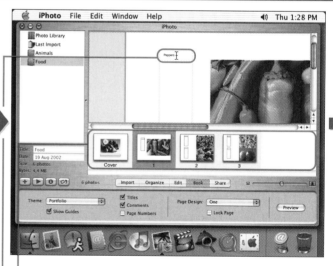

9 These options display titles, comments and page numbers on the pages in the book. You can click an option to display (☑) or hide (☐) the information on the pages.

■ The pages in the book immediately display the changes you make.

Note: If you selected the Picture Book or Story Book theme in step 5 on page 175, selecting the Titles or Comments option will not affect the appearance of the pages in the book.

10 To edit the title(s) or comments on a page in the book, click the page you want to edit.

11 Click in the blue box for the title or comments area.

Note: The Picture Book and Story Book themes do not display title or comments areas.

■ When you click in the title or comments area, iPhoto may automatically magnify the page so you can view the area more clearly.

How can I hide the blue boxes that appear on the pages in a book?

To hide the blue boxes that indicate where you can enter information, such as titles or comments, click the **Show Guides** option (☑ changes to ☐). To once again display the blue boxes, click the **Show Guides** option again.

How can I change the order of the pages in a book?

To change the order of the pages in a book, position the mouse ▶ over the page you want to move and then drag the page to a new location. You cannot move the Cover page.

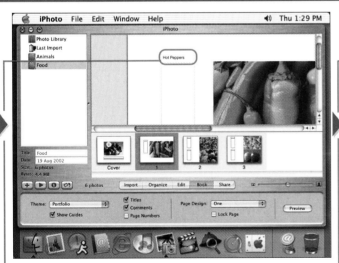

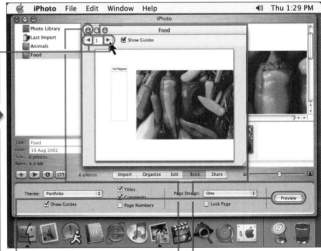

12 Type a title or comments for the photo.

Note: To delete an existing title or comments, drag the mouse I over the existing text until you highlight the text. Then press the delete *key.*

13 You can repeat steps **10** to **12** for each page that contains text you want to edit.

Note: Editing a photo's title and comments changes the title and comments in your photo library and in every album that contains the photo.

14 To view the book in a separate window, click **Preview**.

■ A window appears, displaying the current page in the book.

15 To move backward or forward through the pages in the book, click ◀ or ▶.

■ To display a specific page in the book, double-click this area and type a page number. Then press the return key.

16 When you finish viewing the pages in the book, click ⬤ to close the window.

PRINT PHOTOS

You can produce a paper copy of your photos.

iPhoto offers four different styles you can use to print your photos.

1 Click **Photo Library** to view all your photos or click the album that contains the photos you want to print.

2 Click **Organize**.

■ This area displays the photos in your photo library or the album you selected.

3 Click the photo you want to print.

■ To print more than one photo, press and hold down the ⌘ key as you click each additional photo you want to print.

4 Click **Share**.

5 Click **Print** to print the photos you selected.

■ The Print dialog box appears.

■ This area displays the printer iPhoto will use.

6 To select a print setting for your printer, click this area to display a list of the available settings.

7 Click the setting you want to use.

Can I use iPhoto to order professionally printed copies of my photos?

Yes. When your computer is connected to the Internet, you can use iPhoto to order prints or a book of your photos from an online print service.

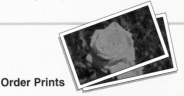

Order Prints

To order prints of your photos, perform steps 1 to 4 below to select the photos you want to order prints of. Then click **Order Prints**. The Order Prints window appears, displaying an order form you can fill out to order the prints.

Order a Book

Before ordering a book, you should design the book you want to order. To design a book, see page 174. Make sure the book contains at least 10 pages of photos. To order a book, perform steps 1 and 4 below, selecting the album you used to create the book in step 1. Then click **Order Book**. The Order Book window appears, displaying an order form you can fill out to order the book.

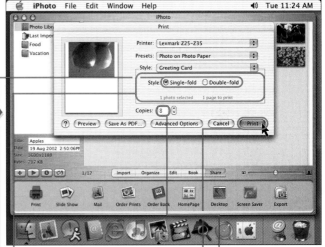

8 To select a print style, click this area to display a list of the available styles.

9 Click the style you want to use.

■ This area shows a preview of how the photos will print.

■ This area displays the options for the style you selected in step 9. In this example, the Greeting Card options are displayed.

10 Click an option to specify if you want to use the single-fold or double-fold style for your greeting cards (◯ changes to ◉).

11 To specify the number of copies you want to print, double-click this area and type the number of copies.

12 Click **Print**.

E-MAIL PHOTOS

You can e-mail your photos to a friend, colleague or family member.

You need to be connected to the Internet to e-mail your photos. To connect to the Internet, see page 238.

E-MAIL PHOTOS

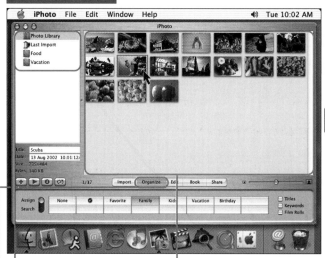

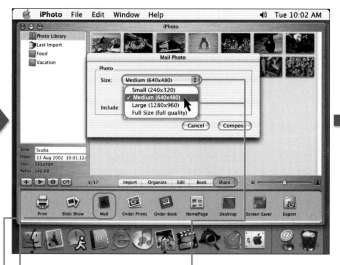

1 Click **Photo Library** to view all your photos or click the album that contains the photos you want to e-mail.

2 Click **Organize**.

■ This area displays the photos in your photo library or the album you selected.

3 Click the photo you want to e-mail.

■ To e-mail more than one photo, press and hold down the ⌘ key as you click each additional photo you want to e-mail.

4 Click **Share** to be able to share the photos in an e-mail message.

5 Click **Mail** to e-mail the photos you selected.

■ The Mail Photo dialog box appears.

6 To select a size for the photos, click this area to display the available sizes.

7 Click the size you want to use.

Note: Smaller photos transfer faster over the Internet and fit better on the recipient's screen.

What are some other ways that I can use my photos?

Display as a Desktop Picture

To display a photo on your desktop, perform steps 1 to 4 below, selecting the photo you want to display in step 3. Then click **Desktop**. The photo you selected immediately appears on your desktop. For more information on changing the desktop picture, see page 73.

Use as a Screen Effect

To use the photos in an album as a screen effect, perform steps 1 and 4 below, selecting the album that contains the photos you want to use in step 1. Then click **Screen Saver**. In the dialog box that appears, click **OK** to use the photos in the album as a screen effect. A screen effect appears on your screen when you do not use your computer for a period of time. For more information on changing the screen effect, see page 70.

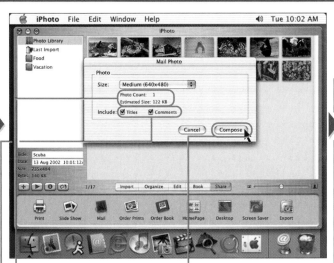

■ This area displays the number of photos you selected and the estimated file size of the photos.

8 These options display the titles and comments for the photos in the e-mail message. You can click an option to display (☑) or hide (☐) the titles or comments.

Note: To add titles and comments to photos, see page 168.

9 Click **Compose** to compose the e-mail message.

■ A window appears, allowing you to send the photos in an e-mail message.

10 Click this area and type the e-mail address of the person you want to receive the photos.

11 To type a subject for the message, drag the mouse I over the existing subject until you highlight the subject. Then type a new subject.

12 Click this area and type the message you want to accompany the photos.

13 Click **Send** to send the message.

PUBLISH PHOTOS TO THE WEB

You can publish photos to the Web to allow people from around the world to view the photos.

When you publish photos to the Web, iPhoto creates a Web page, called a HomePage, to display your photos.

You need to be connected to the Internet and have a .Mac membership to publish photos to the Web. To connect to the Internet, see page 238. If you do not have a .Mac membership, you can obtain a membership at the www.apple.com Web site.

PUBLISH PHOTOS TO THE WEB

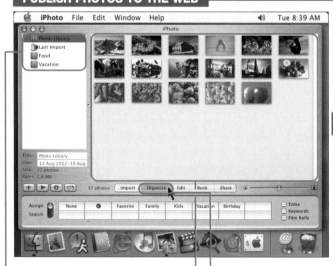

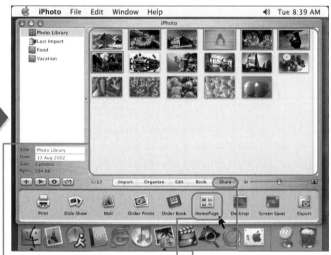

1 Click **Photo Library** to view all your photos or click the album that contains the photos you want to publish to the Web.

2 Click **Organize**.

■ This area displays the photos in your photo library or the album you selected.

3 Click a photo you want to publish.

■ To publish more than one photo, press and hold down the ⌘ key as you click each additional photo you want to publish.

4 Click **Share** to be able to share the photos on the Web.

5 Click **HomePage** to publish the photos you selected.

■ The Publish HomePage window appears, displaying the photos you selected to publish.

Can I make changes to my HomePage?

Yes. When viewing your HomePage on the Web, click the **Created using .Mac** link at the bottom of the page to be able to make changes to the page. For example, you can remove photos, edit text and add a theme to your HomePage. You may need to enter the member name and password for your .Mac membership to make changes to your HomePage.

Is there another way I can show my photos to other people?

Yes. You can display a slide show of your photos on your computer. Perform steps **1** and **4** below and then click **Slide Show**. In the dialog box that appears, click **OK** to start the slide show. To stop the slide show at any time, you can click anywhere on your screen.

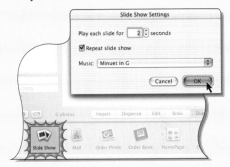

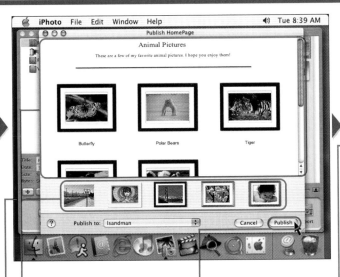

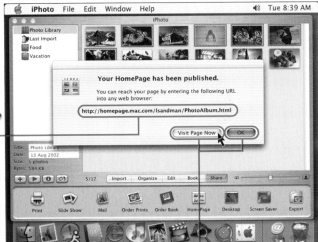

6 To edit the information that will be displayed on the Web page, drag the mouse I over the text you want to change until the text is highlighted. Then type the new text.

7 Click the border style you want to use for the photos.

■ The photos immediately display the new border style.

8 Click **Publish** to publish the photos to the Web.

■ A dialog box appears, stating that your HomePage has been published.

■ This area displays the address where you can view the Web page.

Note: You should write down the Web page address for future reference. Your HomePage address begins with homepage.mac.com/yourmembername.

9 To view the HomePage now, click **Visit Page Now**.

■ To close the dialog box, click **OK**.

CHAPTER 8

Create Movies Using iMovie

Read this chapter to find out how to use iMovie to create and work with movies on your computer. You will learn how to transfer video from a digital video camera, rearrange video clips and add sound effects and music to your movies.

You can use iMovie to transfer video from a digital video camera to your computer. Transferring video to your computer allows you to view and edit the video on your computer.

Before you start transferring video from a digital video camera, make sure the camera is turned on and in VTR mode. Also make sure the tape is at the point where you want to begin transferring the video.

TRANSFER VIDEO FROM A DIGITAL VIDEO CAMERA

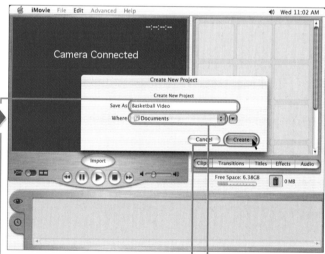

■1 Connect the video camera to your computer.

■2 Click the iMovie icon to start iMovie.

■ iMovie opens on your screen.

■ The first time you start iMovie, a dialog box appears.

■3 Click **New Project** to start a new project.

Note: If the dialog box does not appear and you want to transfer video to a new project, see page 192 to create a new project. Then skip to step 6.

■ The Create New Project dialog box appears.

■4 Type a name for the project.

■ This area shows the location where iMovie will store the project. You can click this area to change the location.

■5 Click **Create** to create the project.

How do I play a video clip?

To play a video clip, click the video clip and then click ▶. You can click ▶ again to stop playing the video clip. Playing video clips can help you determine which video clips you want to include in your movie.

 How can I delete a video clip?

To delete a video clip you do not plan to use in your movie, click the video clip and then press the delete key. The video clip will no longer appear in iMovie.

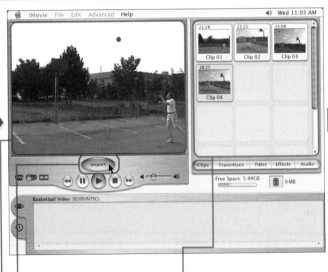

6 Click **Import** to start transferring video to your computer.

■ This area displays the video iMovie is transferring.

■ As iMovie transfers the video, the video clips for the video appear in this area.

Note: Video clips are smaller, more manageable segments of a video you transfer into iMovie. A video clip is created each time iMovie detects a different scene in a video, such as when you switch from pause to record.

7 When you want to stop recording the video, click **Import** again.

■ To save the video clips for the video, see page 190.

8 When you finish working with video in iMovie, click **iMovie**.

9 Click **Quit iMovie**.

ADD A VIDEO CLIP TO A MOVIE

You must add each video clip you want to include in a movie to the clip viewer.

The clip viewer displays the order in which video clips will play in a movie.

ADD A VIDEO CLIP TO A MOVIE

1 Click **Clips** to view all the video clips in the current project.

■ The shelf displays the video clips.

2 Position the mouse ▶ over the video clip you want to add to your movie.

3 Drag the video clip to the clip viewer.

Note: You can add a video clip before, after or between any existing video clips in the clip viewer.

■ The video clip appears in the clip viewer.

■ You can repeat steps **2** and **3** for each video clip you want to add to your movie.

■ If you no longer want a video clip to appear in your movie, drag the video clip back to the shelf.

188

REARRANGE VIDEO CLIPS

You can change
the order of video
clips in the clip
viewer to change
the order in which
the clips will play
in your movie.

REARRANGE VIDEO CLIPS

1 Position the mouse ▶
over the video clip that
you want to move to a
different location in your
movie.

2 Drag the video clip
to a new location in
your movie.

■ The video clip appears
in the new location.

■ The surrounding
video clips automatically
move to make room for
the video clip.

SAVE AND OPEN A PROJECT

You should regularly save changes you make to a project to avoid losing your work. You can also open a saved project to work with the contents of the project.

A project stores the video clips for a video you transferred from a video camera and a rough draft of a movie.

SAVE A PROJECT

■ This area displays the name of the current project.

1 To save the project, click **File**.

2 Click **Save Project**.

■ iMovie saves the changes you made to the project.

OPEN A PROJECT

■ You can work with only one project at a time. Before opening a project, make sure you save your current project.

1 Click **File**.

2 Click **Open Project**.

■ The Open Existing Project dialog box appears.

Where does iMovie store my projects?

By default, iMovie stores each project you create in a separate folder within your Documents folder. Each project folder contains a project file that opens the project, as well as a Media folder, which stores the sound and video clips for the project. For more information on the Documents folder, see page 26.

Can iMovie automatically open the last project I worked with?

Yes. When you start iMovie, the last project you worked with automatically appears on your screen. This allows you to immediately begin working with the project.

■ This area displays the location of the current folder in relation to the disks, folders and files on your computer. The current folder is highlighted.

■ To display the contents of a different folder, click the folder.

Note: The leftmost column shows the disks on your computer. Each of the following columns shows the contents of the item selected in the previous column.

3 Click the folder for the project you want to open.

4 Click the project file you want to open. Project files display the ☆ symbol.

5 Click **Open** to open the project.

■ The project opens and the video clips in the project appear on your screen.

CREATE A NEW PROJECT

When you want to transfer new video from a digital video camera to your computer, you can create a new project to store the video.

A project stores the video clips for a video you transfer from a video camera and a rough draft of a movie.

CREATE A NEW PROJECT

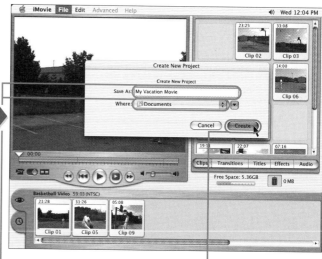

■ You can work with only one project at a time. Before creating a new project, make sure you save your current project. To save a project, see page 190.

 **1** Click **File**.

2 Click **New Project**.

■ The Create New Project dialog box appears.

3 Type a name for the new project.

■ This area shows the location where iMovie will store the project. You can click this area to change the location.

4 Click **Create** to create the project.

Note: To transfer video from a video camera into the new project, see page 186.

CROP A VIDEO CLIP

You can crop the beginning and end of a video clip to remove parts of the clip you do not want to play in your movie.

CROP A VIDEO CLIP

1 Click the video clip you want to crop.

2 Drag the mouse ▶ just below the progress bar.

■ The crop markers (◿ and ◺) appear.

3 To specify where you want the video clip to start, drag the first crop marker (◿) to the location in the video clip.

4 To specify where you want the video clip to end, drag the second crop marker (◺) to the location in the video clip.

■ A yellow area on the progress bar indicates the part of the video clip that iMovie will keep. iMovie will remove the parts of the video clip outside of the yellow area.

5 Click **Edit**.

6 Click **Crop**.

ADD A TRANSITION BETWEEN VIDEO CLIPS

You can add an interesting transition from one video clip to another in your movie. Adding transitions between video clips blends the end of one video clip with the beginning of the next video clip.

ADD A TRANSITION BETWEEN VIDEO CLIPS

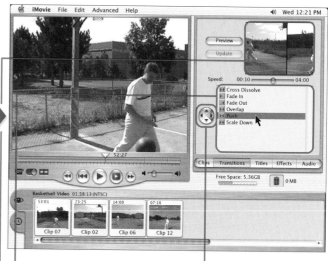

1 Click **Transitions** to add a transition.

■ This area lists the available transitions.

Note: The symbol beside a transition indicates if the transition will affect the video clip before the transition (◄), the video clip after the transition (►) or both (►◄).

2 Click the transition you want to add.

■ This area displays a preview of the transition you selected.

Note: You can repeat step 2 to select a different transition.

■ If you selected the **Push** transition, click an arrow in this area to specify the direction you want the video clip to move off the screen.

What transitions can I add to the beginning or end of my movie?

You can add the Fade In transition to the beginning of your movie and the Fade Out transition to the end of your movie. To add one of these transitions, perform steps **1** to **5** below. When adding the Fade In transition, drag the transition to the area before the first video clip in your movie in step **5**. When adding the Fade Out transition, drag the transition to the area after the last video clip in your movie in step **5**.

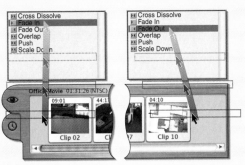

How do I remove a transition from my movie?

To remove a transition, click the transition symbol (▶◀, ▶ or ◀) for the transition you no longer want to use. Then press the delete key to remove the transition from your movie.

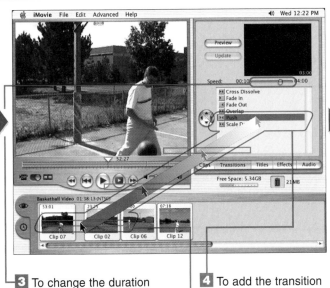

3 To change the duration of the transition, drag this slider (◯) left or right.

4 To add the transition you selected to video clips in your movie, position the mouse ▶ over the transition.

5 Drag the transition to the area between the video clips you want to use the transition.

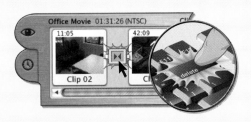

■ A transition symbol (▶◀, ▶ or ◀) appears between the video clips.

6 To play the transition between the video clips, click the transition symbol.

7 Click ▶ to play the transition.

■ The transition plays in this area.

ADD A SOUND EFFECT

You can add sound effects, such as a drum roll, applause or laughter, to your movie.

iMovie comes with two sound tracks that you can add sound effects to. You can add sound effects to both sound tracks to overlap sounds in your movie.

ADD A SOUND EFFECT

■ This slider (▽) indicates the current location in your movie.

1 To specify the location in your movie where you want a sound effect to play, drag the slider (▽) to the location.

■ This area shows the current frame in the movie.

2 Click 🕐 to display the timeline viewer.

■ The timeline viewer appears.

■ To once again display the clip viewer at any time, click 👁 .

■ This area displays the video clips in your movie and both sound tracks for the movie. A slider (▽) indicates the current location in your movie.

3 Click **Audio** to display the sound options for your movie.

How can I change when a sound effect will play in my movie?

You can move a sound effect to a new location in your movie to change when the sound effect will play. In the timeline viewer, drag the sound effect to a new location on the sound track. As you drag the sound effect, the frame where the sound effect will play appears in the viewing area. You can also use this method to change when a voice recording or music will play in your movie. To add a voice recording to your movie, see page 198. To add music, see page 200.

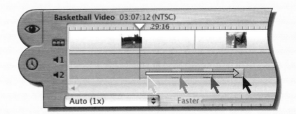

4 Click the sound effect you want to add to your movie. The sound effect you selected plays.

Note: You can repeat step 4 to select a different sound effect.

5 Position the mouse over the sound effect you selected.

6 Drag the sound effect to the location on a sound track where you want the sound effect to play.

Note: You should line up the yellow line (|) with the slider (▽).

■ The sound effect appears as a blue square (■) or as two connected blue squares on the sound track.

■ To add other sound effects to your movie, perform steps 1 to 6 for each sound effect.

■ To delete a sound effect, click the blue square for the sound effect and then press the delete key.

RECORD VOICE

While we were at the family picnic, Jim had a chance to show us his new bicycle.

You can create a voice recording that will play in a movie. Recording your voice is useful when you want to add comments to a home movie or presentation.

You need to connect a microphone to your computer to record your voice.

RECORD VOICE

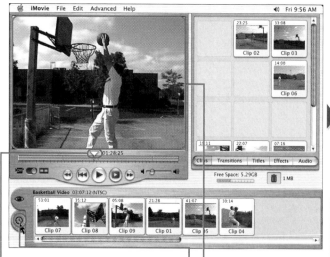

■ This slider (▽) indicates the current location in your movie.

1 To specify the location in your movie where you want your voice recording to start playing, drag the slider (▽) to the location.

■ This area shows the current frame in the movie.

2 Click 🕐 to display the timeline viewer.

■ The timeline viewer appears.

■ To once again display the clip viewer at any time, click 👁.

■ This area displays the video clips in your movie and both sound tracks for the movie. A slider (▽) indicates the current location in your movie.

3 Click **Audio** to display the sound options for your movie.

Can I change the volume of my voice recording?

Yes. In the timeline viewer, click the orange bar for the voice recording you want to change the volume of. Position the mouse over the volume control slider ( ) at the bottom of your screen and then drag the slider left or right to adjust the volume of the recording. You can also use this method to change the volume of a video clip, sound effect or music you added to the movie.

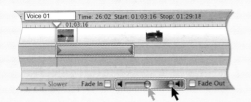

Can I mute some sounds in my movie so I can hear a specific sound more clearly?

You can mute your video clips or all the sounds on a sound track in your movie. For example, you can mute your video clips so you can hear a voice recording more clearly. In the timeline viewer, click the box (☑) next to the video clips or sound track you want to mute (☑ changes to ☐). You can click the box again to once again play the sound.

4 Click **Record Voice** to start recording your voice.

5 Speak into your microphone to record your voice. Make sure you speak clearly and loudly, but do not shout.

■ While you speak, bars in this area indicate the sound level of your voice.

Note: The bars should be green. If red bars appear, you are speaking too loudly.

■ As you record your voice, this area displays the movie.

■ iMovie adds an orange bar for your voice recording on the first sound track.

6 When you want to stop recording your voice, click **Stop**.

■ To delete the voice recording, click the orange bar for the voice recording and then press the delete key.

ADD MUSIC FROM A CD

You can add music from a CD to your movie to enhance the movie.

iMovie comes with two sound tracks that you can add music to. You can add music to both sound tracks to overlap sounds in your movie.

ADD MUSIC FROM A CD

■ This slider (▽) indicates the current location in your movie.

1 To specify the location in your movie where you want music to start playing, drag the slider (▽) to the location.

■ This area shows the current frame in the movie.

2 Click 🕐 to display the timeline viewer.

■ The timeline viewer appears.

■ To once again display the clip viewer at any time, click 👁.

■ This area displays the video clips in your movie and both sound tracks for the movie. A slider (▽) indicates the current location in your movie.

3 Click **Audio** to display the sound options for your movie.

4 Insert a music CD into your computer's CD drive.

Note: If the iTunes window appears, click 🔘 to close the window.

How do I play the songs on a CD in iMovie?

You can use the controls displayed below the list of songs in iMovie to play the songs on a CD. Playing the songs on a CD can help you decide which songs you want to add to your movie.

⏮	Move to the previous song.
⏭	Move to the next song.
▶	Play the selected song.
⏸	Pause the song.

Can I add only part of a song to my movie?

Yes. To add only part of a song to your movie, perform steps **1** to **5** below. Then click ▶ to play the song. When the song reaches the beginning of the part you want to add, click **Record Music**. When the song reaches the end of the part you want to add, click **Stop**. The part of the song appears as a purple bar on the second sound track.

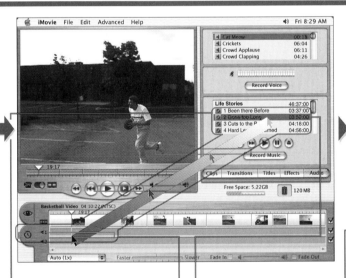

■ This area lists the songs on the CD and the amount of time each song will play.

5 Click the song you want to add to your movie.

6 Position the mouse ▶ over the song.

7 Drag the song to the location on the sound track where you want the song to start playing in the movie.

Note: You should line up the yellow line (|) with the slider (▽).

■ The song appears as a purple bar on the sound track.

■ To add other songs from the CD to your movie, perform steps **1** to **7** for each song.

8 When you finish adding songs from the CD to your movie, click ⏏ to eject the CD.

■ To delete a song from your movie, click the purple bar for the song and then press the delete key.

PREVIEW A MOVIE

After you add the video clips you want to include in your movie, you can preview how the movie will play.

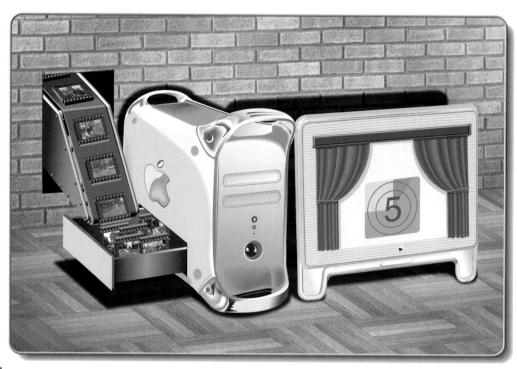

PREVIEW A MOVIE

■1 To preview a movie, click 🔘 to move to the beginning of the movie.

■ To preview only one video clip in the movie, click the video clip. The video clip is highlighted.

■2 Click ▶ to preview the movie.

■ The movie plays in this area.

■ You can click ▶ again to stop playing the movie.

■ This slider (▽) indicates the progress of the movie. The amount of time the movie has been playing appears beside the slider.

Note: Lines on the progress bar indicate where each video clip begins and ends in the movie.

How can I quickly move to a specific location in a movie?

To quickly move to a specific location in your movie, click the location you want to move to on the progress bar. The slider (▽) moves to the new location. To preview the movie starting from the new location, click ▶ .

Can I preview a movie using the entire screen?

Yes. You can click ⊙ to preview a movie using the entire screen. To return to iMovie, click anywhere on your screen.

■ A red marker in the video clips also indicates the progress of the movie.

3 To adjust the volume, drag this slider (⬤) left or right to decrease or increase the volume.

Note: To quickly turn off the sound, click ◀ . To quickly turn the volume to full capacity, click ◀)) .

4 To play the movie backwards, click ◀◀ .

Note: You can click ◀◀ again to stop playing the movie backwards.

5 To fast forward through the movie, click ▶▶ .

Note: You can click ▶▶ again to stop fast forwarding through the movie.

SAVE A MOVIE AS A QUICKTIME MOVIE

After you finish creating a movie, you can save the movie as a QuickTime movie on your computer.

Saving a movie as a QuickTime movie allows you to play the movie on your computer at any time and share the movie with other people. You cannot make changes to a movie you have saved. To play a QuickTime movie, see page 140.

SAVE A MOVIE AS A QUICKTIME MOVIE

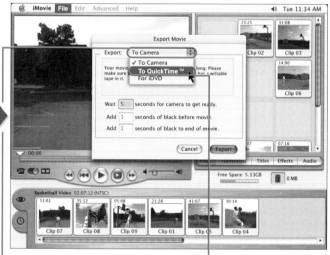

1 To save the video clips in the clip viewer as a QuickTime movie, click **File**.

2 Click **Export Movie**.

■ The Export Movie dialog box appears.

3 To specify how you want to save your movie, click this area to display a list of the available save options.

4 Click **To QuickTime** to save your movie as a QuickTime movie.

Which format should I select for my movie?

The format you should select depends on how you intend to use the movie.

Format	Intended Use
Web Movie	Publish the movie to the Web.
Email Movie	Send the movie in an e-mail message.
Streaming Web Movie	Publish the movie to a QuickTime streaming Web server, which plays movies on the Web as they are downloading.
CD-ROM Movie	Copy the movie to a recordable CD.
Full Quality	Work with the movie in another application.

Is there another way to save a movie?

Yes. In step 4 below, you can choose to save a movie to your digital video camera or for iDVD.

✓ Select **To Camera** to save a movie to the tape in your video camera. This is useful if you want to play the movie on your television.

✓ Select **For iDVD** to save a movie for the iDVD application. iDVD allows you to prepare a high-quality movie that you can copy to a recordable DVD. Some computers do not support iDVD.

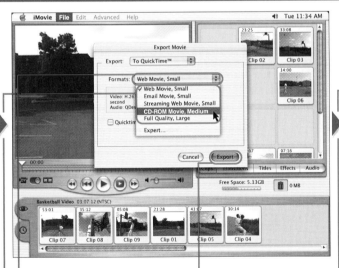

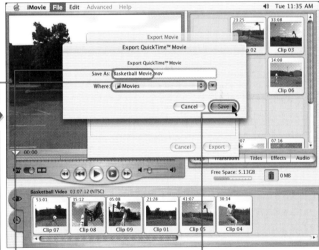

5 To specify the format you want to use for your movie, click this area to display a list of the available formats.

6 Click the format you want to use.

Note: For information on the available formats, see the top of this page.

7 Click **Export** to save the movie.

■ The Export QuickTime Movie dialog box appears.

8 Type a name for the movie.

■ This area shows the location where iMovie will store the movie. You can click this area to change the location.

Note: By default, iMovie stores your movie in the Movies folder, which is located in your home folder.

9 Click **Save** to save the movie.

■ The Progress dialog box will appear on your screen until iMovie has finished saving your movie.

CHAPTER 9

Share Your Computer

If you share your computer with other people, you can create a separate user account for each person. In this chapter, you will learn how to create and manage user accounts on your computer.

ADD A USER ACCOUNT

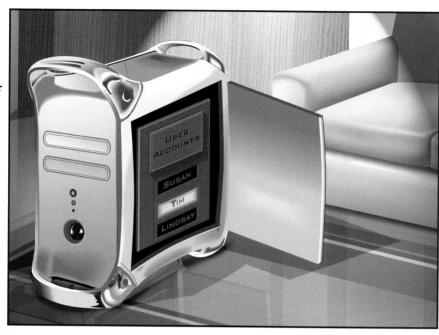

If you share your computer with other people, you can create a separate user account for each person.

You must have an administrator account to add a user account to your computer.

ADD A USER ACCOUNT

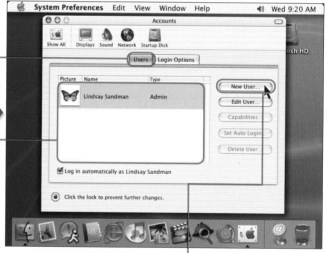

1 Click the System Preferences icon to access your system preferences.

■ The System Preferences window appears.

2 Click **Accounts** to work with the user accounts on your computer.

■ The Accounts window appears.

3 Click the **Users** tab.

■ This area lists the names of the user accounts that are currently on your computer.

Note: When Mac OS was installed on your computer, an administrator account was created.

4 Click **New User** to add a new user account to your computer.

Will Mac OS keep my personal files separate from the files of other users?

Yes. Mac OS will keep your personal files separate from the personal files created by other users. For example, your Home folder contains only the files you have created. Internet Explorer also keeps your lists of recently viewed Web pages and favorite Web pages separate from the lists of other users.

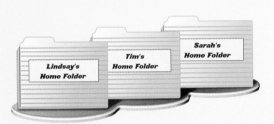

How can I personalize Mac OS for my user account?

You can personalize the appearance of Mac OS for your user account by changing the screen saver, desktop picture, appearance of the Dock and many other computer settings.

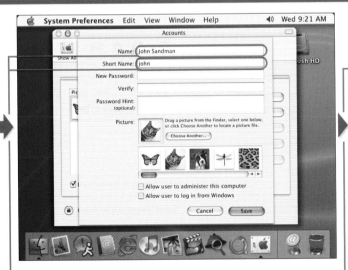

■ A dialog sheet appears.

5 Type the full name of the person who will use the new user account.

6 Click this area and type a short name for the person. A short name cannot contain spaces.

Note: Mac OS automatically enters a short name for the person. If you do not want to use this name, drag the mouse I over the name until the name is highlighted and then type the short name you want to use.

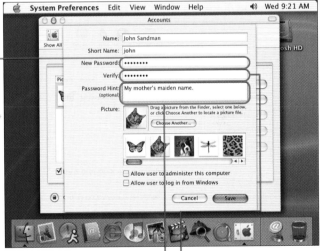

7 Click this area and type a password for the user account.

Note: A password will prevent unauthorized people from accessing the user account. A password must contain at least 4 characters.

8 Click this area and type the password again to confirm the password.

9 Click this area and type a password hint that can help the person remember the password.

Note: Typing a password hint is optional.

CONTINUED **209**

ADD A USER ACCOUNT

When adding a user account to your computer, you can select the picture you want to use for the account.

By default, the picture you select for a user account will appear on the login window each time you log in to Mac OS.

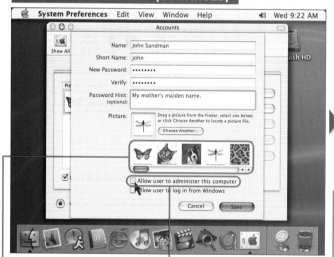

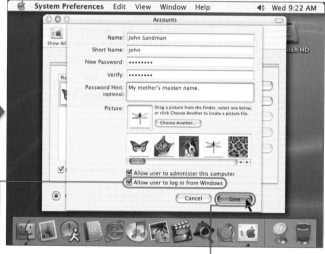

■ This area displays the pictures you can use for the user account.

10 Click the picture you want to use for the user account.

11 To allow the person to perform administrative tasks on the computer, click this option (□ changes to ☑).

Note: An administrator can perform any task on the computer, such as installing new programs and adding user accounts. A regular user can perform only some tasks on the computer, such as personalizing some settings.

12 To allow the person to log in to the computer from a Windows-based computer to access your shared files, click this option (□ changes to ☑). For more information on sharing, see page 228.

13 Click **Save** to add the new user account to your computer.

What does the automatic login option do?

The automatic login option automatically logs a specific user in to Mac OS each time you turn on your computer. By default, your computer uses the account that was created when Mac OS was installed to automatically log in. If you turn off the automatic login option, the login window will appear each time you turn on your computer so you can specify your account name and password to log in. To later change the user account your computer uses to automatically log in or turn off the automatic login option, see page 216.

Can I edit the information for a user account?

If you have an administrator account, you can make changes to any user account on your computer. To edit the information for a user account, perform steps **1** to **13** starting on page 208, except double-click the name of the user account you want to edit in step **4**. You cannot change the short name for a user account. If you change the password, a dialog box will appear. Click **OK** to close the dialog box.

■ A dialog box may appear, asking if you want to turn off the automatic login option.

14 Click a button to specify if you want to turn off or keep the automatic login option.

Note: For more information on the automatic login option, see the top of this page.

■ The new user account appears in the list of user accounts.

15 To quit System Preferences, click **System Preferences**.

16 Click **Quit System Preferences**.

DELETE A USER ACCOUNT

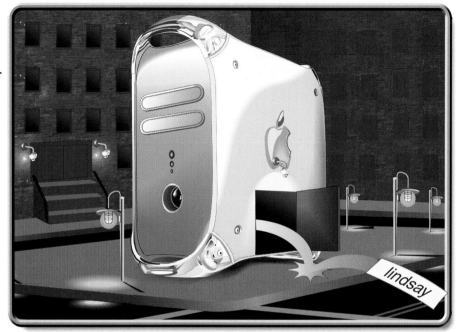

If a person no longer uses your computer, you can delete the person's user account from the computer.

You must have an administrator account to delete a user account.

DELETE A USER ACCOUNT

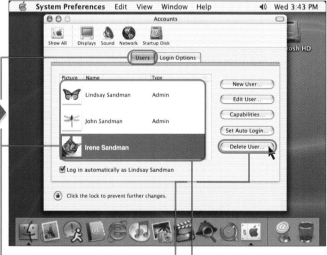

1 Click the System Preferences icon to access your system preferences.

■ The System Preferences window appears.

2 Click **Accounts** to work with the user accounts on your computer.

■ The Accounts window appears.

3 Click the **Users** tab.

■ This area lists the names of the user accounts on your computer.

4 Click the name of the user account you want to delete.

5 Click **Delete User**.

After I delete a user account, can I access the user's files?

Yes. When you delete a user account, Mac OS saves the contents of the home folder for the account in the Deleted Users folder. To open the Deleted Users folder, double-click your hard disk icon on the desktop. In the window that appears, double-click the **Users** folder and then double-click the **Deleted Users** folder. In the Deleted Users folder, double-click the icon for the user account containing the files you want to access. Mac OS places a disk icon for the user account on your desktop. Double-click the disk icon to access the contents of the home folder for the user account.

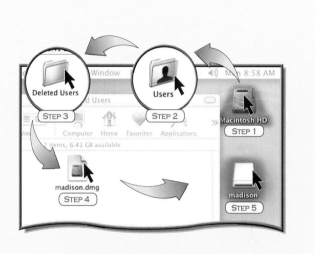

■ A confirmation dialog sheet appears.

6 Click **OK** to permanently delete the user account from your computer.

■ The user account disappears from the Accounts window.

7 To quit System Preferences, click **System Preferences**.

8 Click **Quit System Preferences**.

LOG OUT OR LOG IN

When you finish using your computer, you can log out so another person can log in to use the computer.

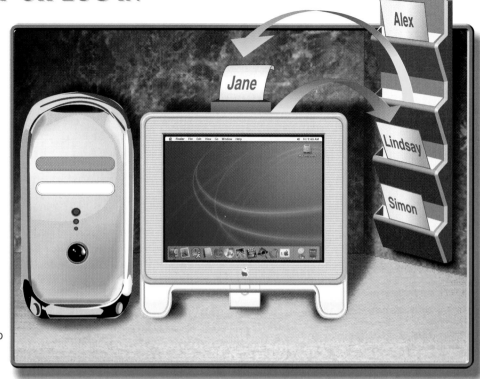

Logging out leaves the computer on, but exits your user account. Logging in allows you to specify the user account you want to use when Mac OS starts.

LOG OUT

■ Before you log out, make sure you close any applications you have open.

1 Click  to display the Apple menu.

2 Click **Log Out** to log out.

■ A dialog box appears, confirming that you want to log out.

3 Click **Log Out** to log out.

■ The login window appears, allowing another person to log in to use the computer.

Why does my login window look different than the login window shown below?

Your login window will look different if you chose to have each user enter both their account name and password to log in. For information on changing the login options, see page 218.

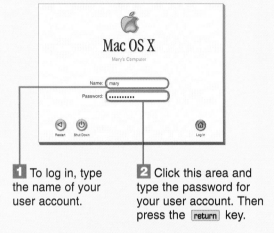

1 To log in, type the name of your user account.

2 Click this area and type the password for your user account. Then press the [return] key.

Why did the login window shake when I tried to log in?

The login window shakes when you enter an incorrect password. If you enter an incorrect password three times, a dialog sheet may appear, displaying a password hint. Click **OK** to close the dialog sheet and then try entering your password again.

LOG IN

■ When you log out, the login window appears.

Note: The login window also appears each time you turn on your computer if the automatic login option is turned off. To turn off the automatic login option, see the top of page 217.

■ This area displays the names of the user accounts on your computer.

1 Click the name of your user account.

■ A box appears that allows you to enter the password for your user account.

2 Type your password and then press the [return] key.

Note: A bullet (●) appears for each character you type to prevent other people from seeing your password.

■ If you accidentally selected the wrong name, you can click **Go Back** to select another name.

■ Mac OS starts, using your personalized settings.

AUTOMATICALLY LOG IN A USER

If you have more than one user account on your computer, you can specify which account you want your computer to use to automatically log in to Mac OS each time you turn on the computer.

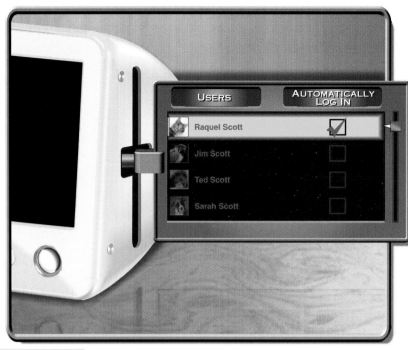

Specifying a user account your computer will use to automatically log in saves you from having to enter an account name and password each time you turn on the computer.

By default, your computer uses the account that was created when Mac OS was installed to automatically log in.

AUTOMATICALLY LOG IN A USER

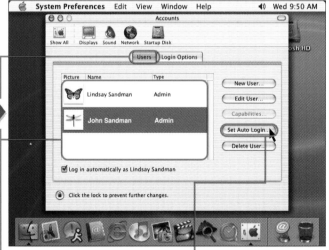

■ You must have an administrator account to change the account your computer uses to automatically log in to Mac OS.

1 Click the System Preferences icon to access your system preferences.

■ The System Preferences window appears.

2 Click **Accounts** to work with the user accounts on your computer.

■ The Accounts window appears.

3 Click the **Users** tab.

4 To specify the user account you want your computer to use to automatically log in, click the name of the user account.

5 Click **Set Auto Login**.

Note: If the Set Auto Login button is dimmed, the computer currently uses the user account to automatically log in.

216

Can I turn off the automatic login option?

Yes. You can turn off the automatic login option so that every user must specify their account name and password to log in before being able to use the computer. Requiring every user to log in helps ensure that users can access and modify only their own files and computer settings. To turn off the automatic login option, perform steps **1** to **3** below and then click **Log in automatically as** *name* (☑ changes to ☐).

If the computer uses my account to automatically log in, how can other users log in using their accounts?

When you finish using the computer, you can log out so another user can log in using their account. Logging out exits your user account, but leaves the computer on. Another user can log in to use the computer. For information on logging out or logging in, see page 214.

■ A dialog sheet appears.

■ This area displays the name of the user account you selected.

6 Type the password for the user account.

7 Click **OK** to confirm the information you entered.

■ The name of the user account you specified appears in this area. This option automatically logs in the user account each time you turn on your computer.

8 To quit System Preferences, click **System Preferences**.

9 Click **Quit System Preferences**.

CHANGE THE LOGIN OPTIONS

You can change the login options to customize the window that appears each time you log in to Mac OS.

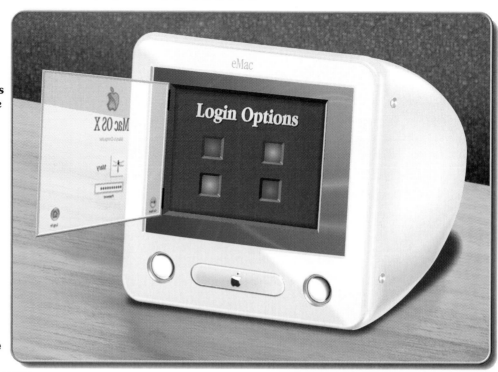

The login window allows you to specify the user account you want to use to log in to Mac OS.

You must have an administrator account to change the login options.

CHANGE THE LOGIN OPTIONS

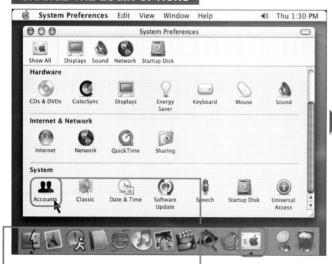

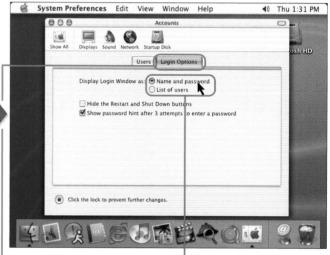

1 Click the System Preferences icon to access your system preferences.

■ The System Preferences window appears.

2 Click **Accounts** to work with the user accounts on your computer.

■ The Accounts window appears.

3 Click the **Login Options** tab to change the login options.

4 Click an option to specify if you want each user to log in by entering their account name and password or by selecting their account name from a list of user accounts (○ changes to ●).

Which login options can I select to help prevent unauthorized users from accessing my computer?

You can select the Name and password option to have each user enter both their account name and password to log in. You can also choose to disable the Restart and Shut Down buttons that appear in the login window. If your computer automatically logs in to Mac OS each time the computer is turned on, unauthorized users can use these buttons to restart the computer and automatically log in. You may also want to avoid displaying a password hint, which can help people guess your password.

Why didn't the login window appear when I started my computer?

By default, your computer uses a specific user account to automatically log in to Mac OS each time you turn on the computer. You can turn off the automatic login option to display the login window each time you turn on your computer. To turn off the automatic login option, see the top of page 217.

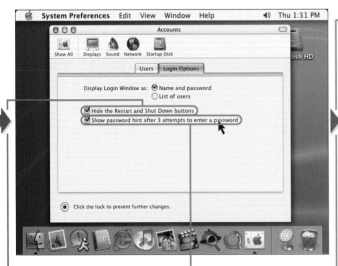

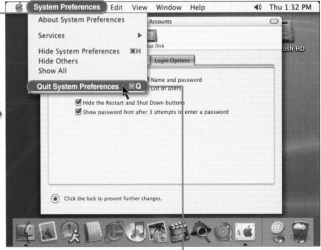

5 This option disables the Restart and Shut Down buttons in the login window. You can click this option to turn the option on (☑) or off (☐).

6 This option shows the password hint after three attempts to log in with an incorrect password. You can click this option to turn the option on (☑) or off (☐).

7 To quit System Preferences, click **System Preferences**.

8 Click **Quit System Preferences**.

CHANGE THE CAPABILITIES FOR A USER ACCOUNT

You can change the capabilities for a regular user to specify the tasks the user can perform on your computer.

Changing the capabilities for a user is useful when you share your computer with a person, such as a child, who you do not want to be able to access all the features and applications on the computer.

You must have an administrator account to change the capabilities for a user.

CHANGE THE CAPABILITIES FOR A USER ACCOUNT

1 Click the System Preferences icon to access your system preferences.

■ The System Preferences window appears.

2 Click **Accounts** to work with the user accounts on your computer.

■ The Accounts window appears.

3 Click the **Users** tab.

4 Click the name of the regular user account you want to change the capabilities for.

*Note: You cannot change the capabilities for an administrator account. Administrator accounts display the word **Admin**.*

5 Click **Capabilities**.

What is the Simple Finder?

The Simple Finder increases the security of your computer and provides a simpler working environment for a user by limiting the items available in the Finder menu bar and the Dock. When a user can access only the Simple Finder, the Dock displays the following items.

Finder	My Applications	Documents	Shared	Trash
Displays the Finder menu bar, which includes limited versions of the Apple, Finder and File menus.	Provides access to the applications that are available to the user.	Provides a convenient place for the user to store files.	Stores files shared by other users on the computer.	Stores files the user deletes.

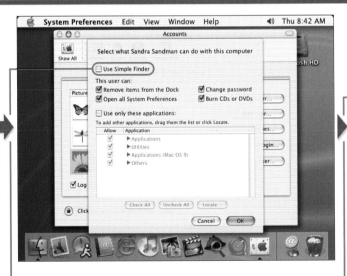

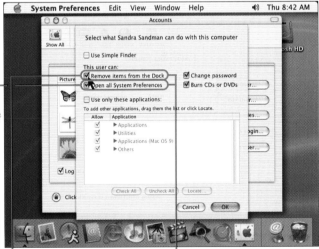

■ A dialog sheet appears.

6 This option allows the user to access only the Simple Finder. You can click this option to turn the option on (☑) or off (☐).

Note: If you selected Use Simple Finder, skip to step 10.

■ This option allows the user to remove items from the Dock.

■ This option allows the user to access all the features available in the System Preferences window.

7 You can click an option to turn the option on (☑) or off (☐).

CONTINUED

CHANGE THE CAPABILITIES FOR A USER ACCOUNT

You can specify the applications you want a regular user to be able to access on your computer.

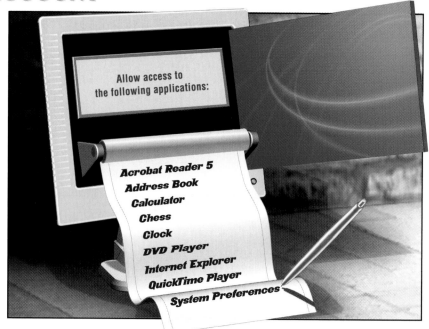

Allow access to the following applications:

Acrobat Reader 5
Address Book
Calculator
Chess
Clock
DVD Player
Internet Explorer
QuickTime Player
System Preferences

CHANGE THE CAPABILITIES FOR A USER ACCOUNT (CONTINUED)

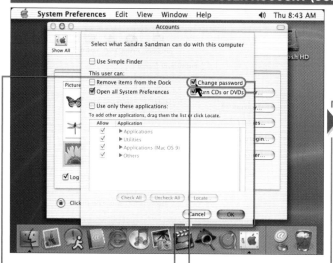

■ This option allows the user to change the password for their own user account.

Note: Change password is available only if you selected Open all System Preferences in step 7.

■ This option allows the user to copy files to CDs or DVDs.

8 You can click an option to turn the option on (✓) or off (▢).

9 This option allows the user to access only the applications you specify. You can click this option to turn the option on (✓) or off (▢).

Note: If you selected Use Simple Finder in step 6, this option is named Show these applications in "My Applications" folder and is automatically turned on.

Can I change a regular user account to an administrator account?

Yes. If you want a regular user to be able to perform any task on your computer, you can edit the user's account and select the Allow user to administer this computer option (□ changes to ☑). To edit a user account, see the top of page 211.

How can I add (☑) or remove (□) check marks for all the applications at once?

To add check marks to all the applications, click **Check All**. To remove the check marks from all the applications, click **Uncheck All**. You may want to remove the check marks from all the applications so you can quickly select only a few applications. To select an application after removing all the check marks, you must first click the box beside the category for the application (□ changes to ☑).

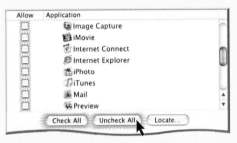

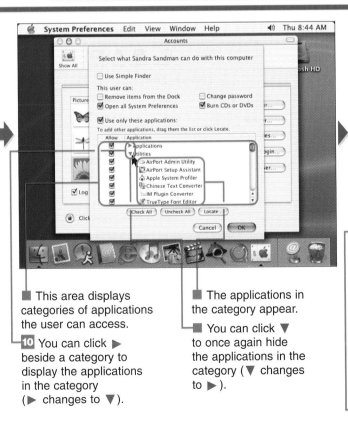

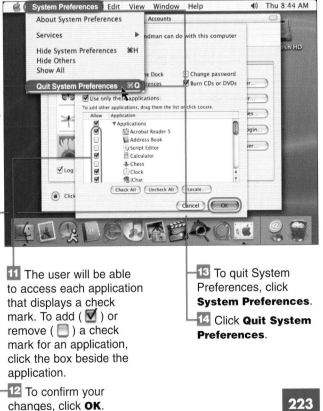

■ This area displays categories of applications the user can access.

10 You can click ▶ beside a category to display the applications in the category (▶ changes to ▼).

■ The applications in the category appear.

■ You can click ▼ to once again hide the applications in the category (▼ changes to ▶).

11 The user will be able to access each application that displays a check mark. To add (☑) or remove (□) a check mark for an application, click the box beside the application.

12 To confirm your changes, click **OK**.

13 To quit System Preferences, click **System Preferences**.

14 Click **Quit System Preferences**.

VIEW SHARED FILES

You can view the files shared by every user on your computer.

VIEW SHARED FILES

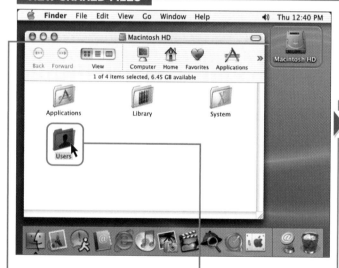

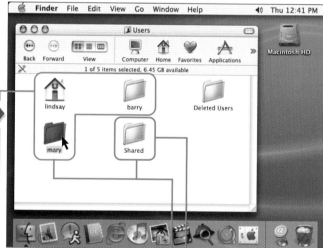

1 Double-click your hard disk icon on the desktop to view the contents of your hard disk.

■ A window appears, displaying the contents of your hard disk.

2 Double-click **Users** to view the home folder for each user account on your computer.

■ The Users window appears, displaying the home folder for each user account on your computer. The home folder for your user account displays a house icon (🏠).

■ The Shared folder contains files shared by the users on your computer. Every user can use this folder to share files.

3 To display the contents of a folder, double-click the folder.

Which folder should I use to share files with other users?

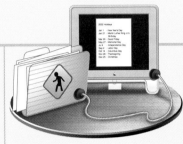

Shared

To share files with every user on your computer, add the files to the Shared folder. Every user can view, add and change files stored in this folder. You cannot delete files that other users add to this folder.

Public

Add files to your Public folder that you want every user on your computer to be able to view, but not change or delete. You cannot add files to another user's Public folder.

Drop Box

To share files with a specific user, add the files to the user's Drop Box folder. Only the user who owns the Drop Box folder can open the folder to view, change or delete files.

■ In this example, the personal folders for the **mary** user account appear.

Note: If you are viewing the personal folders for a user account other than your own, you can access only the contents of the Public and Sites folders. You cannot access folders that display the ⊖ symbol.

■ The Public folder contains files shared by the owner of the current user account.

4 To display the contents of the Public folder, double-click the folder.

■ The contents of the Public folder appear.

■ The Drop Box folder contains files other users have shared with the owner of the current user account. Only the owner of the Drop Box folder can open this folder.

■ You can click **Back** or **Forward** to move backward or forward through the folders you have viewed.

5 When you finish browsing through the shared files on your computer, click ⬤ to close the window.

225

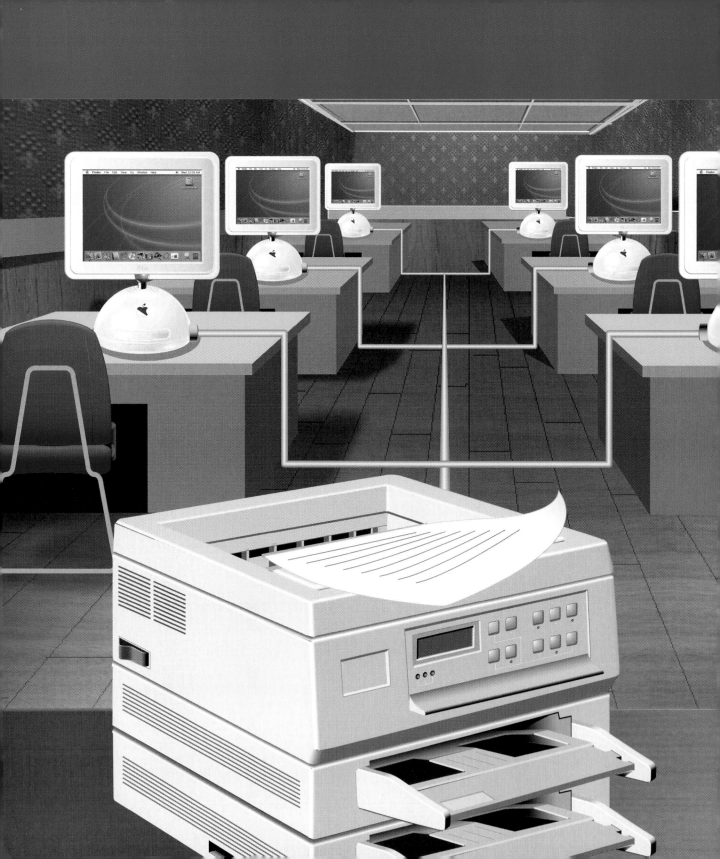

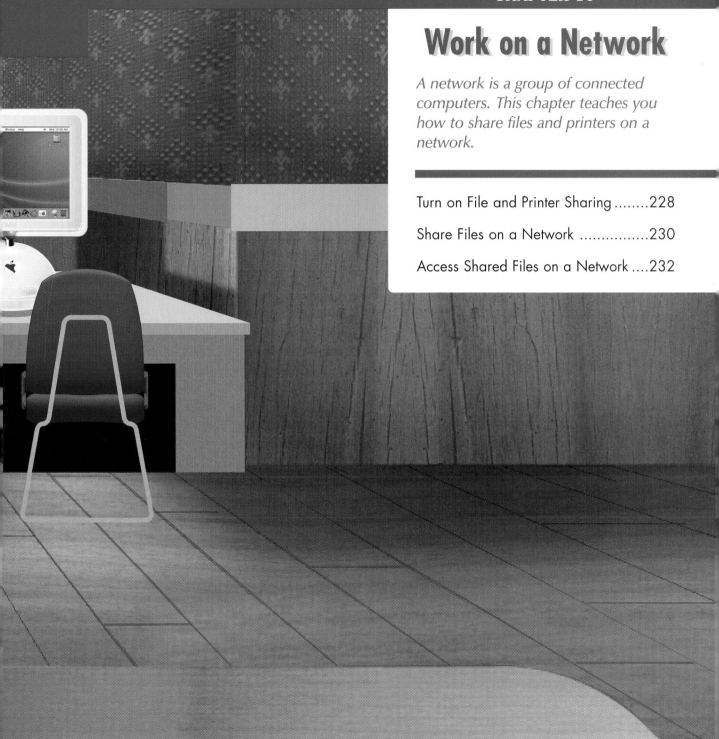

CHAPTER 10

Work on a Network

A network is a group of connected computers. This chapter teaches you how to share files and printers on a network.

TURN ON FILE AND PRINTER SHARING

If you want to share your files and printer with other people on your network, you must turn on file and printer sharing.

Sharing files is useful when other people on your network need to access your files. Sharing a printer allows you to reduce costs since several people on a network can use the same printer.

TURN ON FILE AND PRINTER SHARING

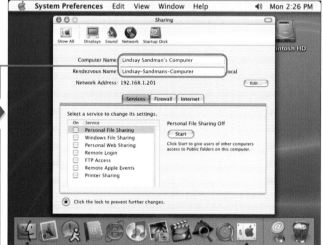

1 Click the System Preferences icon to access your system preferences.

■ The System Preferences window appears.

2 Click **Sharing** to share your files and a printer connected to your computer.

■ The Sharing window appears.

■ This area displays your computer name and Rendezvous name on the network. To change a name, drag the mouse I over the current name until the name is highlighted. Then type a new name.

Note: The Rendezvous name is used to identify your computer to Rendezvous-compatible services and applications, such as iChat.

**How can I print files using a
shared printer on my network?**

You can print files to a shared
printer on your network as if the
printer was directly connected to
your computer. When you print
a file, the shared printer will
automatically appear in the list
of available printers. To print a
file, see page 52.

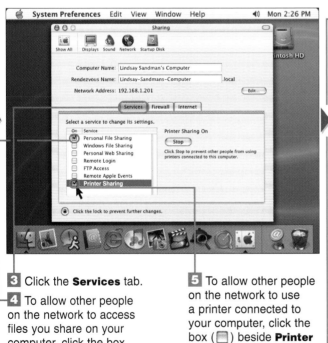

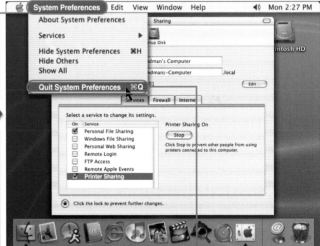

3 Click the **Services** tab.

4 To allow other people
on the network to access
files you share on your
computer, click the box
(☐) beside **Personal
File Sharing** (☐ changes
to ☑).

5 To allow other people
on the network to use
a printer connected to
your computer, click the
box (☐) beside **Printer
Sharing** (☐ changes
to ☑).

■ Everyone on the network
can now access files in
the Public folder on your
computer and use your
printer to print documents.

*Note: To add files you want to share
to your Public folder, see page 230.*

6 To quit System
Preferences, click **System
Preferences**.

7 Click **Quit System
Preferences**.

■ To turn off file and
printer sharing, perform
steps **1** to **7** (☑ changes
to ☐ in steps **4** and **5**).

SHARE FILES ON A NETWORK

You can share files with other people on your network by adding the files to the Public folder on your computer. Everyone on the network can access files stored in your Public folder.

Everyone on the network can open and copy, but not change or delete files in your Public folder.

SHARE FILES ON A NETWORK

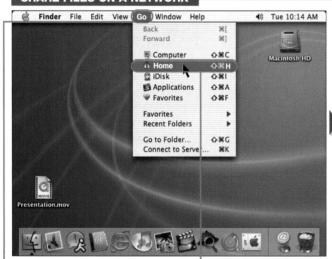

■ To allow other people on your network to access files you share on your computer, you must turn on file sharing. To turn on file sharing, see page 228.

Note: If Go is not available, click a blank area on your desktop to display the Finder menu bar.

2 Click **Home** to view your personal folders.

■ A window appears, displaying your personal folders.

3 To display the contents of your **Public** folder, double-click the folder.

1 Click **Go**.

What is the purpose of the Drop Box folder in my Public folder?

The Drop Box folder provides a location where other people on the network can place files they want to share with you. You are the only person who can open your Drop Box folder to view and work with its contents.

How can I stop sharing a file?

To stop sharing a file, you must remove the file from your Public folder. To display the contents of your Public folder, perform steps 1 to 3 below. Position the mouse ▶ over the file you no longer want to share and then drag the file out of the Public window.

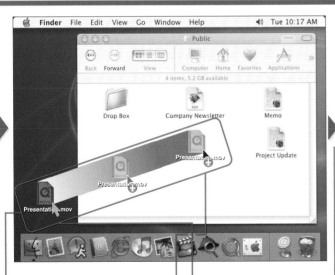

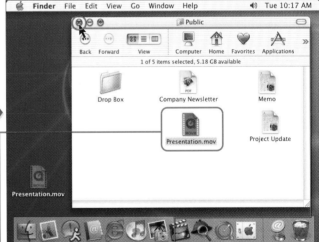

■ The Public window appears, displaying the contents of your Public folder.

4 Locate the file on your computer that you want to share with other people on your network.

5 Position the mouse ▶ over the file.

6 Press and hold down the option key as you drag the file to the Public window (▶ changes to ⊕).

■ A copy of the file appears in the Public window.

■ You can repeat steps 4 to 6 for each file you want to share.

Note: You can copy folders to your Public folder the same way you copy files.

7 When you finish copying the files you want to share to your Public folder, click ⬤ to close the Public window.

ACCESS SHARED FILES ON A NETWORK

You can view the
files shared by
other people on
your network.

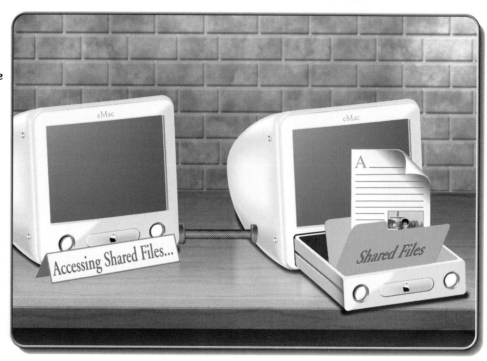

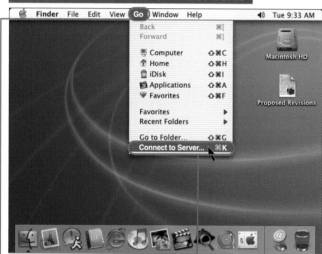

1 Click **Go**.

*Note: If Go is not available,
click a blank area on your
desktop to display the Finder
menu bar.*

2 Click **Connect to
Server**.

■ The Connect to Server
dialog box appears.

3 Click **Local**.

■ This area displays
the computers on your
network.

4 Click the computer
that contains the shared
files you want to access.

5 Click **Connect** to
connect to the computer.

What files can I access on my network?

You can access only the files that users on your network have added to their Public folders. A user's Public folder contains all the files that the user has chosen to share. To access the shared files in a user's Public folder, the computer that stores the files must be turned on and have file sharing turned on. For information on adding files to the Public folder, see page 230. For information on turning on file sharing, see page 228.

■ A dialog box appears, asking how you want to connect to the computer.

6 Click **Guest** to connect to the computer as a guest (◯ changes to ◉).

7 Click **Connect** to connect to the computer.

■ A dialog box appears, asking you to select the user account you want to access on the computer.

8 Click the name of the user account that shared the files you want to access.

9 Click **OK** to continue.

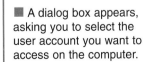

ACCESS SHARED FILES ON A NETWORK

When viewing shared files on a computer on your network, you can open, but not change or delete the files.

ACCESS SHARED FILES ON A NETWORK (CONTINUED)

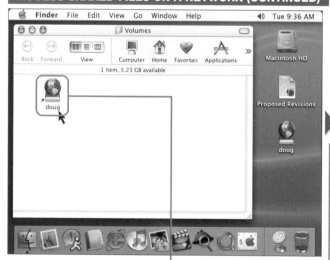

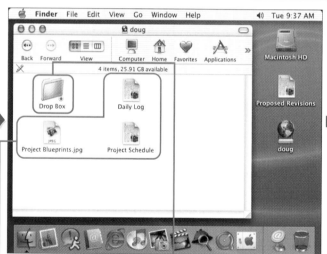

■ The Volumes window appears, displaying an icon for the user account you selected in step 8.

Note: If you previously accessed files shared by other user accounts on the network, an icon for each account you accessed may also appear in the window.

10 To view the files shared by the user account, double-click the icon for the account.

■ The files shared by the user account appear.

■ To open a file, double-click the file.

ADD FILES TO THE DROP BOX FOLDER

■ The Drop Box folder provides a location where you can place files you want to share with only the owner of the user account.

Note: Only the owner of the user account can open the Drop Box folder to view and work with its contents.

How can I make changes to a shared file on my network?

You cannot make changes to a shared file, but you can make a copy of the file on your computer and then make changes to the copy. To copy a shared file, position the mouse ![pointer] over the file and then drag the file to your desktop.

How can I immediately remove the icon for a user account from my desktop?

If you no longer want to access the files shared by a user account, you can immediately remove the icon for the account from your desktop. Position the mouse ![pointer] over the icon for the user account you no longer want to access and then drag the icon to the Trash icon in the Dock.

11 To share a file on your computer with only the owner of the user account, position the mouse ![pointer] over the file.

12 Drag the file to the Drop Box folder (![pointer] changes to ![pointer]).

■ A dialog box appears, stating that you do not have permission to see the results of the copy.

13 Click **OK** to copy the file to the Drop Box folder.

14 When you finish working with the shared files, click ![close] to close the window.

QUICKLY ACCESS SHARED FILES ON A NETWORK

■ After you view the files shared by a user account, an icon for the account appears on your desktop.

1 To quickly display the files shared by the user account, double-click the icon for the account.

Note: The account's icon will no longer appear on the desktop after you shut down, restart or log out of your computer.

235

CHAPTER 11

Browse the Web Using Internet Explorer

This chapter explains how to use Internet Explorer to view and work with Web pages. Learn how to save a picture displayed on a Web page, add a Web page to your Favorites list, quickly redisplay a Web page you have recently viewed and more.

CONNECT TO THE INTERNET

If you use a modem to connect to the Internet, you will need to connect to the Internet before you can access information on the Web.

When you connect to the Internet, your modem dials in to a computer at your Internet Service Provider (ISP), which gives you access to the Internet.

Your Internet connection is usually set up when you install Mac OS on your computer.

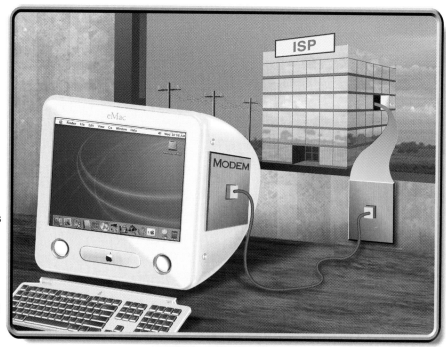

CONNECT TO THE INTERNET

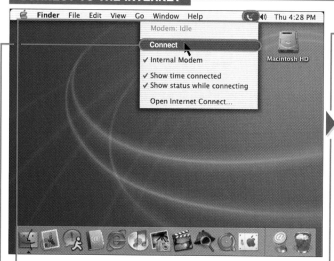

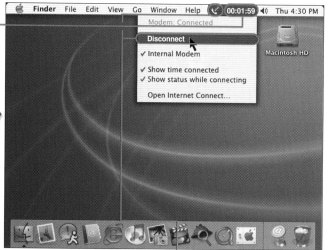

1 Click 📞 when you want to connect to the Internet.

2 Click **Connect**.

Note: A dialog box may appear, asking you to enter your password to connect to the Internet. Type the password for your Internet account and then press the return *key.*

■ After a few moments, you are connected to the Internet. You can now browse the Web and exchange information on the Internet.

■ This area displays the amount of time you have been connected to the Internet.

DISCONNECT FROM THE INTERNET

1 Click 📞 when you want to disconnect from the Internet.

2 Click **Disconnect**.

START INTERNET EXPLORER

You can start Internet Explorer to browse through information on the Web.

Web pages contain links that allow you to easily browse through information on the Web. A link connects text or a picture on one Web page to another Web page. When you select the text or picture, the linked Web page appears.

START INTERNET EXPLORER

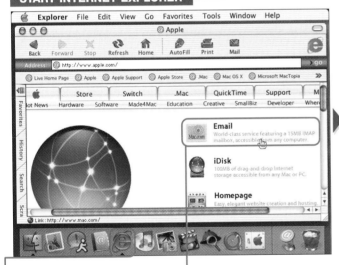

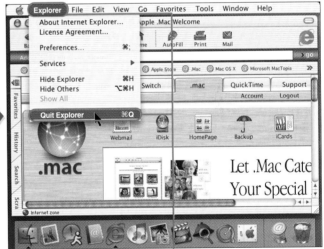

■ You must be connected to the Internet to work with Internet Explorer. To connect to the Internet, see page 238.

1 Click the Internet Explorer icon to start Internet Explorer.

■ A window appears, displaying your home page.

■ When you position the mouse ▶ over a link, the mouse ▶ changes to 🖑.

2 To select a link, click the link.

■ The linked Web page appears.

■ You can repeat step **2** to continue browsing through information on the Web.

QUIT INTERNET EXPLORER

1 When you finish browsing through information on the Web, click **Explorer**.

2 Click **Quit Explorer**.

DISPLAY A SPECIFIC WEB PAGE

You can display a page on the Web that you have heard or read about.

You need to know the address of the Web page that you want to display. Each page on the Web has a unique address, called a Uniform Resource Locator (URL).

DISPLAY A SPECIFIC WEB PAGE

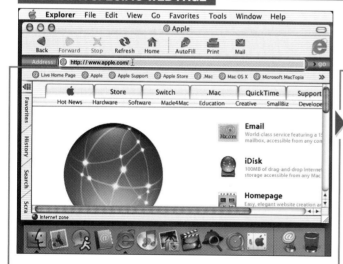

1 Click this area to highlight the current Web page address.

2 Type the address of the Web page you want to display and then press the return key.

Note: If you begin typing the address of a Web page you have recently viewed, a list of matching addresses appears. To display a Web page in the list, click the address of the Web page and then press the return key.

■ The Web page appears on your screen.

STOP TRANSFER OF A WEB PAGE

If a Web page is taking a long time to appear on your screen, you can stop the transfer of the page.

You may also want to stop the transfer of a Web page if you realize the page contains information that does not interest you.

STOP TRANSFER OF A WEB PAGE

■ This icon is animated as a Web page transfers to your computer.

■ This area shows the progress of the transfer.

1 Click **Stop** to stop the transfer of the Web page.

Note: The Stop button is available only while a Web page is transferring to your computer.

■ If you stopped the transfer of the Web page because the page was taking too long to appear, you may want to try displaying the page at a later time.

You can easily move backward and forward through the Web pages you have viewed since you last started Internet Explorer.

MOVE THROUGH WEB PAGES

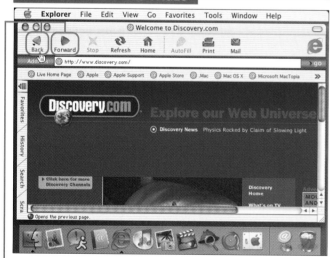

1 Click **Back** or **Forward** to move backward or forward through the Web pages you have viewed.

Note: The Forward button is available only after you use the Back button to return to a Web page.

DISPLAY A LIST OF VIEWED WEB PAGES

1 To display a list of the Web pages you have viewed, position the mouse ▶ over **Back** or **Forward** and then press and hold down the mouse button.

■ A list appears, displaying the addresses of the Web pages you have viewed.

2 Click the address of the Web page you want to view again.

SAVE A PICTURE DISPLAYED ON A WEB PAGE

You can save a picture displayed on a Web page so you can use the picture on your computer.

After you save a picture displayed on a Web page, you can view and work with the picture as you would view and work with any picture stored on your computer.

SAVE A PICTURE DISPLAYED ON A WEB PAGE

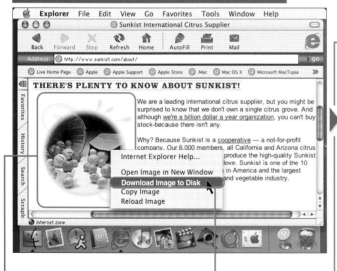

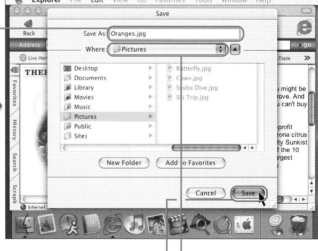

1 To save a picture displayed on a Web page, press and hold down the control key as you click the picture you want to save. A menu appears.

2 Click **Download Image to Disk**.

■ The Save dialog box appears.

3 Type a name for the picture.

■ This area shows the location where Internet Explorer will store the picture. You can click this area to change the location.

4 Click **Save** to save the picture on your computer.

DISPLAY AND CHANGE YOUR HOME PAGE

You can display and change the Web page that appears each time you start Internet Explorer. This page is called your home page.

DISPLAY AND CHANGE YOUR HOME PAGE

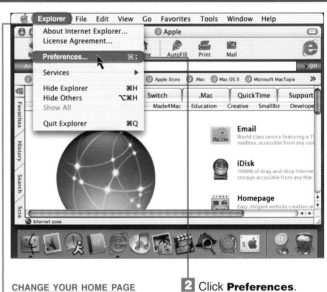

DISPLAY YOUR HOME PAGE

■1 Click **Home** to display your home page.

■ Your home page appears.

Note: Your home page may be different than the home page shown above.

CHANGE YOUR HOME PAGE

■1 Click **Explorer**.

■2 Click **Preferences**.

Which Web page should I set as my home page?

You can set any page on the Web as your home page. The page you choose should be a page you want to visit frequently. You may want to choose a page that provides a good starting point for exploring the Web, such as www.google.com, or a page that provides information about your personal interests or work.

How can I stop using a home page?

Choosing not to use a home page is useful if you do not want to wait for a home page to appear each time you start Internet Explorer. To stop using a home page, perform steps **1** to **3** below and then click **Use None**. To confirm your change, click **OK**.

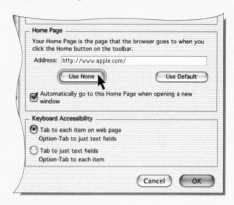

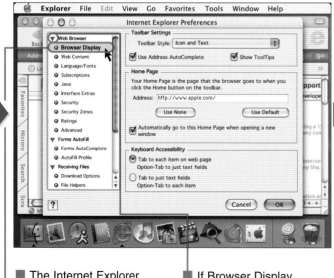

■ The Internet Explorer Preferences dialog box appears.

3 Click **Browser Display** to view the display settings for Internet Explorer.

■ If Browser Display is not available, click ▶ beside **Web Browser** (▶ changes to ▼).

4 To select the current home page address, drag the mouse I over the text until all the text is highlighted.

5 Type the address of the Web page you want to set as your new home page.

6 Click **OK** to confirm your changes.

ADD A WEB PAGE TO FAVORITES

You can use the Favorites feature to create a list of Web pages you frequently visit. The Favorites feature allows you to quickly display a favorite Web page at any time.

Selecting Web pages from your list of favorites saves you from having to remember and constantly retype the same Web page addresses.

ADD A WEB PAGE TO FAVORITES

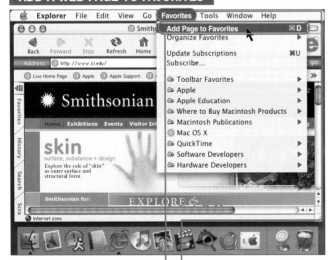

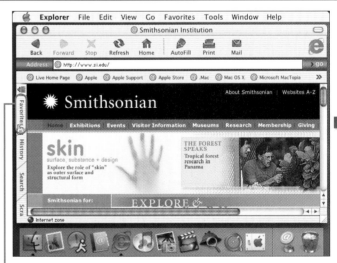

1 Display the Web page you want to add to your list of favorite Web pages.

Note: To display a specific Web page, see page 240.

2 Click **Favorites**.

3 Click **Add Page to Favorites**.

VIEW A FAVORITE WEB PAGE

1 Click the **Favorites** tab to display a list of your favorite Web pages.

How do I remove a Web page from my Favorites list?

To remove a Web page from your Favorites list, position the mouse ▶ over the Web page you want to remove and then drag the Web page to the Trash icon in the Dock. Removing Web pages you no longer visit from your Favorites list can help keep the list from becoming cluttered.

Does Internet Explorer automatically add Web pages to my Favorites list?

Yes. To provide quick access to information that could help you use your computer, Internet Explorer automatically adds the Mac OS X Web page and several folders containing Web pages to your list of favorites. For example, the Apple folder contains Web pages that provide customer support and software updates.

■ The Favorites list appears, displaying your favorite Web pages.

2 To display the favorite Web pages in a folder, click the name of the folder. Folders display the 🖿 symbol.

■ The Web pages in the folder appear. Web pages display the 🔘 symbol.

Note: To once again hide the Web pages in the folder, click the name of the folder.

3 Click the favorite Web page you want to view.

■ The favorite Web page you selected appears in this area.

■ To view another favorite Web page, repeat steps 2 and 3.

4 When you finish reviewing your list of favorite Web pages, click the **Favorites** tab to hide the Favorites list.

DISPLAY HISTORY OF VIEWED WEB PAGES

Internet Explorer uses the History list to keep track of the Web pages you have recently viewed. You can display the History list at any time to redisplay a Web page in the list.

By default, the History list keeps track of the last 300 Web pages you have viewed.

DISPLAY HISTORY OF VIEWED WEB PAGES

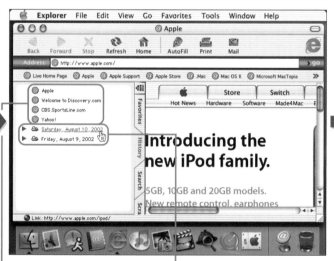

■ **1** Click the **History** tab to display a list of the Web pages you have recently viewed.

■ The History list appears, displaying the Web pages you have recently viewed.

■ The History list is organized by day. Web pages you viewed today appear at the top of the list. Web pages display the @ symbol.

■ Web pages you viewed on previous days are organized into folders. Each day displays a folder symbol ( ).

2 To display the Web pages you viewed during a specific day, click the day.

How do I remove a Web page from the History list?

Position the mouse over the Web page you want to remove from the History list and then drag the Web page to the Trash icon in the Dock. Removing a Web page from the History list is useful if you do not want other people to see a Web page you have recently viewed.

Is there another way that I can view the History list?

Yes. When Internet Explorer is the active application, you can use the Go menu to view the History list and redisplay a Web page you have recently viewed. Click the **Go** menu and then click the Web page you want to view. To display the Web pages you viewed during a specific day, position the mouse ▶ over the day.

■ The Web pages you viewed during the day appear.

Note: To once again hide the Web pages you viewed during a specific day, click the day.

3 Click the Web page you want to view.

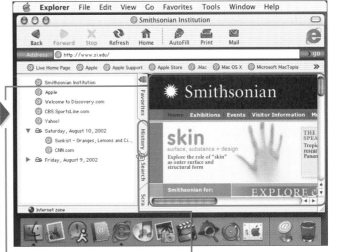

■ The Web page you selected appears in this area.

■ To view another Web page, repeat steps **2** and **3**.

4 When you finish reviewing the list of Web pages you have recently viewed, click the **History** tab to hide the History list.

SEARCH THE WEB

You can search for Web pages that discuss topics of interest to you. You can also search the Web for information such as a person's address, a business or a map.

SEARCH THE WEB

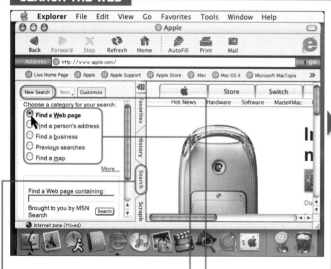

1 Click the **Search** tab.

■ The Search pane appears.

2 Click **New Search** to start a new search.

3 Click the category that describes the type of information you want to search for (○ changes to ●).

■ This area displays the options for the category you selected. In this example, an option for finding a Web page is displayed.

4 Click this area and type the information you want to search for.

*Note: To narrow your search, use specific rather than general words whenever possible. For example, if you want to find Web pages about corvettes, type **corvette** instead of **car**.*

5 Click **Search** to start the search.

Are there other categories I can use to search for information?

Yes. You can also use the **Look up a word** and **Find a picture** categories, which are initially hidden, to search for information. To display these categories, click the **More** link below the list of categories in the Search pane.

How can I view the results of a previous search?

To view the results of a previous search, perform steps 1 to 3 below, selecting **Previous searches** in step 3. A list of the topics you previously searched for appears in the Search pane. Click the topic that you want to once again view the search results for.

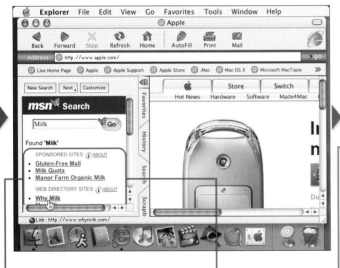

■ A list of matching Web pages appears.

6 Click a Web page of interest.

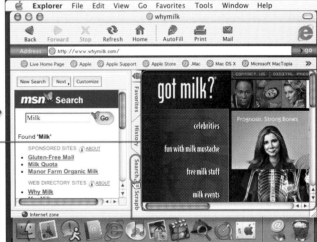

■ The Web page you selected appears in this area.

■ You can repeat step 6 to display another Web page.

■ To perform another search, repeat steps 2 to 6.

7 When you finish searching for information on the Web, click the **Search** tab to hide the Search pane.

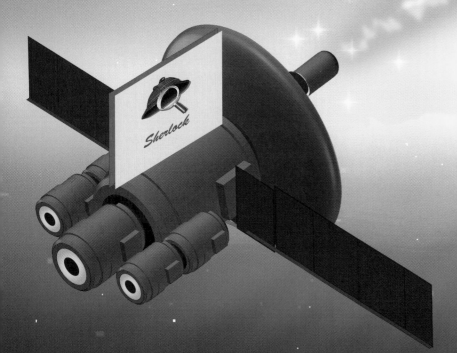

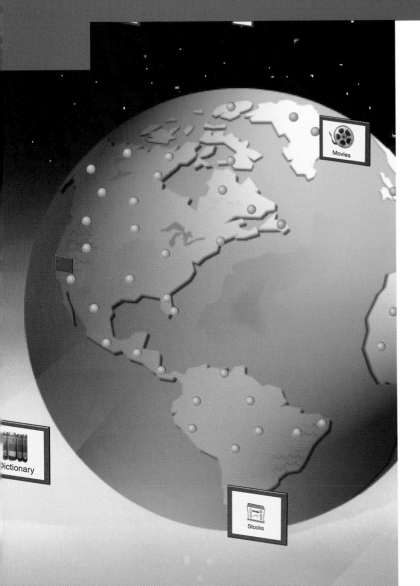

CHAPTER 12

Search the Internet Using Sherlock

Read this chapter to find out how to use Sherlock to search the Internet for information of interest, such as stock information, driving directions to a local business or movies playing in your area.

Internet

You can start Sherlock to search the Internet for information of interest.

Sherlock includes several channels you can use to search for information, including the Pictures, Stocks, Movies and Yellow Pages channels.

You need to be connected to the Internet to use Sherlock to search for information on the Internet. To connect to the Internet, see page 238.

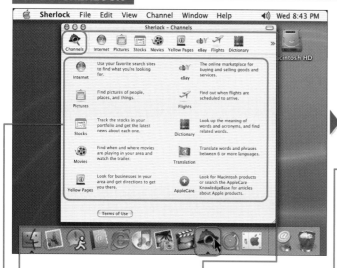

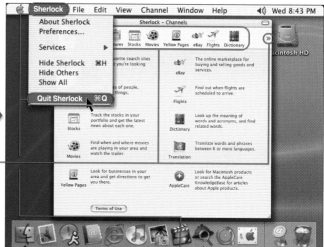

■1 Click the Sherlock icon to start Sherlock.

■ The Sherlock window appears.

■ This area displays a description of each channel Sherlock offers.

■ If the descriptions do not appear, click **Channels** to display the descriptions.

Note: The channels Sherlock offers may change at any time. The channels displayed above may be different than the channels displayed on your screen.

■ This toolbar displays a button for each channel. You can click a button to display the channel.

■ If the button for a channel is not displayed on the toolbar, you can click » to display a menu of the hidden buttons and then select the button you want to use.

QUIT SHERLOCK

■1 When you finish using Sherlock, click **Sherlock**.

■2 Click **Quit Sherlock**.

SEARCH FOR WEB SITES

You can use the
Internet channel
to search for
Web sites that
discuss topics of
interest to you.

SEARCH FOR WEB SITES

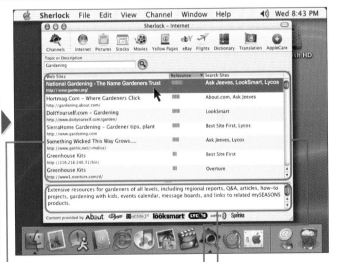

1 Click **Internet** to
search for Web sites
of interest.

2 Click this area
and type the word or
phrase you want to
search for.

3 Click 🔍 to start
the search.

■ This area lists the Web
sites that contain the word
or phrase you specified and
the search site Sherlock
used to find each Web site.
A bar beside each Web site
indicates the relevance of
the Web site to the word or
phrase you specified.

4 Click a Web site of
interest.

■ This area displays
a description of the
Web site.

■ To display a Web
site in your Web
browser, double-click
the Web site.

SEARCH FOR PICTURES

The Pictures channel allows you to search the Internet for pictures of people, places and things.

SEARCH FOR PICTURES

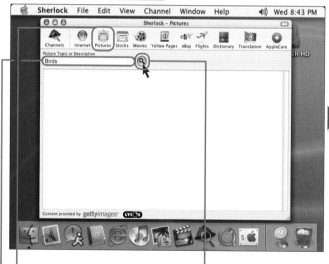

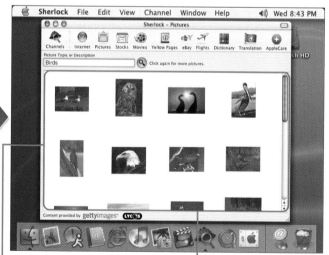

1 Click **Pictures** to search the Internet for pictures.

2 Click this area and type a word or phrase that describes the subject of the pictures you want to search for.

3 Click 🔍 to start the search.

■ This area displays the pictures that match the word or phrase you specified.

Note: You may be able to click 🔍 again to display additional pictures that match the word or phrase you specified.

■ You can double-click a picture to display the Web page that contains the picture in your Web browser.

Note: To save a picture displayed on a Web page so you can use the picture on your computer, see page 243.

SEARCH FOR APPLECARE DOCUMENTS

You can use the AppleCare channel to search the AppleCare Knowledge Base for documents about Apple products.

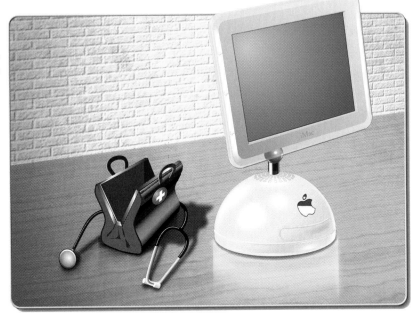

The AppleCare Knowledge Base contains thousands of documents that can help you troubleshoot the applications and hardware on your computer.

SEARCH FOR APPLECARE DOCUMENTS

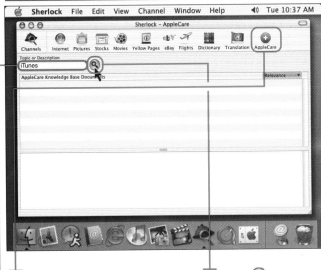

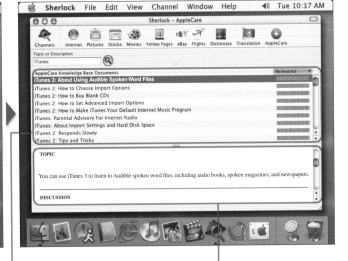

1 Click **AppleCare** to search for AppleCare documents.

2 Click this area and type the information you want to search for.

3 Click 🔍 to start the search.

■ This area lists the documents in the AppleCare Knowledge Base that contain the information you specified. A bar beside each document indicates the relevance of the document to the information you specified.

■ This area displays the contents of the currently selected document.

Note: To display the contents of another document, click the document.

SEARCH FOR STOCK INFORMATION

The **Stocks channel** allows you to search for information on stocks you want to monitor.

The stock quotes Sherlock displays are delayed by 15 minutes.

Sherlock automatically adds Apple Computer, Inc. to your list of stocks.

SEARCH FOR STOCK INFORMATION

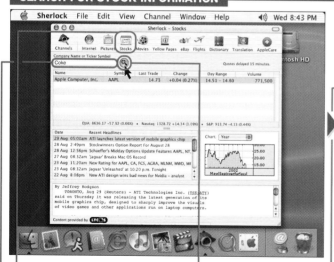

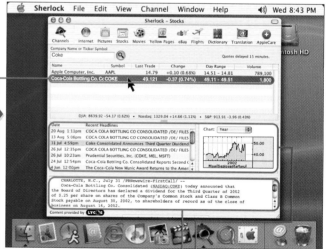

1 Click **Stocks** to search for stock information.

2 Click this area and type the company name or stock symbol for the stock you want to search for.

3 Click the magnifying glass to start the search.

*Note: If you specify a company name that matches more than one stock, a dialog sheet will appear. To display information for a stock that appears in the dialog sheet, click the stock and then click **Add**.*

■ This area displays the name of the stock and information about the stock.

4 To display headlines and a graph for a stock, click the stock.

■ This area displays recent headlines about the stock and a graph of the stock's performance.

■ This area displays the story for the currently selected headline.

Note: To delete a stock you added to your list of stocks, click the stock and then press the delete *key.*

SEARCH FOR BUSINESSES

You can use the Yellow Pages channel to find out where a business in your area is located.

When you search for a business, Sherlock uses your current location to determine driving directions to the business. Your current location is the address that was specified when Mac OS was installed on your computer.

SEARCH FOR BUSINESSES

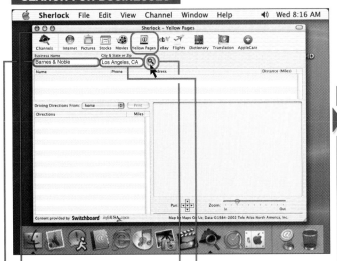

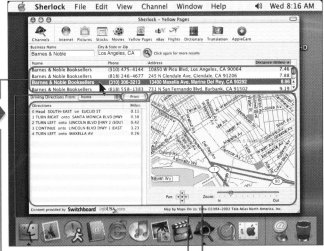

1 Click **Yellow Pages** to search for a business in your area.

2 Click this area and type all or part of the name of the business you want to search for.

3 Drag the mouse ⌶ over the text in this area and type the city and state or the zip code where the business is located.

4 Click 🔍 to start the search.

◼ This area lists the businesses that match the information you specified.

5 To display driving directions and a map for a business, click the business.

◼ This area displays driving directions to the business and a map showing the location of the business.

◼ To print the driving directions and map, click **Print**.

Note: For more information on printing, see page 52.

SEARCH FOR MOVIES

The Movies channel allows you to search for movies playing in your area.

SEARCH FOR MOVIES

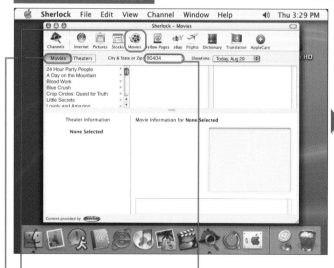

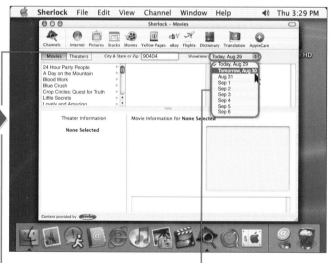

1 Click **Movies** to search for movies playing in your area.

2 Click **Movies** to search by movie name.

3 Drag the mouse over the text in this area and type the city and state or the zip code for the area where you want to search for movies.

Note: Sherlock may have already filled in your zip code for you.

4 To specify the date the movies you want to find are playing, click this area.

5 Click the date of interest.

■ Sherlock automatically starts the search.

Can I search for movies playing at a particular theater?

Yes. Searching by theater is useful when you want to go to a particular theater to see a movie. Perform steps **1** to **5** below, except click **Theaters** in step **2**. In the list of theaters that appears, click a theater of interest to display the movies playing at the theater. Then click a movie of interest to display information about the movie.

Can the Movies channel help me buy tickets for a movie?

Some theaters use an online ticketing service, which allows you to buy tickets for movies on the Web. After you select the movie you want to see and the theater where the movie is playing, you can click **Buy Tickets** below the theater information to display a Web page you can use to buy tickets for the movie. If **Buy Tickets** is not available, the theater does not use an online ticketing service.

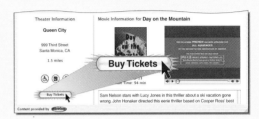

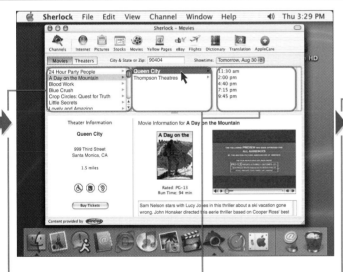

■ This area lists the movies that match the information you specified.

6 Click a movie of interest.

■ This area lists the theaters where the movie is playing.

7 Click a theater of interest.

■ This area lists the times the movie is playing at the theater you selected.

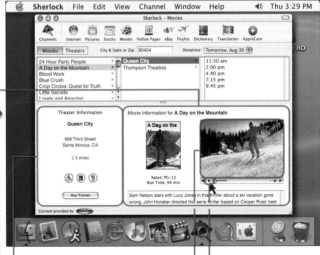

■ This area displays information about the theater you selected, including the name and address of the theater.

■ This area displays information about the movie you selected, including the rating, length and description of the movie.

8 To play the trailer for the movie, click ▶.

■ The trailer plays in this area.

SEARCH FOR GOODS AND SERVICES

You can use the eBay channel to search for goods and services you want to purchase on the Internet.

SEARCH FOR GOODS AND SERVICES

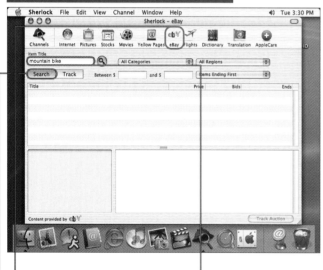

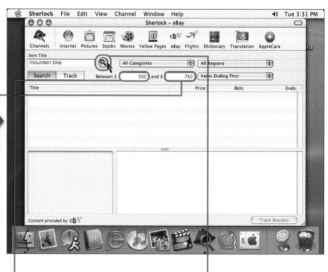

1 Click **eBay** to search for goods and services.

2 Click **Search** to search for an item you want to purchase.

3 Click this area and type a word or phrase that describes the item you want to purchase.

4 To specify the minimum price you want to pay, click this area and type a price.

5 To specify the maximum price you want to pay, click this area and type a price.

6 Click 🔍 to start the search.

Can I sort the items Sherlock found?

Yes. You can sort the items by title, price, number of bids or when the bidding will end. To sort the items, click the heading for the column you want to use to sort the items. To sort the items in the reverse order, you can click the heading again.

How can I view the auctions I selected to track?

To view the auctions you selected to track, click **Track**. A list of the auctions you selected to track appears. To remove an auction you no longer want to track from the list, click the auction and then press the delete key.

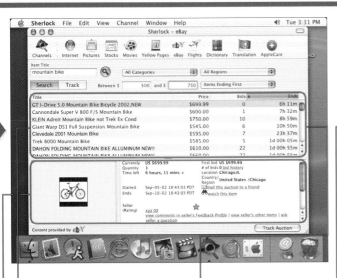

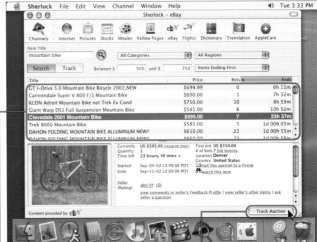

■ This area lists the items that match the information you specified and information about each item, including the current price, number of bids and when the bidding will end.

■ This area displays a picture and details for the currently selected item.

Note: To display a picture and details for another item, click the item.

■ To view additional information or bid on an item, double-click the item to display the eBay Web site.

TRACK AN AUCTION

1 To track the auction for an item, click the item.

Note: Tracking an auction allows you to see the current status of the auction at any time. Sherlock will also notify you when an auction you are tracking is about to end.

2 Click **Track Auction**.

■ Sherlock adds the auction to the list of auctions you want to track.

Note: To view the auctions you selected to track, see the top of this page.

SEARCH FOR FLIGHT INFORMATION

The Flights channel allows you to search for the arrival time and status of a flight.

Flight # 115 Arrival Time: 14:35

SEARCH FOR FLIGHT INFORMATION

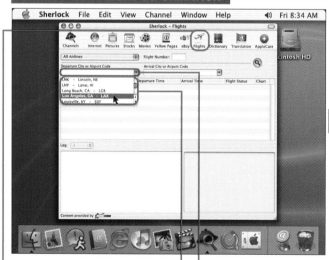

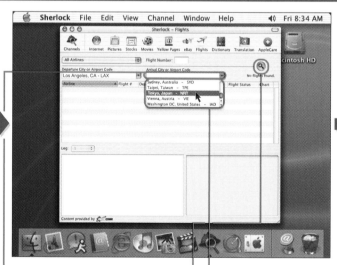

1 Click **Flights** to search for flight information.

2 To specify the city the flight departed from, click ⊡ in this area to display a list of city names and airport codes.

3 Click the city the flight departed from.

4 To specify the city where the flight will arrive, click ⊡ in this area to display a list of city names and airport codes.

5 Click the city where the flight will arrive.

6 Click 🔍 to start the search.

Is there another way to search for a flight?

If you know the name of the airline and the number of the flight you want to find, you can use this information to search for the flight.

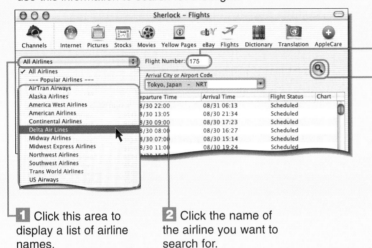

3 Click this area and type the flight number of the flight you want to search for.

4 Click 🔍 to start the search.

1 Click this area to display a list of airline names.

2 Click the name of the airline you want to search for.

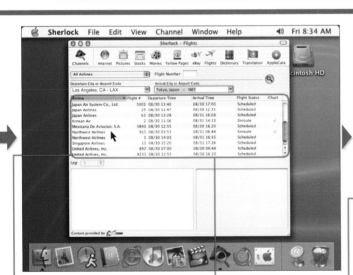

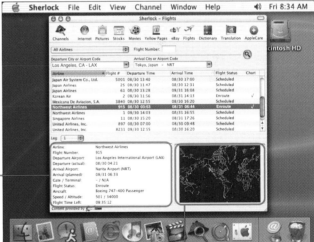

■ This area lists the flights that match the information you specified and information about each flight, including the airline name, flight number, departure time, arrival time and flight status.

Note: The Chart column displays a check mark (√) if a chart showing the route of the flight is available.

7 To display details for a flight, click the flight.

■ This area displays details for the flight, including the aircraft type and amount of time before the flight lands.

■ If a chart is available, this area displays a chart showing the location of the airplane and the route of the flight.

SEARCH FOR A DEFINITION

You can use the Dictionary channel to look up the definition of a word.

The Dictionary channel also allows you to search for the names of important people and places.

SEARCH FOR A DEFINITION

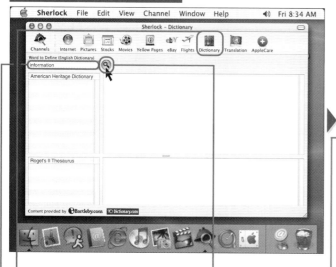

1 Click **Dictionary** to search for the definition of a word.

2 Click this area and type the word you want to look up.

3 Click 🔍 to start the search.

■ This area displays a list of words and phrases that match the word you specified.

4 Click a word or phrase of interest.

■ This area displays the definition of the word or phrase.

■ This area displays words related to the word you specified in step **2** and the definition of the currently selected word.

Note: To display the definition of another related word, click the word.

TRANSLATE TEXT

You can use the Translation channel to translate words and phrases from one language to another.

When translating text, keep in mind that the translation is performed by an application and may not always be accurate. If you need to translate important information, you may want to have a professional translator perform the translation.

TRANSLATE TEXT

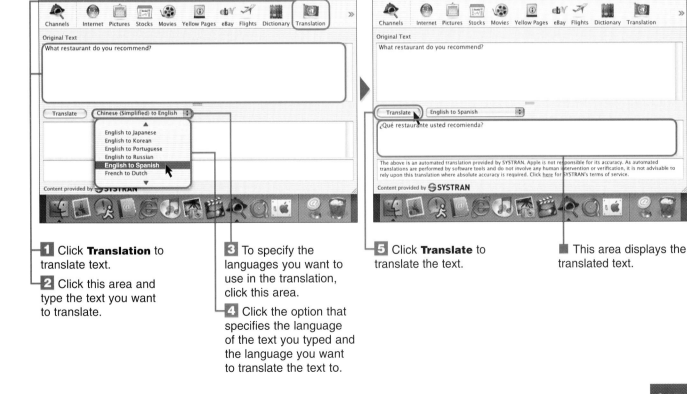

1 Click **Translation** to translate text.

2 Click this area and type the text you want to translate.

3 To specify the languages you want to use in the translation, click this area.

4 Click the option that specifies the language of the text you typed and the language you want to translate the text to.

5 Click **Translate** to translate the text.

■ This area displays the translated text.

CHAPTER 13

Exchange E-mail Using Mail

Mail allows you to exchange e-mail messages with people around the world. In this chapter, you will learn how to read, send and work with e-mail messages.

READ MESSAGES

You can use Mail to read the contents of your e-mail messages.

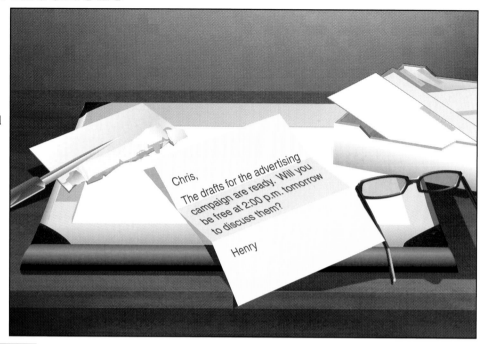

Chris,
The drafts for the advertising campaign are ready. Will you be free at 2:00 p.m. tomorrow to discuss them?

Henry

READ MESSAGES

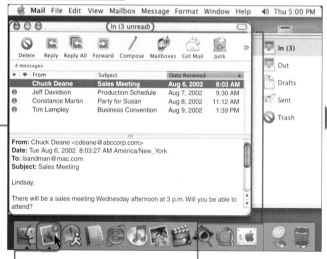

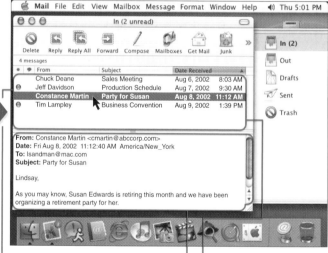

1 Click the Mail icon.

■ A window appears, displaying the messages in the current mailbox.

■ This area displays the name of the current mailbox. If the mailbox contains unread messages, the number of unread messages in the mailbox appears in brackets beside the mailbox name.

■ This area displays the messages in the current mailbox. Unread messages display a dot (●).

Note: Messages considered to be junk mail appear brown in color. For more information on junk mail, see page 286.

2 Click the message you want to read.

■ This area displays the contents of the message you selected.

■ To display the contents of another message, repeat step **2**.

What mailboxes does Mail use to store my messages?

	In	Stores messages sent to you.
	Out	Temporarily stores messages that have not yet been sent.
	Drafts	Stores messages you have not yet completed.
	Sent	Stores copies of messages you have sent.
	Trash	Stores messages you have deleted.

Note: Mail creates the Trash mailbox the first time you delete a message.

Can I sort my messages?

Yes. You can sort your messages by name, subject or date received. To sort your messages, click the heading for the column you want to use to sort the messages. To sort the messages in the reverse order, you can click the heading again.

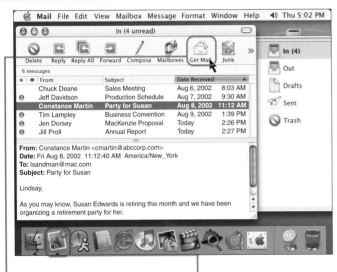

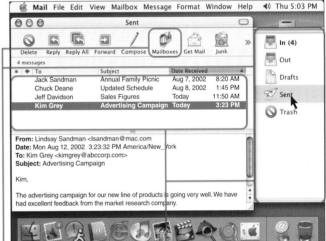

GET NEW MESSAGES

1 Click **Get Mail** to immediately check for new messages.

Note: When you are connected to the Internet, Mail automatically checks for new messages every five minutes.

■ When you have new messages, the Mail icon indicates the total number of new messages.

SWITCH BETWEEN MAILBOXES

■ The Mailbox drawer displays a list of mailboxes.

■ To hide or display the Mailbox drawer at any time, click **Mailboxes**.

Note: If you cannot see the Mailbox drawer, reduce the size of the window. To resize a window, see page 13.

1 Click the mailbox that contains the messages you want to view.

■ The messages in the mailbox you selected appear.

271

SEND A MESSAGE

You can send a message to express an idea or request information.

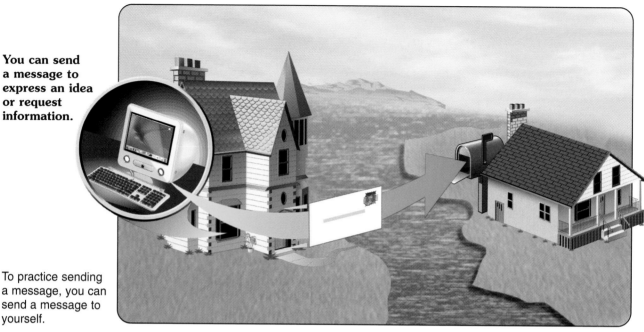

To practice sending a message, you can send a message to yourself.

SEND A MESSAGE

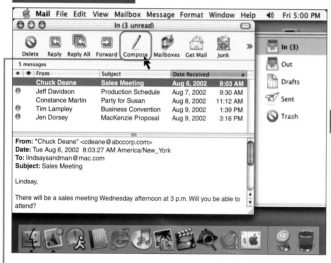

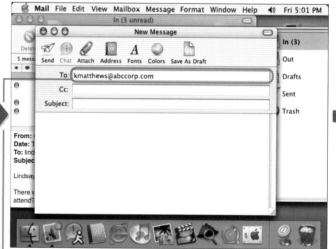

1 Click **Compose** to send a new message.

■ The New Message window appears.

2 Type the e-mail address of the person you want to receive the message.

Note: If you start typing the name or e-mail address of a person in Address Book, Mail will automatically complete the person's e-mail address for you. To add a person to Address Book, see page 128.

How can I express emotions in my e-mail messages?

You can use special characters, called emoticons, to express emotions in e-mail messages. These characters resemble human faces if you turn them sideways. Emoticons are also called smileys.

Cry	:'-(
Frown	:-(
Indifferent	:-I
Laugh	:-D
Smile	:-)
Surprise	:-0
Wink	

Can Mail help me correct a spelling error in a message?

Yes. To get help correcting a spelling error in a message, press and hold down the control key as you click the misspelled word. A menu appears, displaying suggestions to correct the spelling error. Click the suggestion you want to use to correct the spelling error.

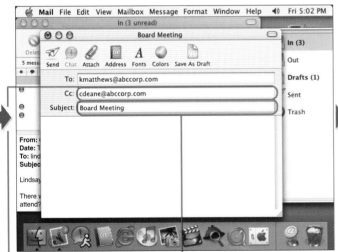

3 To send a copy of the message to a person who is not directly involved but would be interested in the message, click this area and then type the person's e-mail address.

Note: To send the message to more than one person in step 2 or 3, separate each e-mail address with a comma (,).

4 Click this area and then type the subject of the message.

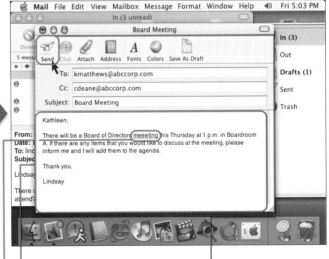

5 Click this area and then type the message.

■ Mail checks your spelling as you type and displays a dotted red underline under potential spelling errors. The person who receives the message will not see the dotted red underlines.

6 Click **Send** to send the message.

■ Mail sends the message and stores a copy of the message in the Sent mailbox.

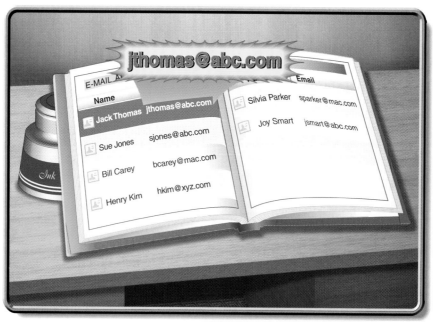

When sending a message, you can select the name of the person you want to receive the message from Address Book.

Address Book allows you to store information about people you frequently contact. To send a message to a person in Address Book, you must have entered an e-mail address for the person in Address Book. To add a person to Address Book, see page 128.

SELECT A NAME FROM ADDRESS BOOK

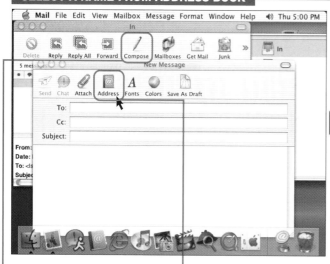

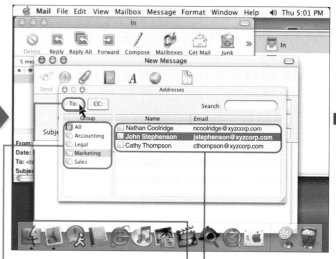

1 Click **Compose** to send a new message.

■ The New Message window appears.

2 Click **Address** to select a name from Address Book.

■ The Addresses window appears.

3 Click the group that contains the person you want to receive the message.

■ To send the message to every person in a group, click the group and then skip to step **5**.

*Note: The **All** group contains all the people you have added to Address Book.*

4 Click the name of the person you want to receive the message.

5 Click **To:**.

■ You can repeat steps **4** and **5** for each person you want to receive the message.

I accidentally selected a name from Address Book. How can I remove the name from the message?

To remove the name of a person you accidentally selected from Address Book, drag the mouse I over the name and e-mail address of the person until the information is highlighted and then press the `delete` key.

The person I want to select does not appear in Address Book. How can I quickly add the person to Address Book?

You can quickly add the name and e-mail address of a person who sent you an e-mail message to Address Book. Click a message you received from the person you want to add to Address Book and then press and hold down the `⌘` key as you press the `Y` key. The person's name and e-mail address will now appear in Address Book.

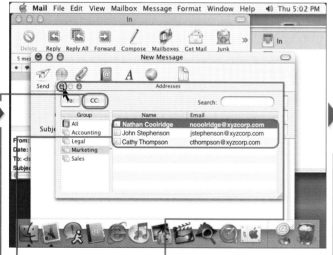

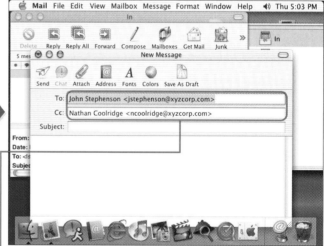

6 To send a copy of the message to a person who is not directly involved but would be interested in the message, click the name of the person.

7 Click **CC:**.

■ You can repeat steps **6** and **7** for each person you want to receive a copy of the message.

8 When you finish selecting names from Address Book, click ◯ to close the Addresses window.

■ This area displays the name and e-mail address of each person you selected from Address Book.

■ You can now finish composing the message.

Note: To finish composing a message, perform steps 4 to 6 on page 273.

SAVE A DRAFT OF A MESSAGE

If you are not ready to send a message, you can save a draft of the message so you can finish the message at a later time.

Saving a draft of a message allows you to later review and make changes to the message.

SAVE A DRAFT OF A MESSAGE

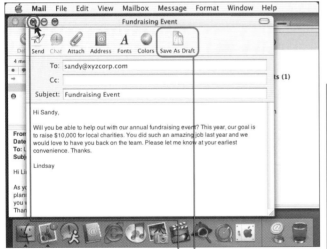

1 To create a message, perform steps 1 to 5 starting on page 272.

2 Click **Save As Draft** to save the message as a draft so you can send the message at a later time.

3 Click ⬤ to close the message window.

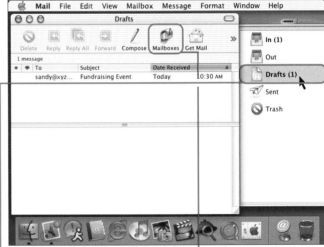

SEND A DRAFT MESSAGE

■ When you save a draft of a message, Mail stores the message in the Drafts mailbox until you are ready to send the message.

1 Click **Drafts** to display the messages in the Drafts mailbox.

■ If the list of mailboxes is not displayed, click **Mailboxes** to display the list.

Note: You may also need to reduce the size of the window to display the list of mailboxes.

How can I save time when typing a message?

You can use abbreviations for words and phrases to save time when typing messages. Here are some commonly used abbreviations.

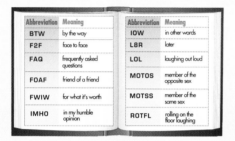

Abbreviation	Meaning
BTW	by the way
F2F	face to face
FAQ	frequently asked questions
FOAF	friend of a friend
FWIW	for what it's worth
IMHO	in my humble opinion

Abbreviation	Meaning
IOW	in other words
L8R	later
LOL	laughing out loud
MOTOS	member of the opposite sex
MOTSS	member of the same sex
ROTFL	rolling on the floor laughing

I no longer want to send a message I saved as a draft. How can I delete the message?

If you no longer want to send a message you saved as a draft, you can delete the message from the Drafts mailbox. To delete the message, click the message and then press the delete key.

■ This area lists the messages you have saved as drafts.

2 Double-click the message you want to send.

■ A window appears, displaying the contents of the message. You can review and make changes to the message.

3 To send the message, click **Send**.

■ Mail sends the message and stores a copy of the message in the Sent mailbox.

REPLY TO A MESSAGE

You can reply to a
message to answer
a question, express
an opinion or
supply additional
information.

When you reply to
a message, Mail
includes a copy
of the original
message to help
the reader identify
which message
you are replying to.
The original message
appears in blue.

After you reply to a message,
a curved arrow (↩) appears
beside the message.

REPLY TO A MESSAGE

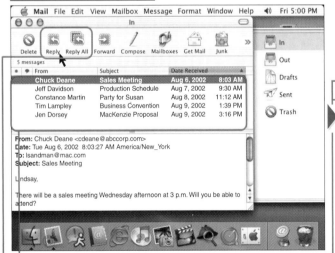

1 Click the message
you want to reply to.

2 Click the reply option
you want to use.

Reply
Sends a reply to only
the author.

Reply All
Sends a reply to the
author and everyone
who received the
original message.

■ A window appears
for you to compose
your reply.

■ Mail fills in the e-mail
address(es) for you.

■ Mail also fills in the
subject, starting the
subject with **Re:**.

3 Click this area and
then type your reply.

4 Click **Send** to send
the reply.

■ Mail stores a copy
of the message in the
Sent mailbox.

After reading a message, you can add comments and then forward the message to another person who would be interested in the message.

After you forward a message, an arrow (➡) appears beside the message.

FORWARD A MESSAGE

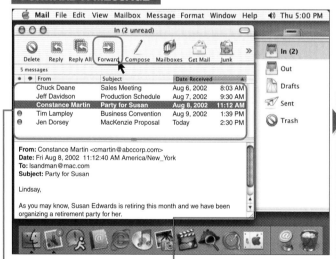

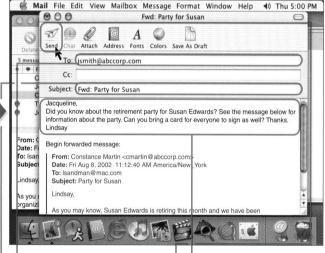

1 Click the message you want to forward.

2 Click **Forward**.

■ A window appears, displaying the contents of the message you are forwarding.

3 Type the e-mail address of the person you want to receive the message.

■ Mail fills in the subject for you, starting the subject with **Fwd:**.

4 Click this area and then type any comments about the message you are forwarding.

5 Click **Send** to forward the message.

PRINT A MESSAGE

You can produce
a paper copy of
a message.

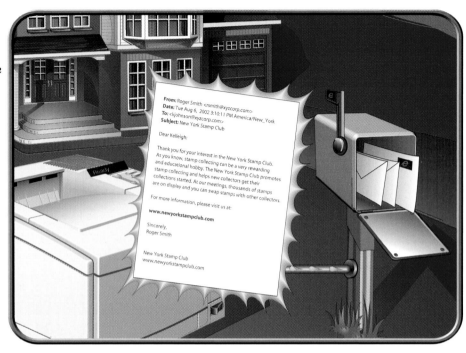

Before printing,
make sure your
printer is turned
on and contains
paper.

PRINT A MESSAGE

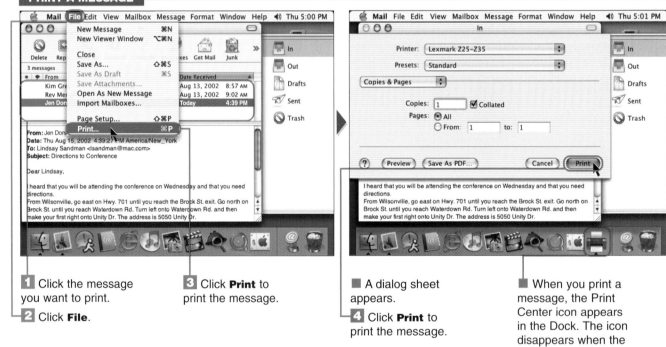

1 Click the message
you want to print.

2 Click **File**.

3 Click **Print** to
print the message.

■ A dialog sheet
appears.

4 Click **Print** to
print the message.

■ When you print a
message, the Print
Center icon appears
in the Dock. The icon
disappears when the
message has finished
printing.

DELETE A MESSAGE

You can delete a message you no longer need. Deleting messages frees up storage space on your computer and helps prevent your mailboxes from becoming cluttered.

DELETE A MESSAGE

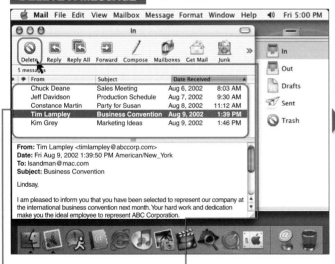

1 Click the message you want to delete.

2 Click **Delete** to delete the message.

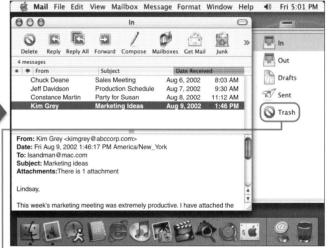

■ Mail removes the message from the current mailbox and places the message in the Trash mailbox.

Note: Deleting a message from the Trash mailbox will permanently remove the message from your computer. To view the contents of the Trash mailbox, see page 271.

ATTACH A FILE TO A MESSAGE

You can attach a file to a message you are sending. Attaching a file to a message is useful when you want to include additional information with the message.

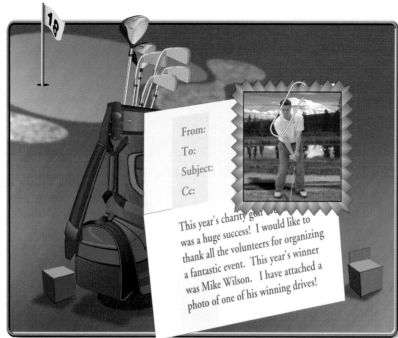

You can attach many types of files to a message, including documents, pictures, videos and sounds. The computer receiving the message must have the necessary software installed to display or play the file you attach.

ATTACH A FILE TO A MESSAGE

1 To create a message, perform steps **1** to **5** starting on page 272.

2 Click **Attach** to attach a file to the message.

■ A dialog sheet appears.

■ This area displays the location of the current folder in relation to the disks, folders and files on your computer. The current folder is highlighted.

Note: The leftmost column shows the disks on your computer. Each of the following columns shows the contents of the item selected in the previous column. You can use the scroll bar to browse through the columns.

■ To display the contents of a different folder, click the folder.

Can I attach a large file to a message?

The company that provides your e-mail account may limit the size of the messages that you can send and receive over the Internet. Most companies do not allow you to send or receive messages larger than 2 MB, which includes all attached files. Some companies provide premium services you can purchase that will allow you to send and receive messages larger than 2 MB.

How can I remove a file I accidentally attached to a message?

To remove a file you accidentally attached to a message, click the icon for the file you want to remove and then press the delete key. The file disappears from the message.

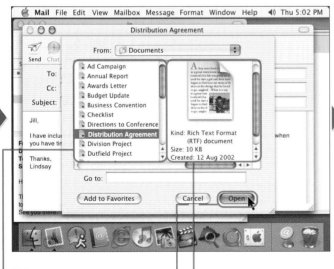

■ **3** Click the name of the file you want to attach to the message.

■ Information about the file appears in the last column.

■ **4** Click **Open** to attach the file to the message.

■ An icon for the file appears in the message. The name and size of the file appears below the icon.

Note: If you attached a picture to the message, the picture appears in the message.

■ To attach additional files to the message, perform steps **2** to **4** for each file you want to attach.

■ **5** Click **Send** to send the message.

■ Mail sends the message and stores a copy of the message in the Sent mailbox.

ADD A SIGNATURE TO MESSAGES

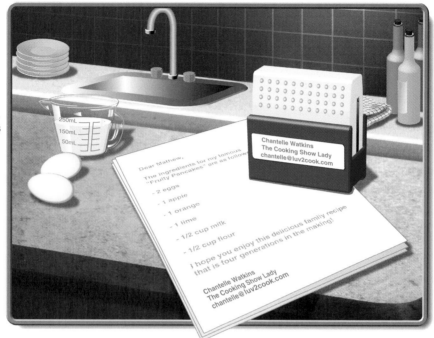

You can have Mail add personal information to the end of every message you send. This information is called a signature.

A signature saves you from having to type the same information in every message you send.

ADD A SIGNATURE TO MESSAGES

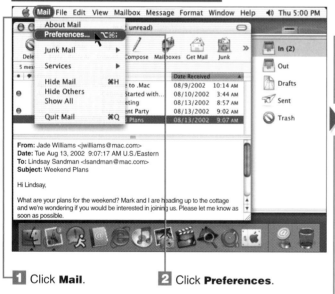

1 Click **Mail**.

2 Click **Preferences**.

■ A window that allows you to change your e-mail preferences appears.

3 Click **Signatures** to work with signatures.

4 Click **Add Signature** to create a signature.

What can I include in a signature?

A signature can include information such as your name, e-mail address, occupation, favorite quotation or Web page address. As a courtesy to people who will receive your messages, you should limit your signature to four or five lines.

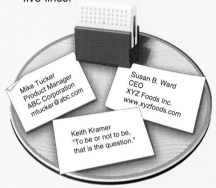

Mike Tucker
Product Manager
ABC Corporation
mtucker@abc.com

Susan B. Ward
CEO
XYZ Foods Inc.
www.xyzfoods.com

Keith Kramer
"To be or not to be,
that is the question."

How can I remove a signature?

If you no longer want to add a signature to the messages you send, perform steps **1** to **3** below to display your signatures. Click the description for the signature you want to remove and then click **Remove**. In the confirmation dialog sheet that appears, click **OK** to remove the signature. The next time you start Mail, the signature will no longer appear in the messages you send.

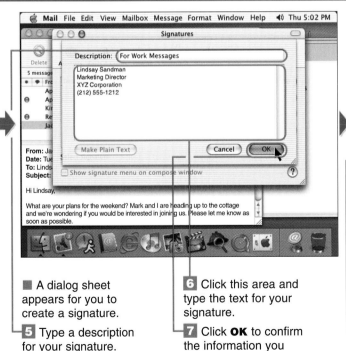

■ A dialog sheet appears for you to create a signature.

5 Type a description for your signature.

6 Click this area and type the text for your signature.

7 Click **OK** to confirm the information you entered.

■ The description for the signature you created appears in this area.

■ This area displays the description for the signature Mail will use in all your messages. You can click this area to select a different signature.

8 Click ◯ to close the window.

■ Mail will now add the signature to the end of every new message you send.

SORT JUNK MAIL

Mail can examine messages you receive to determine if the messages are junk mail.

By default, Mail changes the color of potential junk e-mail messages so you can easily recognize junk mail when reading your messages.

After training Mail to correctly identify junk e-mail messages, you can have Mail automatically move all new junk mail you receive to the Junk mailbox.

SORT JUNK MAIL

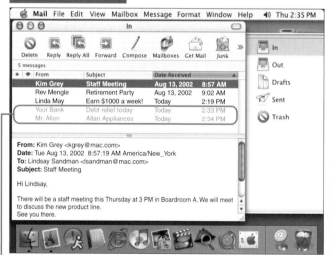

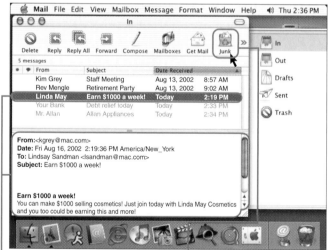

■ By default, Mail starts in training mode. When in training mode, potential junk e-mail messages appear brown in color.

■ You can improve Mail's ability to properly identify junk mail by correctly marking messages as junk mail or not junk mail.

MARK A MESSAGE AS JUNK MAIL

■1 Click the message you want to mark as junk mail.

■ This area displays the contents of the message.

■2 Click **Junk**.

■ The message will appear brown in color.

*Note: The first time you mark a message as junk mail, a dialog box appears, providing information about junk mail. To close the dialog box, click **OK**.*

How can I switch back to training mode?

If you find that Mail is not automatically moving most of the new junk mail you receive to the Junk mailbox, you can switch back to training mode to try to improve Mail's ability to identify junk mail. To return to training mode, perform steps **1** to **3** in the last screen below, except select **Training** in step **3**.

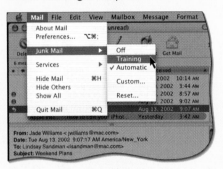

Can I stop Mail from identifying and sorting junk mail?

Yes. You can turn off the junk mail feature to stop Mail from automatically identifying and sorting junk mail. To turn off the junk mail feature, perform steps **1** to **3** in the last screen below, except select **Off** in step **3**.

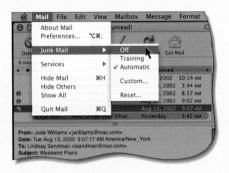

MARK A MESSAGE AS NOT JUNK MAIL

1 Click the message that Mail incorrectly identified as junk mail.

■ This area displays the contents of the message.

Note: A bar appears at the top of the message, indicating that Mail thinks the message is junk mail.

2 Click **Not Junk**.

■ The message will no longer appear brown in color.

AUTOMATICALLY SORT JUNK MAIL

1 To have Mail automatically move junk mail to the Junk mailbox, click **Mail**.

2 Position the mouse over **Junk Mail**.

3 Click **Automatic**.

■ A dialog box appears, asking if you want to move all junk e-mail messages to the Junk mailbox.

4 Click **No** or **Yes** to specify if you want to move the junk e-mail messages.

Note: To display the contents of the Junk mailbox, see page 271.

CHAPTER 14

Exchange Instant Messages Using iChat

You can use iChat to exchange instant messages with your friends and family. This chapter shows you how to add a person to your Buddy List, send an instant message and send a file.

You can use iChat to see when your friends are available and exchange instant messages and files with them.

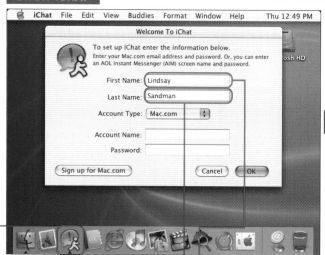

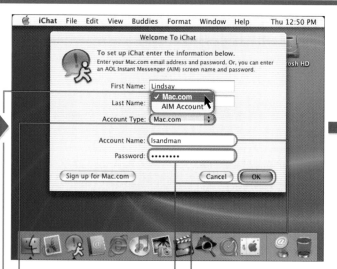

1 Click the iChat icon to start iChat.

■ The first time you start iChat, the Welcome To iChat dialog box appears, allowing you to set up iChat.

2 Click this area and type your first name.

3 Click this area and type your last name.

Note: Part or all of the information in the dialog box may already be filled in for you.

4 To specify if you want to use a Mac.com or AIM (AOL) account with iChat, click this area.

5 Click the type of account you want to use.

6 Click this area and type your account name.

7 Click this area and type your account password.

8 Click **OK** to continue.

How do I obtain an account that I can use with iChat?

Mac.com

You can use a Mac.com account with iChat. If you do not have a Mac.com account, click **Sign up for Mac.com** in the Welcome To iChat dialog box. Your Web browser opens, displaying a Web page that allows you to obtain a Mac.com account.

AIM Account

If you use the AIM (AOL Instant Messenger) application, you can use the screen name and password for your AIM account with iChat. If you use AOL (America Online) to access the Internet, you can use the screen name and password for your AOL account with iChat.

■ A dialog box appears, asking if you want to turn on Rendezvous messaging. If you are connected to a network, Rendezvous messaging allows you to exchange messages and files with other people using iChat on the network.

9 Click **No** or **Yes** to specify if you want to turn on Rendezvous messaging.

■ The Buddy List window appears. You can add people to your Buddy List so you can quickly send them instant messages.

Note: To add a person to your Buddy List, see page 292.

■ If you chose to turn on Rendezvous messaging in step **9**, the Rendezvous window also appears, displaying each person currently using iChat on your network.

10 When you finish using iChat, click **iChat**.

11 Click **Quit iChat**. **291**

ADD A PERSON TO YOUR BUDDY LIST

You can add a person to your Buddy List so you can see when the person is available to exchange instant messages.

ADD A PERSON TO YOUR BUDDY LIST

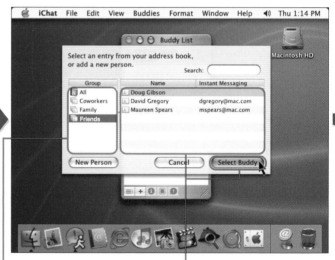

1 Click the iChat icon to start iChat.

■ The Buddy List window appears, displaying each person you have added to your Buddy List.

■ Each person who is available displays a green dot (🟢). Each person who is not available appears dim or displays a red dot (🔴).

2 Click ➕ to add a person to your Buddy List.

■ A dialog sheet appears, listing the people in Address Book.

Note: For information on Address Book, see page 128.

3 Click the group that contains the person you want to add to your Buddy List.

*Note: The **All** group contains all the people in Address Book.*

4 Click the person you want to add to your Buddy List.

5 Click **Select Buddy**.

Can I add a person who is not listed in Address Book to my Buddy List?

Yes. Click  in the Buddy List window. In the dialog sheet that appears, click **New Person** and then perform steps **6** to **8** below. You can also enter the person's first name, last name and e-mail address to provide additional information for Address Book. Click **Add** to add the person to your Buddy List and to Address Book.

How do I remove a person from my Buddy List?

In the Buddy List window, click the name of the person you want to remove and then press the delete key. In the confirmation dialog box that appears, click **OK** to delete the person from your Buddy List.

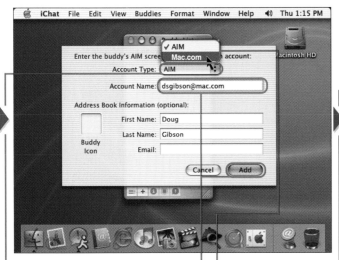

■ If Address Book does not contain an instant message account for the person, a dialog sheet appears, asking you to enter the person's account name.

6 Click this area to select the type of account the person uses.

7 Click an option to specify if the person uses an AIM (AOL) account or a Mac.com account.

8 Click this area and type the person's account name.

9 Click **Add** to add the person to your Buddy List.

■ The person appears in your Buddy List.

SEND AN INSTANT MESSAGE

You can send an instant message to a person in your Buddy List.

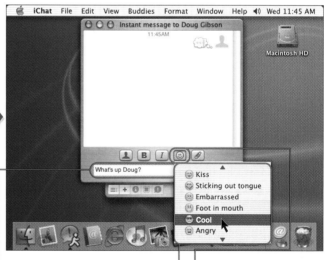

■ You can send an instant message to a person in your Buddy List who is available. Each person who is available displays a green dot (●).

Note: To add a person to your Buddy List, see page 292.

1 Double-click the person you want to send an instant message to.

■ A chat window appears.

2 Click this area and type your message.

3 To express an emotion in your message, click 🙂 to display the available smileys.

4 Click the smiley you want to include in your message.

5 To send the message, press the `return` key.

What should I consider when sending an instant message?

A MESSAGE WRITTEN IN CAPITAL LETTERS IS ANNOYING AND DIFFICULT TO READ. THIS IS CALLED SHOUTING. Always use uppercase and lowercase letters when typing an instant message.

How can I bold or italicize text in an instant message?

When typing an instant message, drag the mouse I over the text you want to bold or italicize until the text is highlighted. To bold the text, click B. To italicize the text, click I.

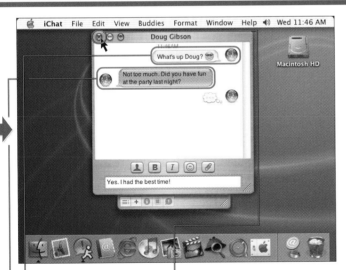

■ This area displays the message you sent.

■ The other person's response appears below the message you sent.

Note: When you or the other person is typing a message, a new icon with an empty balloon appears in the chat window.

6 When you finish exchanging instant messages, click ○ to close the chat window.

RECEIVE AN INSTANT MESSAGE

■ When you receive an instant message that is not part of an ongoing conversation, a window appears, displaying the message.

1 To respond to the message, click anywhere in the window.

■ An area appears, allowing you to type a reply.

2 Click this area and type your reply.

3 To send the reply, press the return key.

SEND A FILE

While exchanging instant messages with another person, you can send the person a file.

You can send many types of files, including documents, pictures, videos and sounds. The computer receiving the file must have the necessary software installed to display or play the file.

There is no limit on the size of files you can send in your instant messages, but larger files will take longer to transfer.

SEND A FILE

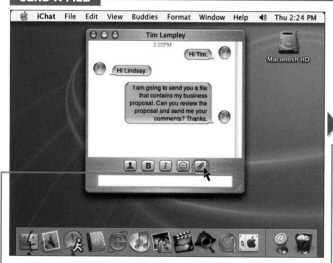

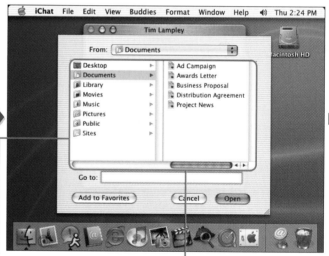

1 While exchanging instant messages with another person, click 🖉 to send a file.

Note: For information on sending instant messages, see page 294.

■ A dialog sheet appears.

■ This area displays the location of the current folder in relation to the disks, folders and files on your computer. The current folder is highlighted.

Note: The leftmost column shows the disks on your computer. Each of the following columns shows the contents of the item selected in the previous column. You can use the scroll bar to browse through the columns.

■ To display the contents of a different folder, click the folder.

How do I accept a file I receive?

To accept a file you receive, click the name of the file in the chat window. After Mac OS transfers the file to your computer, the Desktop window appears, displaying an icon for the file. You can double-click the icon to open the file. An icon for the file also appears on your desktop.

Is there another way to send a file?

Yes. To quickly send a file, click the area where you type your instant messages. Position the mouse ▶ over the file you want to send and then drag the file into the area. An icon for the file appears in the area. To send the file, press the return key.

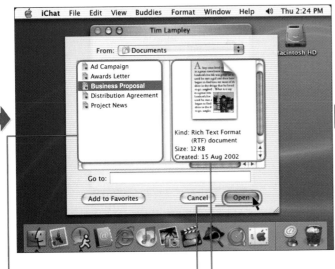

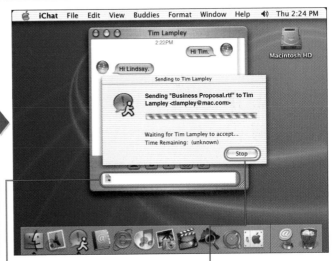

2 Click the name of the file you want to send.

■ Information about the file appears in the last column.

3 Click **Open** to select the file.

■ An icon for the file appears in this area.

4 To send the file, press the return key.

■ A dialog box appears on your screen until the other person accepts the file.

■ To cancel the file transfer at any time, click **Stop**.

Note: If you send a picture, the picture may automatically appear in the chat window without displaying a dialog box.

INDEX

INDEX

INDEX

translate text, using Sherlock, 267
Translation channel, in Sherlock, use, 267
Trash
    appearance, 47
    empty, 48
    item in Dock when using Simple Finder, 221
    move items to, 46-47
Trash mailbox, 271
typeface of text, change, in TextEdit, 124

U

universal access settings, change, 88-91
update software, automatically, 108-111
URLs (Uniform Resource Locators), 240
USB, printer connection type, 97
user accounts
    access files for deleted users, 213
    add, 208-211
    capabilities, change, 220-223
    change regular to administrator, 223
    delete, 212-213
    edit information, 211
    log in automatically, 216-217
    log out or in, 214-215
Users folder, 29

V

video, transfer from digital video camera to computer, 186-187
video clips
    add to movies, 188
    crop, 193
    delete, 187
    mute, 199
    play, 187
    preview, 202-203
    rearrange, 189
    transitions
        add, 194-195
        remove, 195
    volume, change, 199
view. *See also* display
    applications, 26-27
    contents
        of computer, 28-29
        of discs, 30
        of hard disk, 28-29
    folders, personal, 26-27
    fonts, in Key Caps, 138-139
    installed software updates, 111
    of items in windows, change, 32-33
    shared files on computer, 224-225
    songs in iTunes Library, 150
visual effects, display, in iTunes, 149
voice computer uses, change, 104
voice recordings in movies
    add, 198-199
    delete, 199

    location, change, 197
    volume, change, 199
volume
    of movies, adjust, 203
        for components, 199
    of sounds on computer, change, 78-79

W

Web
    pages
        addresses, 240
        display, 240
            list of previously viewed, 242
            recently viewed in History list, 248-249
        Favorites
            add to list, 246
            delete from list, 247
            view, 246-247
        home
            change, 244-245
            display, 244
            stop using, 245
        move through, 242
        pictures, save, 243
        remove from History list, 249
        search for, 250-251
        stop transfer, 241
    publish photos to, 182-183
    search, 250-251
    sites, search for using Sherlock, 255
width of columns, in List view, change, 33
windows
    arrange icons in, 16
    change view of items in, 32-33
    clean up, 17
    close, 11
    effects when minimizing, change, 69
    iTunes, reduce size, 149
    minimize, 14
        Speech Feedback, 103
    move, 12
    overview, 6
    resize, 13, 15
    scroll through information in, 10
    switch between, 18
    toolbar, hide or display, 7
    zoom, 15
wrap of text, in TextEdit, change, 123

Y

Yellow Pages channel, in Sherlock, use, 259

Z

Zoom feature
    turn on or off, 88
    use, 89
zoom windows, 15

Read Less – Learn More™

Visual

Simplified®

Simply the Easiest Way to Learn

For visual learners who are brand-new to a topic and want to be shown, not told, how to solve a problem in a friendly, approachable way.

All *Simplified®* books feature friendly Disk characters who demonstrate and explain the purpose of each task.

Title	ISBN	U.S. Price
America Online Simplified, 3rd Ed. (Version 7.0)	0-7645-3673-7	$24.99
Computers Simplified, 5th Ed.	0-7645-3524-2	$27.99
Creating Web Pages with HTML Simplified, 2nd Ed.	0-7645-6067-0	$27.99
Excel 97 Simplified	0-7645-6022-0	$27.99
Excel 2002 Simplified	0-7645-3589-7	$27.99
FrontPage 2000 Simplified	0-7645-3450-5	$27.99
FrontPage 2002 Simplified	0-7645-3612-5	$27.99
Internet and World Wide Web Simplified, 3rd Ed.	0-7645-3409-2	$27.99
Microsoft Excel 2000 Simplified	0-7645-6053-0	$27.99
Microsoft Office 2000 Simplified	0-7645-6052-2	$29.99
Microsoft Word 2000 Simplified	0-7645-6054-9	$27.99
More Windows 98 Simplified	0-7645-6037-9	$27.99
Office 97 Simplified	0-7645-6009-3	$29.99
Office XP Simplified	0-7645-0850-4	$29.99
PC Upgrade and Repair Simplified, 2nd Ed.	0-7645-3560-9	$27.99
Windows 98 Simplified	0-7645-6030-1	$27.99
Windows Me Millennium Edition Simplified	0-7645-3494-7	$27.99
Windows XP Simplified	0-7645-3618-4	$27.99
Word 2002 Simplified	0-7645-3588-9	$27.99

Over 10 million *Visual* books in print!